"Gold Nuggets or Fool's Gold?"

Magazine and Newspaper Articles on the (Ir)relevance of Proverbs and Proverbial Phrases

Edited by

Wolfgang Mieder and Janet Sobieski

"Proverbium"
in cooperation with the
Department of German and Russian

The University of Vermont
Burlington, Vermont
2006

Supplement Series

of

Proverbium
Yearbook of International Proverb Scholarship

Edited by Wolfgang Mieder

Volume 22

Cover illustration:
"All that glitters is not gold" (#XCI)
Grace Frank and Dorothy Miner (eds.),
*Proverbes en Rimes. Text and Illustrations
of the Fifteenth Century from a French Manuscript.*
Baltimore, Maryland: The Johns Hopkins Press, 1937.

ISBN 0-9770731-4-9

Manufactured in the United States of America
by Queen City Printers Inc.
Burlington, Vermont

Contents

Introduction

Modern scholarship in the social sciences and humanities is to a large degree informed by theoretical considerations, with one innovative theory and its guru following another. To a certain extent this is also true for the field of folklore, although there have always been scholars who also checked with what the folk itself has to say about its narratives, riddles, jokes, proverbs, etc. It obviously makes sense to find out what people in general think about proverbs and proverbial expressions as they continue to make ample use of them in their oral and written communication. High-powered intellectual theories are one thing, but valid as they might be, they say little about the perception and thoughts of the actual tradition bearers. To remedy this situation regarding proverbial folk speech, Wolfgang Mieder published an essay on "Popular Views of the Proverb" some twenty years ago in *Proverbium: Yearbook of International Proverb Scholarship*, 2 (1985), 109-143. Its major purpose was to find out what the general public rather than scholars think about the definition, purpose, significance, use, and function of proverbs. Realizing that there exist dozens of theoretical proverb definitions, the author asked fifty-five Vermont informants how they would define a proverb. A word analysis of the most frequently used nouns, verbs, adjectives, and adverbs resulted in the following composite definition: "A proverb is a short, generally known sentence of the folk which contains wisdom, truth, morals, and traditional views in a metaphorical, fixed, and memorizable form and which is handed down from generation to generation." This wordy definition could be reduced even more to a mere "A proverb is a short sentence of wisdom" by including only the words with the highest frequency counts. Looking also at how journalists and popular writers have defined and discussed proverbs in the mass media, Mieder was able to show that they basically agree with the "folk" definition just stated. The natural conclusion of this investigation was that people in general know quite well what a proverb is without knowing any of the erudite definition attempts by folklorist, linguists, and paremiologists (proverb scholars).

As stated, this one article was primarily concerned with definitional questions of proverbs by the folk and the mass media. However, there is another aspect to the deliberations about proverbs in popular magazines and newspapers that deserves further investigation. After all, the essays that appear in the mass media on proverbial matters from time to time deal not only with the question of definition. They are in fact much more informed by the widespread notion that traditional proverbs might not be suitable any longer in modern technological societies. In other words, popular writers tend to question the validity and value of proverbs, arguing that their wisdom does not hold water when checked against scientific knowledge. Many of the essays refute the truth of well-known proverbs, often manipulating standard texts in such a way that innovative so-called anti-proverbs comment humorously or satirically on the old-fashioned proverbs. And yet, there are also those commentaries in the mass media that stress the fact that people will always employ formulaic language in the form of proverbs, proverbial expressions, proverbial comparisons, proverbial exaggerations, etc. Speakers and writers of the modern age need clichés and idioms to add metaphorical expressiveness to their statements, and they most certainly also rely on proverbial wisdom from long ago and now. To be sure, there are new proverbs to replace some of the old ones, showing clearly that it is a natural phenomenon for people to couch their experiences and observations into wisdom sayings. Never mind if a particular proverb might not be true in a unique situation! That does not necessarily devalue the proverb, since it will doubtlessly prove to be appropriate in another context. Proverbs are not based on a logical philosophical system, and they often contradict each other, as can be seen from such contrasting pairs as "Absence makes the heart grow fonder" and "Out of sight, out of mind" or "Look before you leap" and "He who hesitates is lost." Such proverb duels simply reflect the contradictions of life itself. Concerning the use and appropriateness of proverbs we might simply state: "If the proverb fits, use it, and if it doesn't, choose another one!"

The vast research results on the multifaceted aspects of proverbs have been recorded in the four volumes of Wolfgang Mieder's *International Proverb Scholarship: An Annotated Bibliography* (New York: Garland Publishing and Peter Lang, 1982-2001) and W. Mieder and Janet Sobieski's *Proverbs and the Social Sciences: An Annotated International Bibliography* (Baltmannsweiler: Schneider Verlag Hohengehren, 2003). But with very few exceptions these invaluable bibliographies do not include the popular articles that have appeared in the mass media, varying in length from a few paragraphs to several pages. While they might not represent scholarship in the traditional sense, they are written by informed writers who wish to reach a large audience with their findings and thoughts on proverbs. And that is the point: While scholars might communicate with a small circle of experts, authors of magazine and newspaper articles are writing for thousands or hundreds of thousands readers, thus playing a significant role in getting the folk to think critically about proverbial language. They thus have an incredible influence on the (mis)conceptions that abound among the general population regarding the death or survival of proverbs in today's society.

Popular articles on proverbs and proverbial phrases appear in the mass media throughout the world in various languages. It certainly is not a purely Anglo-American phenomenon. However, the present collection of sixty-four essays includes only texts from American, British, and Canadian magazines and newspapers. All of them have been located and collected during the past thirty-five years and are part of the International Proverb Archives housed at the University of Vermont in Burlington, Vermont (USA). By way of historical research, we were able to locate some isolated essays from 1877, 1890, 1929, 1930, 1941, 1954, 1959, 1961, 1964, 1965, and 1969, but the majority of texts come from the most recent three decades as we have found them by way of our own reading or that of colleagues and friends who know of our deep-rooted interest in all aspects of proverbs. While some of the articles were found in obscure publications, many of them appeared in such major magazines as *Atlantic Monthly, Good Housekeeping, Harper's, People, The Progressive, Punch, Reader's Digest, Saturday Review, Smithsonian, Time*, and *US News & World Report*, others found their way into important newspapers like the *Guardian Weekly, The Montreal Gazette, The New York Times, The Wall Street Journal*, and *The Washington Post*. Quite naturally numerous articles were discovered in our hometown newspaper *The Burlington Free Press*, with some of them having been written by local authors and others having been picked up from the national media services. This is also the case for some of the other magazines and newspapers not enumerated here. But be that as it may, there can be no doubt that the printed mass media must be considered as a major opinion-maker when it comes to raising the consciousness of millions of readers to the fascinating world of proverbs. As professional paremiologists we can only dream about such wide exposure as we sit in our studies

3

writing for the few, of whom, as chance would have it, an even smaller number will actually read our grand theories about the most basic form of wisdom.

The complexities of proverbs, as they have been discussed by scholars, reappear in straightforward, readable, and entertaining ways in the various essays presented in this volume. In fact, the very first paragraph of the first anonymously published article on "The Influence of Proverbs" (1877) from *The New York Times* sets the satirical tone and tells it all:

> The harm done by proverbs, maxims, saws, and catch-phrases, is wholly beyond calculation. They are never quite true, though they are always plausible; they generally contain a fallacy of some sort, and one which it is pleasant to ignore. They are well qualified to deceive, and most of us are very willing to be deceived by them; for, in respect to deception, we are likely to meet them half way. A proverb has been defined as the wit of one and the wisdom of many; it is oftener the sophistry of a few and the unreason of the multitude. The great trouble with a popular adage, or current phrase of any kind, is, that it is commonly accepted as absolute truth. Hardly any one thinks of examining or questioning it; for has it not already received the approval of thousands, if not of generations? It must be sound, especially if it fits our case. It commends itself, mainly by sparing us the trouble of reflection, which is always a relief, even to the most intelligent. Man is a reasoning animal, and, being assured of the fact, he deems it unnecessary to prove it by his practice.
>
> We are well enough aware that there are maxims to suit all tastes and tempers; that some affirm what others deny; that frequently they are direct contradictions. But this does not hinder us from adopting anyone of them as a rule or motive or excuse for something we wish to do, or that we have done. "Too many cooks spoil the broth," is offset by, "In a multitude of counselors there is wisdom." "Two of a trade never agree" flies in the face of "Like pleases like." "A rolling stone gathers no moss," and "A new pasture makes fat sheep," are opposed; so are "Let well-enough alone," and "If to-day be poor,

to-morrow is rich;" "Delays are dangerous," and "Wisdom lies in waiting;" "A little learning is a dangerous thing," and "It is better to know something than nothing;" and so with any number of aphorisms. It is convenient, however, to forget the other side of a question when we want to be directed by the side running parallel with our interest. Consequently, we take what we like as monition or augury, and, for the time being, consider the unwelcome as the unrighteous. To have a proverb at our back, when we incline to a course of meanness or injustice, seems, if not to acquit our conscience, at least to mitigate our offense. We try to believe – and we often succeed in believing – that we can never go entirely wrong while some musty adage covers our behavior. We obey our own will, and throw the responsibility on a seductive saying.

Titles like "Conflicts of Experience" (1890), "Twilight of the Proverbs" (1930), "Parallel Proverbs" (1964), and "Dueling Proverbs" (1992 and 1993) are clear indications that popular writers enjoy pointing out the existence of contradictory (dueling) proverbs, dismissing them far too quickly as useless bits of wisdom. But there are also those claims that proverbs contain statements that are no longer true in the modern age and that they deserve to be or should be on their way out. This rejection of proverbs is clearly signaled in such titles as "Our Toothless Old Saws" (1954), "Are Proverbs Nuggets of Truth or Fool's Gold?" (1988), "Down with Slogans" (1994), "Why Old Proverbs Don't Apply Anymore" (1994), and "The Upside-Down World – When Maxims Mislead" (2005). These and other texts argue against the usefulness of proverbs, but by couching the tirades into humorous or satirical language, there appears to be an unexpressed undercurrent of the fact that proverbs as distilled wisdom will not disappear.

In fact, there are quite a few authors who delight in explaining the origin and meaning of proverbs and proverbial expressions to their readers, thus acknowledging that there is ample interest among the folk to find out more about the metaphors they so often employ automatically without paying any attention to their source, language, and form. Essays like "Clichés – Words of Wisdom on Sayings Like `Raining Cats and Dogs'" (1987), "So They Say ... Finding a Grain of Truth in Old Wives' Tales" (1991), "Dead

Metaphor Society – Colorful Phrases Linger; but Those Who Can Understand Them Are Becoming Scarce as Hen's Teeth" (1995), "Clichés Are Here to Stay – Tired Phrases Put Talkers on Common Ground" (2001), and "'Put a Sock in It!' Wacky, Worn Phrases ... Where Did They Start?" (2004) present interesting mini-etymologies on metaphorical phrases in common use. It is hard to imagine that magazine and newspaper readers would not enjoy these texts explaining some of their favorite expressions! There are, of course, many scholarly and popular books on the market that do the same, but it is the mass media that spreads all of this far and wide. And, to be sure, there is also the internet with its answers for almost any conceivable question. Little wonder then, that the final sentence of the last short essay entitled "Say What?" (2006) states: "For definitions of difficult phrases, go to www.realsimple.com/phrases."

Publishers of magazines and newspapers appear to agree with their popular (free lance) writers that the folk out there loves pieces on proverbs. They are certainly willing to print lists of them that have been obtained from informants, as for example in "Mom's Old Sayings Still Remembered and Quoted" (1993), "Chewing the Rag – Vermonters Say It Right" (1995), and "Getting a Grasp on Idioms" (2006). They are also more than willing to print proverbs from other languages and cultures to illustrate how different their metaphors and worldviews are. Care should, however, be taken that such articles don't draw stereotypical or chauvinistic conclusions, as was the case with a piece on "Japanese Proverbs Apt – They Are Held to Have Had Some Bearing on the War" (1941) that appeared in *The New York Times* during World War II. Some other more or less innocuous articles on the wisdom of other nationalities include "It's a Long March That Has No Turning" (1975; on the Chinese wisdom sayings by Mao Tse-Tung), "Russia's Book of Proverbs – Must Reading for Arms Negotiators" (1985), "Hebrew to Her is Greek to Me" (1997; on French-Canadian proverbs in Montreal), "Proverbial Wisdom" (1998; on African proverbs), and "Not-so-Ancient Chinese Proverb: Glib Truisms Gloss Over Reality" (1999; dealing with the difficulty of translating Chinese proverbs).

There are also articles on the (lack of) knowledge of proverbs and proverbial phrases, as for example "Age-Old Proverbs That Ring a Bell – And Some That We Don't Recall So Well" (1985) or "Too Many Cooks Mix a Metaphor – As My Mom Never Said"

(1988). With the apparent decline of cultural literacy even in such basic matters as proverbs, it should not be surprising to find some reports that discuss how metaphorical language is taught in schools, among them "[Proverb] Tests Help Pupils: (a) Acquire Words, (b) Become Verbose" (1965) and "Fifth-Graders Find Fun in Proverbs." However, some teachers in Toronto definitely took political correctness a bit too far in trying to change the wording of some harmless phrases, as can be seen from a report on "Teachers Aim to Clean up Clichés" (1994). Manipulating or parodying proverbs for a bit of linguistic humor and also in an attempt to find new proverbs based on old structures makes considerably more sense, as is evident from three articles that must have entertained thousands of readers, quite surely also leading them to create their own anti-proverbs: "The Proverbial Dilemma" (1993), "Fractured Epithets Abound" (1995), and "Proverbial Punch Line – Scrambled Sayings Express Our Satirical, Humorous Sides" (2003).

But not all of the sixty-four popular essays included in this volume are humorous or satirical reactions to the limitations of proverbial lore. There are also plenty of positive articles that do look at proverbs from a more balanced point of view, dealing with questions of definition, origin, history, distribution, use, function, meaning, etc. Titles like "The Art of Proverbs: An Evaluation of the Minds – Wary and Illusionless – that Have Created the World's Wisdom" (1965), "The Wild Flowers of Thought" (1969), "Wisdom of the Tribe – Why Proverbs Are Better Than Aphorisms" (1983), "Words of Wisdom" (1989), "It Never Rains But It Pours! Discovering English Proverbs" (1992), "Words to Live by, or at Least Ponder" (1992), "Speaking of Language – Proverbs are Pithy Purveyors of Wisdom" (1995), "Let's Hear It for the Lowly Sound Bite" (1996), "Words We Live By: What Do Proverbs Really Mean to Us?" (2003), and "Counting Chickens, Milking Cats: The World's Timeless Proverbs Offer Great Wisdom – Which We Sometimes Turn into Folly" (2004) all point to discussions of proverbs and proverbial expressions that stress their continued value as metaphorical expressions based on generational wisdom and expressive language. And to be sure, there are also a few essays in which journalists report on the publications of paremiologists, with the authors having discussed various aspects of proverb research with leading scholars. Reports on "A Proverbial Quest That Intrigues Scholars" (1975), "The Proverbial Collector"

(1992), and "A Proverb Each Day Keeps this Scholar at Play" (1992) all refer to serious probes into the work of proverb scholars, once again explaining the significance of proverbs as signs of human life and communication.

What all of the essays included in this volume show is that proverbs, no matter whether interpreted negatively or positively, are part of the verbal and social interchange among people. They are true "monumenta humana", metaphorical signs of human life, and they will continue to be part of our communicative strategies. Even if at times their value and appropriateness in certain contexts might indeed be questioned or negated, we are still governed by their insights to a certain degree. While some proverbs do disappear from the basic repertoire due to their antiquated values or archaic language, others remain timeless in their wisdom and applicability. And, we must not forget that new proverbs continue to be created, a fact that is often forgotten by those who criticize traditional proverbs. Old and new proverbs and their wisdom confront us every day, and proverb scholars would do well to pay more attention to the present survival and creation of proverbs. Above all, paremiologists can learn much from such popular discussions as presented in this book of essays from magazines and newspapers. They reflect far better than serious scholarship what the people think and make of proverbs as ubiquitous expressions of collective wisdom. While proverbs are not universal truths, they are most certainly appropriate as general guideposts for mastering life's joys and challenges.

We would like to thank David Busker, Peter Daley, Alan Dundes, David Howell, Barbara Mieder, Keith Monley, Ann Park, Karl-Ludwig Selig, Beverly Skinner, Hannelore Spence, Patricia Turner, and Jared Wood for sending us some of the articles included in this volume. The publication of this book was made possible by the much-appreciated financial support of our former student Keir Kleinknecht and his family foundation, Gertraud and Jerry Jacobson, and Hank Schaefer, whose interest in our work and the University of Vermont is indeed exemplary.

Fall 2006   Wolfgang Mieder and Janet Sobieski

Influence of Proverbs (1877)

Anonymous

The harm done by proverbs, maxims, saws, and catch-phrases, is wholly beyond calculation. They are never quite true, though they are always plausible; they generally contain a fallacy of some sort, and one which it is pleasant to ignore. They are well qualified to deceive, and most of us are very willing to be deceived by them; for, in respect to deception, we are likely to meet them half way. A proverb has been defined as the wit of one and the wisdom of many; it is oftener the sophistry of a few and the unreason of the multitude. The great trouble with a popular adage, or current phrase of any kind, is, that it is commonly accepted as absolute truth. Hardly any one thinks of examining or questioning it; for has it not already received the approval of thousands, if not of generations? It must be sound, especially if it fits our case. It commends itself, mainly by sparing us the trouble of reflection, which is always a relief, even to the most intelligent. Man is a reasoning animal, and, being assured of the fact, he deems it unnecessary to prove it by his practice.

We are well enough aware that there are maxims to suit all tastes and tempers; that some affirm what others deny; that frequently they are direct contradictions. But this does not hinder us from adopting anyone of them as a rule or motive or excuse for something we wish to do, or that we have done. "Too many cooks spoil the broth," is offset by, "In a multitude of counselors there is wisdom." "Two of a trade never agree" flies in the face of "Like pleases like." "A rolling stone gathers no moss," and "A new pasture makes fat sheep," are opposed; so are "Let well-enough alone," and "If to-day be poor, to-morrow is rich;" "Delays are dangerous," and "Wisdom lies in waiting;" "A little learning is a dangerous thing," and "It is better to know something than nothing;" and so with any number of aphorisms. It is convenient, however, to forget the other side of a question when we want to be directed by the side running parallel with our interest. Consequently, we take what we like as monition or augury, and, for the time being, consider the unwelcome as the unrighteous. To have a proverb at our back, when we incline to a course of meanness or injustice, seems, if not to acquit our conscience, at least to mitigate our offense. We try to believe – and we often succeed in believing – that we can never go entirely wrong while

9

some musty adage covers our behavior. We obey our own will, and throw the responsibility on a seductive saying.

"Let me make the songs of a people, and I care not who makes the laws," has been worn threadbare. If any man could make the proverbs of a nation, he could better afford to be indifferent to the laws; for those would have more potency than these. Proverbs cause human conduct; laws merely regulate it. They are greater moral agencies than is suspected, and any amount of mischief might directly be traced to them as a source. Once expressed, they refuse to perish; they may fade out of mind and use for a time; but they are sure to grow fresh and find favor again. The maxims of MACHIAVELLI, especially those in *The Prince*, corrupted politically half of mediaeval Europe, and the great pages of pointed cynicism which ROCHEFOUCAULD wrote established his reputation, and to this day serve us with excuses for selfishness. Put your thought into an epigram, spice it with ill-nature, and it will keep longer than any plain and pleasant truth. And thousands who are yet unborn will quote you as an endorser of their sins; perhaps thank you for a pretext to avoid their self-contempt.

Who can estimate the political evil MARCY wrought by declaring that "To the victors belong the spoils." That simple phrase has done more to debauch American politics in this generation than any amount of malfeasance in office. It has come to be regarded as a political right, and has until recently defeated every effort of civil service reform. No intelligent or honest mind believes the principle right; it is impossible not to see, on every hand, the ill effects of its adoption; yet the mass of politicians accept it practically and echo it heartily as a party cry, as an apology for party corruption.

How many times a day do we hear, "The world owes every man a living?" The persons that quote this are usually those who owe, not those to whom anything is owed. Their world is apt to be any kind-hearted or credulous soul they can dupe or borrow from, without any thought of return. Does the world stand so largely indebted? It owes a living to those who work, and are willing to work, and they well-nigh invariably get the living. But it does not owe a living to the sluggards and tricksters from whose lips the phrase most frequently falls. They expect to lie under trees and have fruit fall into their hands; they count themselves privileged to eat the bread which others have earned. They

10

are distinctly the men to whom the world is under no obligations whatever, whom it can well spare, but who won't be spared.

What a monstrous proverb is "All is fair in love and war!" As respects war, perhaps any kind of deception or stratagem is warranted, because one knows the enemy will resort to any means for success, and because artifice is a recognized part of military science. But in love nothing is fair except perfect sincerity and truth; love rests on faith, and to deal dishonestly with love is doubly a crime. Love and war have no connection save figuratively; they are antipodes; they are contradictions. Love comes from love; war comes from hate; and to say they should be treated alike is to exhaust iniquity. The author of the adage could never have known the meaning of love, else he would not have so invited its destruction.

The seeds of deceit, injustice, falsehood, are thickly scattered through many proverbs, and repetition turns them to noxious flower. "Base is the slave who pays;" "Time was made for slaves;" "Silence gives consent;" "Once makes not a habit;" "Young saint, old devil;" "Still waters run deep," and hundreds of others are applied and interpreted mischievously. Be ware of tho man who skulks behind proverbs!

The New York Times (April 29, 1877), p. 6.

Conflicts of Experience (1890)

H.G. Keene

Persons who accept Lord John Russell's definition of a proverb must sometimes be puzzled to find that one and the same community is in the habit of using adages which are diametrically opposed to one another, If it were true that a proverb is the wisdom of the many and the wit of one, we should surely be justified in expecting all accepted proverbs to resemble laws of nature or formulas of mathematics. But we see that this is far from being the case; and no sooner do we think that we have obtained an irrefragable maxim from the crystallization of experience than another, equally authoritative, confronts us with an absolutely opposite direction.

"Take care of the pence, and the pounds will take care of themselves," is a traditional rule that must have been quoted many millions of times by persons disposed to economy. Its principle is reinforced in the proverbial philosophy of other nations besides our own. "Little streams make large rivers," say the French, and the Scots match them with "Many a little makes a mickle." English domestic economists declare that "A pin a day is a groat a year," though it may be doubted whether there was ever a community in which fourpence *per annum* was held a commensurate return for the trouble of stooping to the daily pin. Yet, after we have digested all this mass of concurrent testimony, it is not a little baffling to be checked in our decision by an equally respectable body of evidence which tells us that we must not be "Penny wise and pound foolish." For if a careful husbandry of copper in the integer leads to an idiotic treatment of two hundred and forty pence in the aggregate, where is the wisdom of leaving the pounds to take care of themselves?

"More haste less speed," is one of our English expressions of caution as to the dangers of precipitation. The Hindu has put the same thought in various shapes, after his concrete manner; one of these is, "He took off his shoes before he came to the ford." "He who goes slow has long to go (*Chi va piano va lontano*)," says the melodious Italian; and neither in India nor in Italy does there appear to be much danger from superfluous energy. But our forefathers seem to have been aware of the opposite risk, and to have provided a number of countervailing maxims. Such, for example,

12

are "Take time by the forelock," "Delays are dangerous," "Time and tide for no man bide."

Nowhere is this contradictory tendency more seen than in those sayings which partake of the nature of aphorisms. Aphorisms, if we may trust to etymology, are the marking off or delimitation of experience from the confused reasonings of careless minds. "Use is second nature" has been often cited as an excuse for persons who are opposed to change. Yet many opposite sayings remind us that men love novelty and will welcome "anything for a change."

In Archbishop Whately's edition of Bacon's essays is collected an abundance of saws that the philosophic chancellor had put together under the title of "Antitheta." Ranged in parallel columns we find these conflicting maxims at the foot of the more important papers. Thus, on the subject last mentioned, the following are amongst the "Antitheta" appended to the "Essay of Innovations."

> Time is the great innovator; why then do we not imitate time?

> What innovator imitates time, who so insinuates his innovations that they escape notice?

Here the reformer says plainly that we should imitate time who is the great reformer; while the conservative answers that no reformer can do so, for the reason that time's reforms are imperceptible. A singular commentary on which is given in the essay itself to which these texts are appended. "For otherwise," says Bacon, "if men do not follow the gentle example of time's innovations, whatsoever is new is unlooked for, and ever it mends some and impairs others; and he that is holpen takes it for a fortune and thanks the time; and he that is hurt for a wrong and imputeth it to the author." We are reminded that Bacon stood at the parting of the ways, when the Tudor monarchy had done its work and was perishing in the feeble hands of the first Stuart.

It is unknown from what source Bacon derived the greater portion of these maxims. But, in the authentic deliverances of the philosophers and poets one meets with similar conflicts. A French writer has said that he is able to reconcile two of such utterances: namely, the saying of Tacitus, "The unknown always passes for the marvellous (*Omne ignotum pro magnifico*);" and that of Ovid, "No one cares about the unknown (*Ignoti nulla cupido*);" and evidently there is a sense in which both are true. A due synthesis of such apparently opposite maxims will result, not in a mutual cancelment, but in a composite principle. For men may not desire the unknown yet may admire it when it comes under their observation, when it ceases to be unknown. But there are more startling contradictions to be found in the recorded experience of very great men. When Juvenal conceived his magnificent defiance of fortune he was so pleased with it that he used it twice, each time in the same words. The most familiar and appropriate use is, no doubt, in the grand passage which concludes the tenth satire on the vanity of our wishes. The passage has been translated by Dryden and imitated by Johnson, but neither of those masculine and skilful writers has done justice to Juvenal's meaning. And, what is still more unfortunate, the text itself is unsettled. According to one reading the satirist meant to say: "If one has wisdom one has every deity on one's side." According to the other he says to Fortune: "Thou hast no authority where wisdom is," *i.e.*, it is only the fool who wants luck to befriend him. Great as the difference is, the two readings agree in this, that prudence is worth more than luck; and this is, manifestly, a salutary principle. The difficulty is to reconcile it with such a saying as "Fortune favors the brave," or with the still more audacious law of Bonaparte, "Providence is on the side of the big battalions." One tells us that strength is the criterion and cause of success, the other puts it in wisdom. We think of Horace and his "Mere brute force perishes by its own strength (*Vis concili expers mole ruit sua*)." Athens of old drove in ignominious flight the mighty hosts of Xerxes. Clive at Plassy and elsewhere puffed away the big battalions of Asia with a handful of men formed by European discipline, Wellington, with a force of thirty thousand British troops, pushed the hosts of Napoleon's own marshals out of the peninsula and across the Pyrenees. Here, also, there may be a synthesis such as was supposed in the last case, but it is far from obvious.

Even more irreconcilable appears the conflict if we understand Juvenal's saying in a still deeper sense. Suppose that he meant more than either of the above interpretations, and that his view implied not merely that the wise man had no luck because he had no need for it, but that the weak and foolish had chances without which they could not prosper, or even exist? There is no doubt a specious reasonableness about such a proposition; and it is more than ever opposed to the counter-maxims.

14

No one has contributed more to the aphoristic treasures of his country than Shakespeare. In at least one instance he has supplied a saying upon what, though noticed elsewhere, had never received due notice in English. The saying occurs in "Romeo and Juliet," where we are told that "He jests at scars who never felt a wound." This goes to the very foundation of human sympathy as described by Aristotle; showing that it is only those who have suffered who can really feel for the suffering of others. Our countrymen, as a race, have not been of sufficiently tender mood to trouble themselves over this question enough to make it into a proverb; it was left for gentle Shakespeare to find them a household word on sympathy and its true source. They have been mostly content with sayings that have strengthened their natural hardness; such as, "Keep your breath to cool your own porridge," or (in the most modern form), "Paddle your own canoe." The Hindus, however, have a couplet, as pertinent if not as poetical as the line from Romeo, which may be thus rendered:

Whose heels have never cracked in sun-baked fields,
How can he know what pain my heel-crack yields?

This is almost an equivalent of the truth conveyed in Dido's words: "We must suffer before we can learn to sympathize with suffering (*Haud ignara mali, miseris succurrere disco*)."

There are few proverbs of more wide acceptance than the maxim *Esse quam videre*, showing us the vanity of imposture, but teaching a more subtle lesson still. To be what you seem would indeed be but a poor expedient if what you seem is bad; and it would almost be better, like Johnson, to have nothing of the bear but the skin. An old gentleman, of more wit than manners, is reported to have given a happy turn to the adage. In rebuking the self-assertion of a young Mr. Carr who was boasting of his sincerity, our friend blustered out the following impromptu:

Be what you seem's a good old rule,
You bear it out, my Carr!
You look a most infernal fool,
And so, by G –, you are.

Thus, too, we are bidden to admire him whose "bark is worse than his bite," and so forth. Perhaps the deepest, kindliest, thing on this topic is a remark which was quoted from Fénelon in Diderot's "Hor. Subsc." 2, 129: "Simplicity is the rectitude of a soul which refuses all return to itself and its doings. Many persons are sincere without being simple. They do not want to pass for more than they are, but fear to pass for what they are not. The real simplicity is to have lost the 'I' which causes so much jealousy." Whether this absolute simplicity of the soul that "refuses all return upon itself" is a grace or a weakness may well be discussed. In any case there must always be good men and women who find it easy not to pass for what they are not, but not easy to renounce the fear of being taken for what they are not.

Among Shakespeare's aphorisms another well-known line reminds us that "Uneasy lies the head that wears a crown." This was a king's opinion, while among the oracles of the people were such sayings as "Happy as a king," and the like, showing admiration and envy of royal privileges. Yet we need not go back to Shakespeare's kings for evidence of the peculiar sorrows and cares of regal state. The death of Charles the First, the overthrow of his son James, the fate of several czars of Russia, the miseries of Louis the Sixteenth and his consort, and the tremendous vicissitudes of our current century, and even of its most recent years, are full of matter to justify the poet. If we look back only to the lifetime of persons still young, we cannot but be struck by the tragedies in which heads have fallen which seemed held high above the common chances of humanity. In 1868 the writer of these sentences saw the imperial family of France in the saloons of the Tuileries; the emperor with his cold blue eyes and face of inexpressive reserve, the empress beautiful and splendid, leading her boy by the hand. In a few years the emperor had been defeated, deposed, and had died by a cruel death in a strange land; the empress, bowed beneath the weight of an untimely age, was mourning in exile for her husband and for the brave lad slain in a foreign quarrel. Think of the sufferings of Maximilian in Mexico, the cares of the czar Alexander the Second – each ending in a bloody and public death; the mysterious scene on the shores of the Bavarian lake; the assassination of two American presidents; the protracted agony of the late emperor Frederick; the sorrows of the house of Hapsburg ending – for the present – in the unrevealed horror of the shooting-box at Meyerling!

Do those who have passed through such furnaces of affliction look back on their brighter days with pain? Dante says so, in the memorable lines attributed to Francesca di Rimini which our own poet has adopted, in "Locksley Hall:"

This is truth the poet sings,
That a sorrow's crown of sorrow is remembering happier
   things.

Is it so indeed ? Or are those right who say with Horace:

Cras vel atra
Nube polum pater occupato
Vel sole puro; non tamen irritum
Quodcunque retro est efficiet?

Dryden's masculine paraphrase will be remembered:

Not heaven itself over the past has power,
For what has been has been, and I have had my hour.

This conflicting doctrine – that the memory of past joy is a
possession and not a pain – has been maintained by Alfred de
Musset, a man whose pleasures and pains had been of a less digni-
fied kind than Dante's, but to whom nevertheless joy and sorrow
had been equally known. De Musset does not content himself with
a mere counterstatement; he challenges Dante in plain words and
with a personal appeal.

Why saidst thou, Dante, that 'tis grief's worst sting
To tell, in sorrow, of past happiness?
What spasm from thee that bitter cry could wring,
That insult to distress?
Is then the light less certain or less glad,
And – when night falls – forgotten in the gloom
Is it from thee, Spirit sublimely sad!
From thee; we have such doom?
No! by the splendor of yon rising moon,
Not from thy heart a blasphemy so void:
A happy memory is a truer boon
For life, than bliss enjoyed.

And to Francesca – angel of thy glory –
Thou couldst assign a sentence such us this,
She who broke off, to tell her tragic story,
From an eternal kiss.

For me, I only say, Here, for an hour,
A day, I loved, was loved, and she was fair;

Close to my heart I press the faded flower,
And Death shall find it there.

These stanzas, from the poem written on his rupture with George Sand, show that De Musset regarded past joy quite otherwise than did Dante. He treasured it as a possession, while the older and graver author lamented it as a loss. It cannot be even said that the words *nella miseria* are left out, as in Lord Tennyson's reference. The English poet has undoubtedly weakened the thought; it is not the memory of past joy alone, but its memory in the midst of present suffering, that, according to the great Florentine, makes the woe. But De Musset is earnest and sincere, where Lord Tennyson is but an artist. He expressly includes the Dantean condition, wanting which indeed the plaint is little but a phrase, a commonplace "of little meaning though the words be strong." The difference between the modern Frenchman and the medieval Italian is a deliberate opposition of temperament.

In this fluctuating world all that men can do will barely avail to establish for them a compromise with the unheeding forces about them which, for want of a better word, they are wont to term nature. Hence they learn to encourage and organize a counteracting force for their own use and protection; and the social army fortifies itself with proverbs. They are not infallible weapons; when one breaks the combatants have to betake themselves to another. As the witty and sagacious Whately has pointed out, a proverb will usually be merely a compendious expression of some principle, true or false, applicable or non-applicable, as the case may be in which it is employed. "When, then, a proverb is introduced," says the archbishop, "the speaker employs it as a major premise, and is understood to imply, as a minor, that the principle thus referred to is applicable in the existing case."

It is much the same with the great writers whose conclusions pass into the rank of our household words. When a poet, in his criticism of life, appears to have generalized his wide and kindly observation into a rule of conduct, he must not be regarded as upon his oath. He only means to say that, in given conditions, certain results may be expected to follow. He is a prophet of contingent predictions. Or, we may say, he is a wise judge fully conscious of the fallacy of inapplicable precedents.

Living Age, 185 (May 24, 1890), pp. 483-486.

Proverbs and Popular Similes (1929)

Vernon Rendall

"Have at you with a proverb!" says a servant in one of the dullest of Shakespeare's comedies. But the time has long gone by since a proverb could be regarded as an effective weapon. It is a broad generalization for a world which has become far too subtle to believe in such things, knowing that circumstances alter cases, and that the infinite and mysterious complexity of life cannot be circumscribed by any formula. A man of spirit, even if he be-lieve in proverbs for most people, will feel that he is above them himself, the bright exception to make the general experience look ridiculous. James Howell pleaded:

> The people's voice the voice of God we call;
> And what are proverbs but the people's voice,
> Coined first and current made by common choice?
> Then sure they must have weight and truth withal.

Confronted with the blunders and humbugs of democracy, we cannot be so sure, and certainly the wit claimed for proverbs is gone. Perhaps they were felt to be witty in the days of Solo-mon or Aesop, but now they are stale beyond words, lacking ei-ther surprise or brilliance. Who ever paused over the warning of a proverb? The next minute, if he had a fairly good head, he might think of another that contradicted it. The man of fashion, according to Chesterfield, never uses a proverb, and the clever world, seeing the futility of these guides to wisdom, gained for a while some notice by distorting them. "Nothing succeeds like excess" and "Virtue is its own punishment" had a considerable run and may still be heard. But the good old proverb as an attrac-tive addition to the literary menu is no more prized than the good old pun. Epigram and paradox have taken their place, and the wise have realized that poets, not gnomic writers, are the ideal interpreters of life. Where the proverb does survive with us, it is for a touch of fancy and an unusual setting provided by foreign examples. "No one knows," say the Arabs, "what the camel thinks of the camel-driver." That is not really a new or deep thought, but it pleases because it is so quaintly expressed.

The Far East is even more attractive with personal touches and an adornment of detail which the English mind, hating rheto-

19

ric, and loving brevity, does not reach. What Englishman could have made this proverbial?

> Although mankind number a million millions, and although the desert of Shant-Tzi be boundless, yet here did Li-Hing encounter his mother-in-law.

The familiar English stock might have been made by a collaboration between Benjamin Franklin, Samuel Smiles and Martin Tupper. This general judgment is not disturbed by a collection [i.e., G.L. Apperson, *English Proverbs and Proverbial Phrases. A Historical Dictionary*. London: Dent, 1929] made by a learned antiquary which has taken years to gather and which shows that, if proverbs have gone out of fashion, they have abundant interest historically. Mr. Apperson does not confine himself to didactic sentences but also includes stereotyped metaphors and familiar similes. The abundant display of examples, following a saying down the centuries, notes where a great writer has helped to keep a proverb alive. We warm over a reference to Goldsmith's Vicar or Byron's Letters, and in particular thank the compiler for good rustic stuff, local phrases which have the unspoilt vigour of George Herbert or old Fuller. London is not England, and the country has preserved much that is better than copy-book maxims, though unknown to urban speech. In rural Oxfordshire forty years since the shrewd proverb was current, "It's the fox that spouts." When someone in a company is guilty and no one will speak, the guilty man betrays himself by talking too much, clever though he may think his tactics.

Great and homely writers, Shakespeare, Scott, Dickens, have preserved proverbial lore. To Scott especially the language owes much. Thus he took up Hamlet's "Yeoman's service" and made it familiar English. In general, English maxims are full of prudential morality, largely concerned with the weather. The Scottish proverbs have more salt, 'Rob Roy' alone is a mine of them. Mr. Apperson has delved there for "It's ill taking the breeks off a Hielandman" but not for "Every wight has his weird." Scottish independence breaks away from the standardized English of schoolmasters and journalists. It is some years since a writer or speaker has been able to give currency to a new proverb, or even choose a good old one. Tennyson is, perhaps, the latest writer to add to the popular stock. Within a few line of his 'Morte d'Arthur' come

20

The old order changeth, yielding place to new,

which is classic enough to be perpetually misquoted, and

More things are wrought by prayer
Than this world dreams of.

The Bible is a great source of proverbs, but when "To the pure all things are pure" is cited, few today think of St. Paul. This collection does not show how much that ardent Apostle has contributed to English with the "thorn in the flesh," the "forty stripes save one," the "labour of love," and that trenchant command to the Thessalonians about working before you eat which has been forgotten by a self-indulgent democracy.

The type of expression presented by "As good as gold" is obsolescent but goes to the very heart of the English people, revealing its limitations and real interests. "As clear as mud" is a rare example of humour. "As dead as a doornail" seems an odd saying, as Dickens notes in the passage cited. It refers to the cold feel of iron, and Shakespeare supplies the clue when the corpse of Henry VI is addressed as "Poor key-cold figure of a holy king!" These "Intensifying Similes" have been studied by a Swedish scholar. They hint what more than eight solid pages of this collection confirm: That our forefathers were very concerned about the Devil. Sport in modern times takes the prominent position, and we miss here "not cricket," which a German explainer of London idioms once sadly misinterpreted as "no light affair." It is essentially an English phrase which could hardly be current across the Atlantic.

Foreign sources have not, apart from Greek and Latin, contributed much to the English stock. Schiller's "Against stupidity the very gods fight in vain" has had some run, and Carlyle brought in "Speech is silvern, silence golden," compressing the said silence, as Lord Morley remarked, in thirty-five volumes.

The ancient classics are treated by Mr. Apperson as fairly as one can hope for today. Trimalchio with his "Quod non expectes, ex transverso fit" was of the same opinion as Disraeli about the unexpected, but neither, so far as we can see, has been included. "Virtue is the only true nobility" is a direct rendering of Juvenal, and surely Horace should have been credited with *aurea mediocritas*, which is the "golden mean." He is quoted for "Between the devil and the deep sea," but the real Latin parallel is "Inter sacrum saxumque stare," to "stand between the victim and the

21

stone knife," which takes one back to the earliest rites of Rome. There is the spiritual home of England, with the brevity, practical sense, good fighting qualities and stoicism which distinguish English proverbs and the English character. For poetry, grace and fancy one must look elsewhere. They would be – to quote a rare exception to the national stolidity – "as welcome as flowers in May."

The Saturday Review (October 19, 1929), p. 443.

Proverbs are old going back to Greek + Latin, so they no longer apply

Twilight of the Proverbs (1930)

Anonymous

Science and civilization are hard on old proverbs. Some of them cut a sorry figure in the modern world. It is a wonder that the cynics and realists have not noted their demise.

"Two's company, three's a crowd." there's a mid-Victorian for you! We moderns recognize the triangle as part of the accepted order.

"Rain before seven, clear before eleven." A very loose and inaccurate statement. It all depends on whether you are talking of Standard Time of Daylight Saving.

"As honest as the day is long." But how honest is that if the earth slows up a little sometimes, as the astronomers maintain? Perhaps a man who stole only a few hundred dollars a year would qualify.

Even *tempus fugit* has fallen on evil days. Some of the experts say it just slips around the corner and comes back again.

If that is so, there is at least one proverb that should continue in good standing. Two-way time is certain to give new meaning and force to "All's well that ends well."

The New York Times (May 3, 1930), p. 18.

Old proverbs become
out dated due to science +
changes in civilization

Japanese Proverbs Apt –
They Are Held to Have Had Some Bearing on the War (1941)

Henry F. Woods

Like all peoples of ancient origin, the Japanese have a wealth of proverbs. Homely expressions of the wisdom born of experience, the superstitions, cynicisms, prejudices and popular fallacies, they illustrate the folkways of a people probably better than anything else could. Especially do they provide an insight into the national psychology of the Japanese, and in some instances serve to explain in a measure their engagement in the present war and their manner of launching it upon us.

Among many of their proverbs are several which are peculiarly expressive of their racial philosophy. Some of them are oddly at variance with the principles of Bushido, the knightly ethical code of the Samurai, which is still honored in Japan. In their cynicism some of these popular aphorisms run counter to Bushido's cardinal teachings of honor and truthfulness. This might be puzzling were it not that Bushido also teaches that revenge is desirable and not incompatible with conceptions of honorable conduct.

To the occidental mind, shocked and bewildered by the perfidy and treachery, of a nation whose envoys were speaking formal words of peace almost at the very moment their government was raining death and destruction on the people to whose government they were accredited, at least one of their proverbs may be enlightening. "Who can speak well can lie well," it runs.

Good Job of Lying

How well they lied is attested by the havoc they wrought in Pearl Harbor. Their fortifications of the mandated islands of the Pacific, explained away by lying words, also prove how they took to heart the import of the proverb, which itself is a callous recognition of the advantage of craft and deceit in gaining their ends. That it has a place in their folk sayings is a justification of the distrust felt by occidentals of the surface politeness of the Japanese. That they themselves discount the lip service that has come to be associated with them as a racial characteristic is shown by another of their proverbs, "Too much courtesy is discourtesy."

By now the people of Japan, wearied of the interminable "China Incident," must have realized the truth of yet another of

24

their proverbs. "A journey of a thousand miles begins with one step" perfectly describes how the fateful clash at Marco Polo Bridge some four years ago was the step that began the long journey filled with tragic and inevitable consequences.

"It is difficult to be strong and not rash," a truth apparent to the common people of Japan and incorporated by them in their store of folk sayings, seems to have conveyed no warning to their rulers and the military class. Since their easy victories over the Russians in 1904, when for the first time they began to regard themselves as a world power, they have exulted in their strength, forgetting or defying the caution against rashness.

harmful when not paid attention too

In their power-intoxicated course Japan's rulers have overlooked yet another of their national proverbs that should have given them pause. It runs: "At the first cup man drinks wine; at the second cup wine drinks wine; at the third cup wine drinks man." It is as applicable to the dangers inherent in their rulers' mad course as it is to the folly of overindulgence in the fruit of the vine.

Bushido teaches rectitude and justice, hut an ancient Japanese saying is that "He that steals gold is put in prison; he that steals land is made a king." Japan's rulers seem to have chosen to ignore the proverb's moralistic import and to have adopted it for its realistic truth.

Probable Genesis of War

If the genesis of this war is sought it is probably to be found in their proverb that declares, "Cold tea and cold rice may be endured, but not cold looks and words." We know, of course, that the immediate cause is the aggressive policy of Japan athwart which the democratic powers stand. But Japan's war upon us has been long brewing and that against Britain only a little shorter time. She has never forgiven us the slight put upon her by our exclusion laws, nor has she been able to forgive Britain for the refusal to renew the treaty of alliance with her.

Japan not able to forgive

Nursing her revenge, she allied herself with evil companions. In joining hands with the two men most execrated in the world today. Japan's rulers have been indifferent alike to the judgment of history and to that native proverb that declares, "A man's character depends upon whether his friends are good or bad."

our proverbs prone they're bad

However indifferent her rulers may be to the good opinion of the world, they would be wise to ponder, on purely materialistic grounds if no other, the homely wisdom expressed in their folk

25

saying, "He who hunts two horses leaves one and loses the other." In coveting the mastery of all Asia and seeking to possess it, Japan is hunting not one but a whole herd of horses. A calm appraisal of the mighty forces now arrayed against her should enable her to see that she stands to lose all – what she has and what she seeks to acquire.

If that shall come to pass, Japan's rulers will be in a position to appreciate the truth packed in a single sentence phrased by her people: "Man learns little from victory, but much from defeat."

[Letter to the editor: New York, December 24, 1941]

The New York Times (December 28, 1941), p. E6.

Proverbs should be trusted and considered, as they contain wisdom that will keep you from getting in over your heads. The Japs are bad ppl b/c they didn't listen

Our Toothless Old Saws (1954)

Scott Corbett

Our old saws are fast disappearing under the impact of modern engineering magic. A lot of them don't cut much ice any more. *[haha I use that]*

I am speaking of old saws such as "People who love in glass houses shouldn't throw stones." Nobody would think of going around repeating an adage like that today. Modern structural glass has made it obsolete. People who live in glass houses now may throw all the stones they want to, safe in the knowledge that their dwelling units' building materials are 20.4 times tougher than ordinary old-fashioned materials. The Glass Housing Institute of America, a nonprofit research organization supported by the Glass Manufacturers of America, has proved that people in glass houses can throw up to 45 per cent more stones than people in frame houses, with perfect impunity. *[new tech removes meaning from proverb]*

Another old saw which is definitely out of key with our present period of gracious living is the one which refers to "the pot calling the kettle black." Black pots and kettles are a thing of the past. Anyone who has seen five minutes of TV knows that. Just a touch with any of a dozen miracle scouring pads assisted by one of the countless miracle cleaning powders carried by your friendly neighborhood grocer and all that unpleasant blackness is whisked away down the drain. Today's housewife would not put up with a black pot long enough for it to call anybody anything.

Take, too, the assertion once uttered so confidently, that "you can't make a silk purse out of a sow's ear." Laughable today. Modern engineering magic would merely reduce the sow's ear to its chemical components, and out of them would come Sowcron, a new miracle fabric for purses which would be even finer than ordinary silk and give up to nine times as much wear. *[replace materials]*

Prominent among those products of modern engineering magic that have taken the edge off so many old saws are radio and TV. To mention but one, they have disproved conclusively the ancient misconception which holds that "silence is golden." Nobody is making any money out of silence these days.

To TV alone, however, must go the credit for sending into the discard our final example: "Seeing is believing."

Atlantic Monthly, 193 (March 1954), p. 92.

[new tech takes meaning out of proverbs]

27

A Proverb in the Hand – Is Often Worth a Thousand Words: Herewith an Examination of a Much Used But Seldom Analyzed Form of Homely Literature (1959)

Horace Reynolds

[handwritten: , really?]

"One cannot live without proverbs" is one of several Russian sayings that praise the proverb. As all the world knows, Premier Nikita S. Khrushchev is a devoted subscriber to this adage. "You can expect it when shrimps whistle," "Strong friends cannot be parted – even by water," "Get rid of the devil and the priest will have nothing to do," are some of his favorites. When he arrives on these shores next Tuesday doubtless he will have more in his dialectical armory. His cross-country tour can be expected to put proverbs on many front pages, drawing attention to a homely form of literature we use much but seldom think of.

Like poetry, the proverb is indefinable. There have been some good tries. Francis Bacon called proverbs: "The edged tools of speech." Lord Russell in a much-quoted appraisal called a proverb: "The wisdom of many and the wit of one." But the definition I like best comes from the good old Encyclopaedia Britannica: "A pungent criticism of life." That seems to fit the insight and compassion which mark the prover at its best, in such an ancient observation as "Three things drive a man out of doors: a smoky chimney, a leaky roof and a scolding woman." *[handwritten margin: p ≠ neg]*

One reason the proverb is so hard to define is that it is so many different things. In collections of proverbs we find not only such bits of popular wisdom as "There's more to marriage that four bare legs in bed," but also similes as "Scarce as hen's teeth," such metaphorical phrases as "All buttons and no overcoat," such exclamations as "How's that for high!" such weather lore as "Rain before seven, clear before eleven," such calendar rhymes as "Thirty days hath September," such quotations as "No one ever fergits where he buried the hatchet" and many more varieties.

But one doesn't always find the most interesting proverbs in such collections. They have a way of eluding the net. They are best caught on the fly.

Broadly, there are two kinds of proverbs – national and international. National proverbs are those made by a certain people and not borrowed from some other nation or the Great Common Source, which includes the Bible and the classics. The English proverb "England is a ringing island," a reference to its merry

28

[handwritten: national = only in country ... inter = all countries]

pealing bells; the American "A thunderstorm in January means a death in the White House"; the Spanish "When a Spaniard sings he is either mad or has no money" seem to be national, not borrowed, proverbs.

But a proverb like the French, Italian and Dutch "To give an egg to get an ox" is a horse of a different color. This is one of those saws which reveal the artful dodgeries by which man lives: in pithy form it expresses the device of giving a small gift in the hope of getting a large one in return. You would expect such a proverb to crop up everywhere, and it does. I first came across it in a Scottish Gaelic saying, "To give a loaf to get a shive (sheaf)." The French also have it again in "To one who has a pie in the oven you may give a bit of your cake." Americans say, "Throw a sprat to catch a mackerel"; they and the Germans and the English also say, "Throw a sprat to catch a whale." The pattern is susceptible of much variation. Erasmus has it: "He baits his gifts with a hook." and the Italians say, 'Giving is fishing."

A proverb like this belongs to at least all Western Europe and the Americas. And if you ask whether its spread represents borrowing or parallel coinage, I would be inclined to say some of both, but more of the former.

Let's take a short proverb tour, beginning, in deference to Mr. Khrushchev's visit, with some that appear to be specifically Russian. "He could climb a fir tree and not tear his clothes" well characterizes a maddening type. "A jug that has been mended lasts for 200 years" recognizes the perversity of fate. Mr. Khrushchev's "The dog barks, and the wind carries it away" and "Spit in his eyes and he'll say it's dew from heaven" reflect his approach to practical politics. But the most individual thing about the Russian sayings is the number which praise the proverb. The Spaniard also is traditionally fond of his adages. We think of the typical Spanish saying as bitter-sweet, like the Seville orange. "My teeth before my relations," "To shiver at work and sweat at meals," "The fierce ox becomes tame on strange ground" – these have even in English the sententiousness which is the genius of the Spanish language. But the best of all is the Spanish proverb which reveals the national love of ease and dignity: "How beautiful it is to do nothing and then rest afterward."

If we associate Spanish proverbs with Don Quixote, we connect German sayings with food and cookery. One goes, "Cheese is gold in the morning, silver at noon and lead at night," which may be a development of the old German saw "The morning hour has gold in its mouth." Another individual German proverb is "He who loves neither wine, woman nor song remains a fool all his life long." (I think the man who attributed that to Martin Luther took the same pleasure in mischief as did a Protestant Irishman friend of mine who named his son Martin Luther Murphy.)

French proverbs recognize that there are two sides to every question. "A thought is worthless if the counter-thought is not there," "It takes a bad heart to say a good thing," "He who is never guilty of folly is not as wise as he thinks," "Nothing more closely resembles an honest man than a knave" – these show delight in rubbing antithetic halves together.

Everyone should be leery of attempting to discover national characteristics in a nation's proverbs, but the Irish triad "Three things that serve as well as better things: a wooden sword in the hands of a coward, poor clothes on a drunken man and an ugly woman married to a blind man" contains much of the Irish fantasy of spirit. Of all the Irish proverbs, I especially like the following for its humanity (a quality not only of Irish proverbs but of the proverb in general): "If you give away an old coat, don't cut off the buttons." Incidentally, the Irish adage is more serious than humorous, which would indicate that in his proverbs, if nowhere else, the Irishman speaks from his center of being.

To come back home, the proverbial phrase, as distinct from the proverb, has had an especially rich development in the United States. Offhand one thinks of "See a man about a dog." "Get the hang of," "Fly off the handle." Americans enjoy playing with old proverbs, thus making new ones out of old. One product of this process, "A new broom sweeps clean, but an old one knows the corners," contains some comfort for the old.

Though we amuse ourselves with such play (remember the vaudevillian "She was pure as snow but she drifted"), in general old sayings change less than one would think, even in America. Millions of people on all continents still live by such sayings as "A stitch in time saves nine" and "A bird in the hand is worth two in the bush." These are still to adults everywhere something of what nursery rhymes are to children, constituting, like archetypal myths, a kind of international fund of popular ideas. They will last as long as human nature.

The New York Times (September 13, 1959), p. 74.

Can Anybody Compose a Proverb? (1961)

Anonymous

Francis Wayland of Brown University, one of the greatest of our nineteenth century college presidents, was speaking in class one day of the great wisdom of the Proverbs in the Scriptures. A supercilious student spoke up: "I don't think there's anything very remarkable in the Proverbs. They are rather commonplace remarks of common people." "Very well," said Dr. Wayland. "Make one."

Many people have loved proverbs – in or out of the Scriptures – for the wisdom embedded in them. Others have treasured proverbs for the vividness or earthiness of their imagery. But students of the subject are impressed by still another characteristic of the proverb: its verbal economy. Proverbs are rarely wordy. The usual proverb is spare and austere in expression, and some are marvels of compactness.

For Example, "Know Thyself"

One of the greatest of proverbs is also one of the briefest: "Know thyself." It is at least 2,500 years old, possibly much older. Diogenes Laertius attributed it to Thales.

"Know thyself." Perhaps the best way to appreciate the extraordinary conciseness of that ancient saying is to try an experiment in the spirit of Dr. Wayland. Challenge yourself to invent a profound and memorable two-word sentence. Try it. Don't bother trying to invent one worthy of being handed down for a hundred generations. Just try to devise one worthy of being recalled next week. You will gain a new respect for the spare beauty of the ancient maxim.

Another saying that excels in terse profundity is "*Festina lente*," a Latin maxim that dates at least from the first century of the Christian era. We can say it in two words, "Hasten slowly," but the usual English form is "Make haste slowly." In neither form does it have the rhythmic beauty of the Latin original; but even in three words it stands as one of the marvels of wisdom economically packaged.

"Que Sera, Sera"

A three-word proverb that is familiar in just about every European language appeared several years ago – in its Spanish version – as the title of a popular song: "*Que será, será.*" We say it more wordily in English: "What will be, will be."

31

The French language boasts one of the greatest of three-word proverbs: *"Qui s'excuse, s'accuse."* We have no exact equivalent in English. (Literally it is "He who excuses himself, accuses himself," but that doesn't quite say it. The idea behind the saying comes through most vividly for us in the words of Hamlet's mother, "The lady doth protest too much, methinks."

If we allow ourselves one more degree of wordiness, moving to four-word proverbs, we find innumerable meaty (and salty) items. *"Vox populi, vox Dei"* dates back at least to the eighth century A.D. It is so compactly and perfectly expressed in the original Latin, it has never gained much currency in translated form. And, by the way, the two-part, balanced phrasing of this proverb, with repetition of the key word, is a favorite pattern in proverbs. *"Besser stumm als dumm"* ("Better silent than stupid") is a German proverb in the same pattern.

The Old – and Ever New

Another in this repetitive pattern is "Soon ripe, soon rotten" – a proverb that appears, in one form or another, in a number of languages. Still another is "Soon gotten, soon spent," a venerable saying the theme of which is more familiar to us in one of the most popular of English-language proverbs: "Easy come, easy go." The latter illustrates the astounding capacity of some proverbs to preserve their freshness and youthful quality over the years. A modern teen-ager who wouldn't be caught dead wearing last year's clothes feels quite up to date, even fashionably sophisticated, in saying "Easy come, easy go." It seems to him to have a wonderfully up-to-the-minute flippancy and cynicism. His father thought so too. So did his father's father.

There are many other good four-word proverbs. "First come, first served" sounds like a product of the competitive modern age, but it first appeared in quieter centuries.

A Dash of Cynicism

We could let down the bars against wordiness still further and look at five-word proverbs. But by now the reader will have been so spoiled by the fine, lean beauty of the proverbs we have cited that five words will seem intolerably rambling. Still, there are some choice items. Consider the old English saying, "The bait hides the hook."

The New York Times (November 12, 1961), p. E8.

Parallel Proverbs (1964)

Mario Pei

Proverbs are among the most ancient of human institutions. Numerous proverbs appear in the tongues of which we have the oldest existing records: Egyptian, Akkadian, Chinese, Sanskrit, Greek, and Latin. The Hebrews have contributed to the Bible an entire "Book of Proverbs." Yet, though most countries teem with popular sayings, a few groups have none. Literacy and culture seem to have nothing to do with it. The African Negroes have many proverbs, the American Indians none.

Criticism of life, in brief and pithy form, is characteristic of proverbs, while their popular philosophy is, indeed, proverbial. "Proverbs are the wisdom of peoples" goes an Italian saying. This is perhaps an exaggeration, but there is no doubt that much of a nation's folk-philosophy gets into proverbs, along with the spice of national customs and, above all, the peculiar flavor of the nation's language and phraseology.

How did proverbs originate? No one knows exactly, but if the Greeks have given us a correct etymology in their word for "proverb" (*paroimia*, "by the roadside"), then proverbs are sayings that have grown up "along the road." The Latin equivalent, *proverbium*, means "a word uttered forth" or "publicly." Proverbs are generalizations of human experience, condensations of oft-repeated occurrences of the trial-and-error variety. Above all, they are the fruit of observation and inductive reasoning, two of the great faculties of the human mind.

A sage of ancient Babylon, Palestine, Greece, or Rome, watching the infinite variations of events taking place around him, yet noticing that similar sequences led more or less inevitably to the same outcome, was undoubtedly the one who first spun the generalization. Then he offered it, as the Greek word implies, "along the road," to anyone who cared to listen. The saying caught on, became popular, was passed from mouth to mouth, from generation to generation. Ultimately, it became an integral part of the group's folklore, and was repeated whenever the situation it described recurred.

"Language," says an Arab proverb, "is a steed that carries one into a far country." But for proverbs a distant journey is hardly necessary, because "many minds with but a single thought" is often highly appropriate. Proverbs prove that human nature is one, whether in New York or Moscow, Peking or Timbuctoo. If there is an element of common vicissitude, then many languages will be sure to "have a word for it."

Some sayings are almost prehistoric, others quite modern. "What is healthy to a Russian is death to a German" sounds like something manufactured during the three winter campaigns of the Second World War. Actually, it goes back several centuries and is the Russian way of saying that "one man's meat is another man's poison."

"You can't fool all of the people all of the time" is attributed to Lincoln. It received a vivid demonstration in Fascist Italy, where Mussolini's followers were trying to force their own manufactured slogan down the people's throats: "Mussolini is always right!" "Particularly when he's wrong" was the addition made by an unknown native wit. And that was the way the slogan stuck, to plague the Fascists.

It was not the first time, for Italians specialize in taking internationally known bromides and giving them a humorous twist: "Silence is assent; but if you keep your mouth shut you're not saying anything"; or "Slow but sure – and you never get there."

Many sayings are international, proving that "great minds run in the same-channel," even if the minds are anonymous. But the same idea can be expressed in different ways. Witness our "Too many cooks spoil the broth"; in Russian it runs: "With seven nurses, the child goes blind"; in Persian, "Two captains sink the ship"; in Japanese, "Too many boatmen run the boat up to the top of a mountain"; in Italian, "With too many roosters crowing, the sun never comes up." We "call a spade a spade," but the Spaniards "call bread bread and wine wine." We say, "Don't bite the hand that's feeding you," while the Russians say, "Don't defile the well; you might want to drink from it," and the French, "Don't spit in the air; it might fall back on you." "Pray to God and keep your powder dry" is, in Russian, "Pray to God, but row toward shore."

"Don't put the cart before the horse" has a counterpart in Finnish: "Trees are climbed from the bottom, not from the top." "Don't bite off more than you can chew" is paralleled by Rumania's "Don't stretch yourself till you're longer than your blanket." "Setting a thief to catch a thief" is, in Hungarian, "Setting a dog to watch the bacon." "To have one's cake and eat it" is, in Russian, "Keeping one's innocence and accumulating capital."

34

To the Russian, "a fly in the ointment" is "a spoonful of tar in our cask of honey"; "When in Rome do as the Romans do" is "When living with wolves, howl like a wolf"; "to hit the nail on the head" is "to smite not on the brow, but in the eye"; "to have a heavy heart" is "to have cats scratching on your heart." The old Latin proverb, "In the land of the blind a one-eyed man is king," is curiously paralleled by Korea's "Where there are no tigers, a wildcat is very self-important."

Every proverb tells a story and teaches a lesson. "If the pitcher hits the rock, or the rock hits the pitcher, it's too bad for the pitcher", is a Spanish warning that you should not pit yourself against superior forces. China says the same thing in these words: "Don't set out unarmed to fight a tiger." Our American Southern counterpart is, "The worm is wrong when it argues with the hen." "The palest ink is better than the most retentive memory" is China's admonition to "put it in writing," while Spain urges, "Don't sign papers you don't read, or drink water you don't see." Portugal, in the same vein, reminds you that, "Caution and chicken broth never harmed anyone."

Proverbs are often cynical, especially in money matters. "The coalman is black, but his money is white," says a Portuguese proverb. "The poor man dies waiting for the rich man to make up his mind" is an Albanian expression of skepticism, while Rumania has it: "The rich man makes a mistake, and the poor man hastens to apologize." "When it rains oatmeal, the poor man has no spoon to catch it with" is Sweden's contribution to pessimism, while the Italians assert that "Those who have bread have no teeth, and those who have teeth have no bread." Czechoslovakia sagely advises: "If you have no money, don't go to the inn." Surprisingly, it is Japanese, not Russian, that has the most rabidly anti-capitalistic saying: "A rich man and a spittoon grow dirtier as they accumulate." Japanese further shows its contempt for earthly wealth by saying: "There is no instance of a naked man ever losing anything."

Cynicism appears in other connections. "Those who die are at rest; those who live set their hearts at rest" is Italy's rather bitter reflection on life and death. France is more light-hearted: "You can't make an omelet without breaking eggs." "The pleas of the mighty thunder out like commands," say the Swiss. America says: "When luck gets to running your way, sawdust is as good as brains," and Russia concurs with "Be born neither wise nor fair, but lucky." Highly pessimistic are Russia's "Good luck disappears like our hair; bad luck hangs on like our fingernails," and Spain's "Welcome, evil, if you come alone."

Proverbs of various countries are sometimes contradictory. "To trust is well, but not to trust is better," says Italian, but Spanish counters: "If you lose a knife that doesn't cut, or a friend that doesn't lend, you're not losing much." "Three-tenths according to a man's ability; seven-tenths according to his clothes" is China's way of saying that "Clothes make the man"; but Spain denies this: "Though the monkey wear silk, it's still a monkey." Contradictions may even appear in the same tongue. "A wife and a floor mat are good when fresh and new" and "A wife and kettle get better as they grow older" are both from Japan.

Most proverbs were born at a time when civilization was agricultural and earthy; they seldom speak of machines, often of farm animals. "A big ox plows a crooked furrow," says the Czech. "A donkey's braying does not reach heaven," says the Italian. "Seat a pig at the table and he'll put his feet on it," says the Russian. "Why make an ox or a horse of yourself for posterity?" inquires the Chinese.

There is scarcely any contingency of life that is not covered by some national saying. "With words alone, you don't make the soup" is Rumania's way of reminding you that "Action speak louder than words." The Italian equivalent, "Deeds are masculine, words feminine" has been borrowed, untranslated, as the motto of our Naval Academy at Annapolis. China has it: "Talk cooks no rice," and our Southern Negroes say: "'Mean to' don't pick no cotton."

"A swimmer's real skill is knowing how to keep his eye on his clothes," warns Spanish; and the Chinese gently admonishes: "Don't lean against a bamboo fence; lean against a wall." "Better to be waited for than to wait" is the Japanese excuse for being late to an appointment, while Arabic has a typical lazy man's proverb: "It is better to walk than to run; better to stand than to walk; better to sit than to stand; better to lie than to sit." Czech has a good slogan for salesmen: "When you're trying to catch a bird, sing to it nicely"; while Macedonia warns you to "Be a man, not a mouse" in these words: "If you turn into a lamb, the wolf will eat you up."

Volumes of philosophy are at times wrapped up in one saying. The Arabic "Birth is the messenger of death," the Rumanian

"What man fears he cannot escape," the Italian "Graveyards are full of after-wisdom" are cases in point. For sheer moral grandeur, it is hard to beat Finland's "Fire cannot destroy the truth," Switzerland's "Conscience is a better guide than science," or China's "Those who follow that part of themselves which is great, are great men; those who follow that part of themselves which is small, are small men." A Spanish proverb runs: "God says: 'Take what you want, and pay for it.'" From our South Carolina mountaineers comes: "We ain't what we want to be, and we ain't what we're goin' to be, but we ain't what we wuz."

Philosophy is often interlarded with humor. The Czechs, for instance, say: "Real suffering is not working on a mountaintop; it's working among people." "The cat knows perfectly well whose chops he's licking," say the Portuguese. And the Chinese, with their Confucian background, have this to offer: "The good man, doing good, finds the day too short; the evil man, doing evil, likewise finds the day too short."

God and the devil play conspicuous roles. "The doctor examines you, but God makes you well," says a Polish proverb. "God does not pay off on Saturday, but by Sunday everything's paid up" is the Italian tribute to divine justice.

The devil of proverbial utterances is an imp. "Man makes fun of man, and the devil makes fun of all of them" says Rumanian. "Man is fire; woman is firewood; the devil comes along and blows on them," says Spanish. Albania believes in appeasement: "Light a candle to the devil, too, so he'll do you no harm." But Macedonia thinks it's no use: "The devil doesn't listen to sermons."

Woman is all-powerful in some proverbs. "Man is the product of the women he has known" and "What woman wants, God wants," says the gallant Frenchman; and the Italian agrees by saying: "A woman's hair pulls more than a yoke of oxen." But there are limitations: "The prettiest girl in the world can only give what she's got" is another French saying (the Italian counterpart is "The cask can give only the wine it holds").

The fickleness of woman is celebrated in song and saying. "When she says no, a woman shakes her head lengthwise," say the Japanese; but out of fairness they add: "A man's heart is as changeful as the autumn sky." The Chinese add a touch of domestic cynicism: "Two women in one room are one too many."

The Russians are nasty: "A dog is wiser than a woman; it doesn't bark at its master."

Love and marriage, of course, have their innings. "Keep your eye on people in love, because they are all stone blind," says Portugal. "If you hanker to be a martyr, lead a rich wife to the altar," says Switzerland. "When the bride is in the cradle, the bridegroom should be old enough to ride a horse" is Russia's idea of the proper age difference between the sexes. The Poles are bitter about marriage: "The woman cries before the wedding; the man cries afterwards." But the Russians think they know what to do about it: "Love your wife like your soul, and beat her like your fur coat."

The Dutch are pessimists about remarriage: "To marry once is a duty; twice, an act of foolishness; three times, lunacy." To which the French add: "Divorce is the sacrament of adultery."

The upbringing of children appears not only in our "Spare the rod and spoil the child"; the Danes say, "Give to a pig when it grunts, and to a child when it cries, and you will have a fine pig and a bad child."

Both fools and sages are the object of ridicule. "Giving advice to a fool is like giving medicine to a dead man" is an old American proverb. "A fool can ask more questions than seven wise men can answer," says a German proverb. But a Spanish proverb counters: "There is no foolishness that is not sponsored by some sage." Our "A word to the wise is sufficient" is elaborated by the Czechs: "To a wise man, just whisper; but to a fool you must spell out everything."

Gossips also come in for their share. "He who knows little soon repeats it," say the Spaniards, and the Turks add: "Who gossips to you will gossip about you."

Some proverbs make you feel like arguing the point. Hungary's "Good wine needs no publicity" is quite at variance with America's "It pays to advertise." One could also dispute Albania's "Better to suffer misfortune quickly than to wait too long for good fortune," or Arabia's "All that is hidden is sought after."

"Don't get 'American stomach' by eating too fast" is the gist of several proverbs in many languages, like Italy's "At table you don't grow older," or China's "Work may be hastened, but not food." In addition to proverbs, there are picturesque similes. "For eating, like a wolf; for working, like a log" is Rumania's way of describing some people. "Lucky like a dog in church" is Italy's description of bad luck. "As nice as soot is white" is Russia's expression of disgust, while the Arabic reply to a sympathetic inquiry as to how things are going is "Like tar!" and the Chinese puts it: "Seven kinds of mess, eight kinds of disorder." If you want to be in a desirable spot against the wishes of those in control, you are said by the Italians to be trying to "get into Paradise in spite of the Saints." Other people are said to be "looking for work and praying to God they won't find it."

It is fashionable in some quarters to describe certain groups as backward, ignorant, illiterate. There may be mechanical justification for these epithets, but you certainly cannot prove mental inferiority or lack of philosophical perception by the language or proverbs of many of these groups. Take, as a single example, the Swahili of East Africa. "To speak is good, and not to speak is good" parallels the European "Speech is silver, silence is gold." "He who is there above, await him below" sounds very much like our "Pride goes before a fall." "He who is not here, and his business is not here" reminds you of the Italian "The absent are always in the wrong." There is a world of earthly wisdom in "Whether the cock crows or not, it will dawn"; "Drunkenness takes away sense"; "Whether you have little or much, be content." And what has the West to offer that surpasses this triad in philosophical content: "Profit surpasses pride"; "Understanding surpasses property"; "As for dying, we shall all die"?

Saturday Review, 47 (May 2, 1964), pp. 16-17, and p. 53.

[Proverb] Tests Help Pupils:
(a) Acquire Words
(b) Become Verbose (1965)

Anonymous

Question: What's a sharper way of saying, "An ogled saucepan does not reach 212 degrees Fahrenheit?"

Answer: "A watched pot never boils."

Or, "Lifeless males of the human race communicate negative false truth?"

"Dead men tell no tales," of course.

These are samples of what fifth and sixth graders at West Orange School [Orange, California] came up with when assigned to find more elaborate ways of stating familiar phrases.

Their teacher, Lucile Barker, hoped it would improve the vocabulary of her advanced reading class.

The idea was to re-word proverbs so as to stump others in the class. Here are other examples:

"A solid rotating mass does not accumulate any bryophytic plants" for "a rolling stone gathers no moss."

"Avoidance of speculative enterprise precludes profit" for "nothing ventured, nothing gained."

"A feathered vertebrate that soars aloft, held in the carpus, metacarpus and phalanges, is equal to two feathered vertebrates in the shrubs of the third dimension in proportion" for ... etc., etc., etc.

The New York Times (February 10, 1965), p. 43.

The Art of Proverbs:
An Evaluation of the Minds – Wary and Illusionless – that Have Created the World's Wisdom (1965)

F.L. Lucas

Anyone who strolls through a public library may come, in some corner, on whole shelves of Dictionaries of Proverbs – volumes, often, of formidable fatness, but seldom much thumbed. A proverb is by definition a popular maxim: but today proverbs appear to have lost their popularity. They figure little in our talk, our letters or our books. One does not often hear people daring, or deigning, to use sayings so flat and trite as "A stitch in time saves nine" or "One swallow doesn't make a summer." Occasionally some wit may try to renovate faded aphorisms by turning them facetiously inside out – "One summer does make one swallow." But such bright sallies, too, fade and are forgotten.

Our ancestors, however, seem to have felt differently. Proverbs are among the most ancient literary forms, and among the most universal. Not a country on earth but appears to possess such adages by hundreds and thousands. And they are immemorially old – older than history, older than Homer. They already existed in ancient Egypt, Babylonia and Israel. Classical antiquity made collections of them. They delighted the Middle Ages. And at the Renaissance, scholars as eminent as Erasmus, poets as fastidious as George Herbert, could still run after proverbs as zestfully as entomologists after butterflies.

Then seems to have begun one of those changes in taste that spread through society silently, imperceptibly, almost unnoticed. Growing eager to be thought genteel, people came to despise proverbs as vulgar and "low"; growing eager to be thought original, they came to disdain proverbs as humdrum and banal. Already in antiquity Aristotle had observed that such adages of homespun wisdom were specially dear to rustics. Shakespeare took to raising a laugh at characters like Touchstone or Dogberry by giving them an absurd fondness for apothegms; and in his contemporary, Cervantes, proverbs pour grotesquely from the lips of Sancho Panza like sausages from a machine. "'God curse you!' cried Don Quixote. 'May sixty thousand devils take you and your adages! For an hour you have been piling one on another, and each of them is torture to me.'" By the 18th Century that arbiter of the graces, Lord Chesterfield, could warn that natural son whom he labored so hard to make.unnatural: "A man of fashion never has recourse to proverbs and vulgar aphorisms."

Yet perhaps Lord Chesterfield, as so often, was over-quick with his contempt. It is true that our national proverbs seem trite; but that is because we know only a familiar fraction of them. There are hundreds more which few of us today have ever heard. And the proverbs of other races can turn out surprisingly fresh, and refreshing.

It must, indeed, be owned that folk wisdom is sometimes curiously silly. "God," says the Frenchman, "tempers the wind to the shorn sheep" (not, as in Sterne, "shorn lamb" – who shears lambs?): "God," echoes the Russian, "does not give more beard than soap." But who believes such blind optimism? However, there are other proverbs that provide an amusingly cynical corrective – "God gives nuts to the toothless" (Portuguese) and "God lets the coconut fall when there is none beneath the tree" (Arab) – in the same way that original, Jeremy Bentham, would dourly remark when things went wrong, "Just like Provvy!"

One must also concede that most aphorisms, even in the hands of masters like Bacon or La Rochefoucauld, tend to be inadequate and superficial, falsifying life's complexities with the brevity of epigram. Hence the notorious frequency with which proverbs contradict one another. "A kiss and a drink of water," says the prudent Scot, "make a tasteless breakfast." Yet Solomon said just the opposite – "Better is a dinner of herbs where love is, than a stalled ox and hatred therewith."

But here it can be answered that both maxims are true. Love in a cottage often proves rash; for love is likely to vanish up the empty chimney. Yet to marry simply for money is also rash, as well as disgusting. The mistake lies in expecting any proverb to contain the whole truth. Complex problems cannot be solved in a single sentence. Enough if it holds its measure of truth. It remains for the hearer's own common sense to see when and where it applies. Unfortunately, as another proverb says, "Wise men make proverbs, and fools repeat them." It can easily look silly to have adages too much on one's tongue. Yet it may prove far from silly to keep a few sound ones in one's head.

It must be granted that there are too many proverbs in the world. The collection I have found most stimulating, S. G. Champion's *Racial Proverbs*, runs to no less than 900 pages. Even this is only a skimming. From Germany, Russia, Sweden,

Estonia and Finland alone, compilers are said to have amassed a prodigious total of nearly 2,000,000. To read pages of bad proverbs can be suffocating. All the same, there remain a surprising number of good ones.

Proverbs are the anonymous wisdom-literature of the common man in ages past (just as anonymous ballads are his poetry, and legends and fairy tales his fiction). Yet they often bear the stamp of minds no means common. They can throw fascinating light on human nature, on national character, on life itself. And even when we doubt their wisdom, we can still often admire their trenchancy, their brevity, their imaginative imagery. "A proverb," says the Arab, "is to speech as salt to food."

How do these forgotten proverb makers see the world? Even in countries far apart their tone is often strangely similar. They have, to begin with, certain objects of widespread dislike. Terse themselves, these village sages have a special scorn for wordiness. For the wordy are bores. "As the desert sand to the tired traveler, so is loquacity to the lover of silence" (Oriental). The wordy are also contemptible – it is the worst wheel or the empty barrel that makes the most noise. "One dog barks at nothing, and the rest bark at him" (Chinese). "The dogs bark, but the caravan goes on" (Arab). "The turtle lays a thousand eggs, and no one knows: the hen lays one, and tells the town" (Malayan). "A child learns sooner to talk than to be silent" (Norse).

Then, the wordy are apt to be insincere. "A blethering cow soon forgets her calf" (British). The wordy frustrate themselves – "Every time the sheep bleats, it loses a mouthful" (British). And finally, loquacity is dangerous. "Do not talk like a mountain, it is so easy to fall off" (Burmese). "Walls have mice," observes the Persian, "and mice have ears." Briefer still in Spain and Portugal: "The fish dies by its mouth."

Reticence is correspondingly admired. The Irishman notes that "The stars make no noise" and "Even God did not tell His Mother everything." And the Japanese concludes – "What you want to say, say it tomorrow, silent man is often worth listening to."

It is consistent with this that the world's proverbs should show a persistent dislike for two talkative types of person – lawyers and priests. "God wanted to chasten mankind, so He sent lawyers" (Russian). "When a piece of paper blows into a law court, it may take a yoke of oxen to draw it out again" (Chinese).

"The houses of lawyers are roofed with the skins of litigants" (Welsh). "When two go to law one is left in his shirt; the other, naked" (Sardinian). This shrewdness is eternally repeated yet seldom learned.

More surprising is the proverbial distrust of clerics, even in countries commonly thought devout. "The priest's eyes and the wolf's jaws devour whatever they see" (Russian). "An ounce of mother is worth a ton of priest" (Spanish). "Do not put paper in water, a feather near the fire or a priest near your wife" (Polish).

Nor do pietists in general seem to be loved much better. "Young saint, old devil" (British). "Having sold her skin to the devil, she bequeathes her bones to God" (French). "If your neighbor has made one pilgrimage to Mecca, watch him: if two, shun him; if three, move to another street" (Arab).

Natural enough that the proverb maker, being generally a man of the people, should often be no less sardonically bitter toward governments and officials, the powerful and the rich. "Thieves nowadays are not in forests, but in offices" (Rumanian). "Tiger and buffalo fight – the reeds and bulrushes die" (Bengali). "The rich man and the ashtray grow dirtier as they accumulate" (Japanese). "Even in the next world we shall have to serve the gentry, for they will be in the caldrons, and we shall have to stoke the fires" (Russian).

Consolation is found mainly in a sturdy individualism. "Honor is better than honors" (Flemish). "Better on one's own feet than another's stilts" (German). "The highest price a man can pay for a thing is to ask for it" (British). One might expect to come across more communistic adages, like the Italian, "Peace would be universal if there were neither 'mine' nor 'thine.'" But these dour old village elders whom one pictures coining proverbs seem usually too individualistic, too disillusioned about human nature, too skeptical about collaboration to indulge much in socialist dreams. "The community is strong as water and stupid as a pig" and "If you get into the pack, you need not bark, but wag your tail you must" (Russian).

Equality likewise can provoke ironic aphorisms. "Who seeks equality should go to tho graveyard" (German). "If I am a lady, and you are a lady, who shall bed the sow?" (Galician). This last is amazingly widespread; recurring, with variations, in England, Germany, Estonia, Arabia, Egypt, Turkey and the Punjab. Popular maxims seem to travel from country to country as impalpably and imperceptibly as dust or microbes through the atmosphere.

Honesty, however, must own that for all their wit and wisdom, the harsh realism of proverbs tends at times to a cynical misanthropy – entertaining but rather repellent. An extreme instance of this is the Estonian, "There are two good people; one is dead, the other unborn." Even friendship is viewed with distrust: "Who seeks a constant friend, goes to the graveyard" (Russian). "When you need nothing, go to your friends" (German). Lending is widely regarded as fatal. "If you have had enough of a friend, grant him a loan" (Russian: similarly Portuguese). "Stand and lend: kneel and ask it back" (Chinese). Neighbors, naturally, are not trusted either: "Love your neighbor, yet pull not down your hedge" (British). And guests grow quickly a bore. "Guests and fish stink after three days" (many countries). "Visits always give pleasure –if not the arrival, the departure" (Portuguese).

As for relatives, they are even less reliable than friends or neighbors (Bosnia, Denmark, Poland, Hindustan; some Hindu proverbs, though, say the opposite). "Be brothers, but keep accounts" (Arab). "May our relatives prosper – and may we never find the way to them!" (Polish).

Even toward sons and daughters Everyman may show a deep-rooted bitterness. For, as the Chinese say, "Water runs downhill"; that is, affection usually flows more abundantly from the older to the younger. "Little children, little sorrow: big children, big sorrow" (Danish). "Small children stamp on your lap: big ones, on your heart" (Czech). "One father can support ten children: ten children cannot support one father" (Spanish, similarly Estonian). "Trust your servants, and you will be blind in one eye: trust your sons and daughters, and you will be blind in both" (Burmese).

But this surprisingly misanthropic tendency in proverbs is mild compared with their ubiquitous misogyny. Nothing has so astounded me in reading them as their massed chorus of rage, rancor and derision toward women. No doubt the war of the sexes is old as the Stone Age; yet astounding this virulence remains. I apologize to my women readers; I might even suggest that they skip the next paragraphs. (But would they? No.) Enough to point out that proverbs, it is clear, were seldom composed by women; just as the lion observed that if lions painted, there would be far more pictures of lions killing men instead of men killing lions.

To begin with, there is the mere scream of indiscriminate denunciation. "Pray to God to preserve you from bad women, and preserve yourself from good ones" (Yiddish). "To educate a woman is putting a knife in the hand of a monkey" (Hindi). "Lord, there are so many nasty things in the world, and Thou hast created wives!" (Russian).

Then come the more specific charges. First, it is said, women talk so much. "Ten measures of babble came down from Heaven, and woman took nine of them" (Talmud). "Would you have tough shoes, sole them with a woman's tongue" (Alsatian). "A secret goes only in trousers" (Yiddish).

Secondly, women's vanity. "When men meet, they listen to each other; when women meet, they look at each other" (German). "Tell a woman she is beautiful, and the Devil will repeat it to her ten times more" (Italian). "The three animals that spend the most time at their toilet are cats, flies and women" (French).

Next, continues the indictment, women are so quarrelsome. "Two scythes can lie quiet together, but never two spinning wheels" (Russian). "If you want to be praised, die; if you want to be blamed, marry" (Polish).

Fourth (as Chaucer's Wife of Bath admitted), women always want to domineer. It is extraordinary how many countries, from France to Rumania, Russia to Madagascar, unite to execrate this tendency under the same hateful symbol – the "crowing hen."

Fifth, says the popular voice, women are insatiable. "Women, priests and poultry have never enough" (British). "You may carry your wife on your back all your life, but if you once put her down she will say, 'I am tired'" (Montenegrin).

Sixth, they are as false as Cressida; "Never trust a woman, not though she has borne you seven children" (Japan). "Trust a dog to the end, and a woman till the first opportunity" (British). "A woman is harder to guard than a sackful of fleas" (German). "The dog that will bite, growls; the bee that will sting, buzzes; but a girl merely sparkles her eyes" (Polish).

Finally, say the proverbs, women are incomprehensible idiots. "Three kinds of men fail to understand women – young men, old men and middle-aged men" (Irish). "The tongue is the last means a woman has of making herself understood by her husband" (British). "A woman cuts her wisdom teeth when she is dead" (Rumanian)

Monstrous judgments, yet how bitingly vivid! The essential fallacy lies not only in applying to all women the faults of some, but in so complacently implying that men are better. But, holding such views of the eternal feminine, these jaundiced sages naturally tend to look with sardonic eyes on romance. "Love, love, the beginning is bad and the end worse" (Portuguese). "Love lasts seven seconds, the fantasy seven minutes, the unhappiness a lifetime" (Arab). And marriage is even more scathingly decried. "Love has wings; marriage, crutches" (Russian). "At first they fit into one shirt; later, not into one cottage" (Estonian). "Honest men marry soon; wise men, never" (British). "Marriage has teeth, and him bite very hot" (Jamaican). But the clinching argument comes from Georgia in South Russia: "If wives were good, God would have had one."

Remedy? Apart from celibacy, the most common prescription seems to be Nietzsche's – the whip. "The pretty woman needs three husbands – one to pay her debts, one to love her and on] to beat her" (Slovak). "Love your wife like your soul, and shake her like a pear tree" (Russian).

Only rarely does this popular wisdom produce something more humane. For example: "In bed, man and wife: out of bed, guests" (Chinese). "If your wife is small, stoop and whisper in her ear" (Talmud). And once, from Portugal, one seems to hear the woman's side: "What is marriage, mother? Daughter, it is spinning, childbirth, weeping."

Of life in general one would not expect from such minds as these any rosy views. And in fact proverbs seem often strikingly somber in outlook. "Life is an onion that one peels crying" (French). "I was wise once – that was in crying when I was born" (Welsh). "We do not get even death free – it costs our life" (Russian). "Man's life is like an egg in the hands of a child" (Rumanian). And then there is that audacious saying of the Bulgarians: "God is not sinless – He made the world."

In short, "vanity of vanities." A typically French adage wisely infers from this the need at least for gaiety – "We must laugh before we are happy, lest we die without having laughed."

But as a rule the proverb makers seem to fall back simply on a courageous quietism, as Lao Tzu did in the China of long ago; better is tranquility than fuss and fret about the world's baubles and futilities. "Do not push the river, it flows of itself" (Polish). "Walk fast, and you catch misfortune; walk slowly, and it catches you" (Russian). "Two things a man should never be angry at – what he can help and what he cannot" (British). "Smoke your pipe and be silent – the world is only wind and smoke" (Irish). "Never trouble trouble till trouble troubles you" (Jamaican). "In the hum of the market is money; but under the cherry tree is rest" (Japan). "Nothing but a handful of dust will fill the eyes of a man" (Arab).

What proverbs say remains often less remarkable than the way they say it. Some of these obscure and nameless sages could give many an established writer lessons in style. For their sayings are gifted, at times, with a modest poetry, like violets hidden in the grass. Here, to conclude, is a random selection of adages, various in subject, but all outstanding in their laconic expressiveness. Let anyone who thinks it easy, just try to say so much in so little.

"Who physics himself, poisons a fool" (British). "He's the slave of a slave, who serves none but himself" (Scottish). "Every man complains of his memory; none of his judgment" (French). "The wise make more use of enemies than fools of friends" (German). "Give time time" (Italian). "Tomorrow is often the busiest day of the week" (Spanish). "You lift, and I'll groan" (Latvian). "They came to shoe the Pasha's horse, and the beetle stretched out his leg" (Arab). "The bear knew nine songs: all were about honey" (Turkish). "If a man of Naresh has kissed thee, count thy teeth" (Hebrew). "The sieve says to the needle, 'You have a hole in your tail'" (Bengali). "If a low-bred man gains wealth, he will carry a parasol at midnight" (Tamil). "A wife is like a blanket – its contact irritates; if you cast it aside you are cold" (Oji, Ashanti). "Let your love be like misty rain – light in falling, but flooding the river" (Malagasy). "Believe only half of what you see, and nothing of what you are told" (Cuban). "The dog in the kennel barks at his fleas; the dog that hunts does not feel them" (Chinese).

Now perhaps it grows a little easier to picture by what kind of minds the world's proverbs were mainly composed. Not much, one suspects, by the well-to-do, nor by women, nor by the young. I seem to see, rather, dimly emerging from the shadows of the past, by firesides long extinct, the gnarled faces and furrowed brows of caustic old countrymen in a world far more rustic, less sophisticated, but not therefore less shrewd, than ours; village patriarchs who had seen a good deal of their rulers and betters without much liking what they saw; bitter yet humorous; realistic, not romantic; highly practical, frequently cynical, not at all mystical; not much of philanthropists, largely misogynists, yet at times penetrating psychologists. There is about them often something of Benjamin Franklin, though without his scientific genius or his geniality; something of Thomas Hardy, though without his art, his sensitiveness, his tragic power. There are, indeed, rustic characters of Hardy's that these unknown aphorists may at moments recall, such as Michael the milkman: "a good saying well spit out is a Christmas fire to my withered heart."

Our world grows ever fuller of science; but not of sense. We drag our poor eyes over acres of print, of which a year later we often remember nothing. We go to parties where not a thing may be said worth recalling the morning after. Modern man has become too hustled and bustled to sit and think, or to stand and stare. And so perhaps, despite Lord Chesterfield, there may still be profit, as well as pleasure, in sometimes listening to the good sayings well spit out, which have for some reason stamped themselves on the memories of people all over the world. Homer's wise Odysseus – probably like "Homer" himself – was one who wandered among many peoples and learned their ways of thinking, and so grew wiser still. With a good dictionary of proverbs one may still travel as wisely, and more widely still.

Holiday, 38 (September 1965), p. 8, and pp. 10-13.

The Wild Flowers of Thought (1969)

Anonymous

"Too many cooks spoil the broth" – so goes a proverb that is as familiar to most Americans as its meaning. The Iranians expressed the same thought with different words: "Two midwives will deliver a baby with a crooked head." So do the Italians: "With so many roosters crowing, the sun never comes up." The Russians: "With seven nurses the child goes blind." And the Japanese: "Too many boatmen run the boat up to the top of the mountain."

These lean, didactic aphoristic statements, so varied in their language, seem to distill universal wisdom. In the Samoan fishing culture, which is dependent on the canoe, islanders would have no difficulty in recognizing the kinship of the English proverb, "It never rains but it pours" to one of their own: "It leaks at the gunwale, it leaks in the keel." From the Biblical injunction, "An eye for an eye, a tooth for a tooth" it is only a short and negotiable step to an old saying of the Nandi tribe in East Africa: "A goat's hide buys a goat's hide and a gourd a gourd."

Hidden Code.

Can it be that the proverb – literally, "before the word" – provides a clue to the common denominator of all human thought? The possibility has been raised by George B. Milner, 50, a linguist at the University of London's School of Oriental and African Studies. Many anthropologists and linguists have long suspected that the human mind obeys a hidden code – just as the computer follows instructions programmed into it before it begins to think. In an article for Britain's *New Society* magazine, Milner contends that the proverb may stand breathtakingly near to the source of that code [see George B. Milner, "What is a Proverb?" *New Society*, 332 (February 6, 1969), pp. 199-202].

Milner's interest in the proverb began in 1955, when he flew to the South Pacific to compile the first Samoan dictionary since 1862. There he found a rigidly stratified culture that relied on the proverb as a guide through the thicket of social life.. The Samoans had proverbs for every human exchange, says Milner: "To pay respect, to express pleasure, sympathy, regret, to make people laugh, to blame or criticize, to apologize, to insult, thank, cajole, ask for a favor, say farewell." Intrigued, he collected thousands of these pithy sayings.

50

Back in England, Milner compared the Samoan stock with the proverbs current in Europe, and was struck by the many similarities in structure, rhythm and content. It was almost as if the proverb shared a common source. Since this was culturally impossible, Milner considered another potential origin: the universality of human thought.

Regardless of their genesis, Milner argues, the best proverbs easily transcend ethnic and geographical barriers. They deal in the fundamental stuff of life: love and war, birth and death, sickness and health, work and play. Like the human mind itself, they seek the core meaning of things and the satisfying symmetry of antithesis. They touch the taproots of the mind without requiring the service of the intellect.

Precursor Sage.

Many words in a given language can be traced to their root origins by a skilled lexicographer. The ancestry of proverbs can rarely be determined with scientific accuracy. Aeschylus was as familiar as Solomon with the proverb, "A soft answer turneth away wrath," but no one can say to what precursor sage both men owed the saying. It remains a mystery moreover, why some civilizations are rich in proverbs and others are not. Why id the Incas, the Mayans and nearly all the Indian tribes of North America produce such a meager crop of proverbs, when the Spaniards, the Samoans, the Arabs and the Chinese were minting them by the thousands?

The answers must await further exploration of that greatest mystery of all the processes of the mind. Milner's contention is that the proverb, the wild flower of human wisdom, may now help to direct the search into the deep.

Time (March 14, 1969), pp. 75-76.

A Proverbial Quest That Intrigues Scholars (1975)

Earl Lane

There is an old German proverb, which appears in various forms in dozens of other countries, to the effect that "when the sun shines and it rains at the same time, the devil is beating his wife." The origins of the proverb were relatively obscure until 1957, when a Finnish scholar, Matti Kuusi, tracked it through the ages in a methodic 420-page essay.

Now, to devote 420 pages in the pursuit of a single one-line proverb takes a special flair. Kuusi is a zealot, but he is no nut, at least not in any conventional sense. He is a paroemiologist, a member of a gritty little band of scholars dedicated to the proposition that the short, salty proverb is worth exploring at great length.

Kuusi, at 61, is a sort of grand old man of the field. In addition to his work on "the devil is beating his wife," Kuusi also has compiled the proverbs of the Ovambo people of Africa (a list that runs to 2,483 proverbs and 4,631 variants), is working on a method of classifying and comparing thousands of proverbs from different nations and is the editor of a delightfully obscure little journal called Proverbium, the bible of all hard-core paroemiologists.

But don't rush to sign up for a subscription. A notice on the back cover of each issue, kindly printed in *four* languages, informs the reader that "Proverbium does not accept paid subscriptions." Instead, it is sent free to about 300 institutions with which the journal has an exchange policy. A small number of copies are reserved for active proverb scholars "whose addresses are or will become known to the editor's office."

The number of active researchers has *never* been large (at one time, they could have held a convention in a phone booth) but it has been growing in recent years. About 60 participated in a symposium on proverbs held in Finland last year, the first of its kind. Scholars from a variety of fields dabble in paroemiology from time to time, including literary historians, linguists, anthropologists and folklorists. But as Wolfgang Mieder of the University of Vermont, a prominent student of proverbs, said recently, "There are very few who devote themselves full-time to the study of the proverb ... You can't imagine the work that still remains to be done." Indeed, Kuusi already has identified more than 5,000 proverbial themes in his work, which he considers to be only a beginning.

Francis Bacon, the English philosopher, said iihat "the genius, wit and spirit of a nation are discovered in its proverbs." But modern paroeminologists are wary of attempts to distill the national character from a collection of proverbs.

The American character, for example, might be expected to show up in the pragmatic, economic proverbs of Benjamin Franklin, such sayings from his "Poor Richard's Almanack" as, "Early to bed, early to rise, makes a man healthy, wealthy and wise," or, "God helps them that help themselves." The revisionists have already done old Ben in, however, by pointing out that most of his proverbial wisdom was derived from distinctly non-American (alas, even British) sources.

Rather than trying to bare the soul of a nation in its proverbs, most scholars are content to explore common themes found in the folk wisdom of all nations. One problem has been simply trying to arrive at a good definition of what constitutes a proverb.

"A proverb has a fixed form," Kuusi said recently, "but there are many thousands of definitions." The late Archer Taylor of the University of California, a driving force in the growth of modern proverb studies, shrewdly refused to be pinned down on a precise definition. "An incommunicable quality tells us that this sentence is proverbial and that one is not," Taylor once wrote.

That definition allowed Taylor, a sort of one-man interdisciplinary program, to write scholarly treatises on the classical proverbs of antiquity but also allowed him to include many modern expressions in his works as well. It was Taylor who first welcomed the immortal, "No tickee–no washee," into the fold, and he wrote that the terse, "Put up or shut up," qualified, too, since it "possesses as much vitality as can be demanded of a proverb."

Mieder defines a proverb as "a concise statement of an apparent truth which has currency." Like Taylor before him, Mieder argues passionately that the age of proverb-making has not passed. "What is on the decline," Mieder said, "is the didactic use of proverbs. What 15-year-old kid is going to listen to his father throwing proverbs at him?" Mieder is now studying the ways in which proverbs are used, and sometimes abused, in modern advertising. Psychiatrists have been using proverbs in psychiatric testing, asking patients to tell the meaning of various proverbs. Art scholars have had occasion to study the use of proverbial expressions in the content of paintings, particularly in the work of the 16th Century Flemish master Bruegel.

In one Bruegel painting, "The Blue Cloak" [usually called *Netherlandish Proverbs* (1559)] more than 100 proverbial expressions are portrayed in a busy town scene. Art historians have been vigorously engaged in the game of trying to identify them all.

Some researchers are even talking of pressing the computer into the service of paroemiology, a sure sign that the field aspires to academic greatness. Some of the work in the field, unfortunately, already reads like it was written by a computer, particularly some of the structural analyses of proverb formation. "There is a danger of taking the life out of the work," Mieder said. It is that life, the wit and wisdom of the ages, that is sprinkled through even the driest writings of the paroemiologists. The extent to which various peoples, in their own ways, arrive at similar conclusions on life is striking.

Consider, for example, this common English proverb: "A bird in the hand is worth two in the bush." A brief sample of the equivalents in other tongues includes:

Better a bird in the hand than a thousand on the house. (*Romanian*)
A bird in the snare is worth more than eight flying. (*Latin*)
Better a sparrow in the hand than a crane on the roof. (*German*)
A sparrow in the hand is worth a vulture flying. (*Spanish*)
Better a sparrow in the pan than a hundred chickens in the pastor's yard. (*North Italian*)
Better a wood grouse in the fist than nine or two in the branch. (*Finnish*)
Better a hawk in the hand than two in flight. (*Icelandic*)

Or take this expression: "Too many cooks spoil the broth." In China, it is: "If there are too many cooks, the dog's flesh will never get done." In Sweden: "The house that is built according to every man's advice seldom gets a roof." In Burmese: "Too many doctors and the son dies."

If some of the derivations seem a bit obscure, the scholars would agree. Part of their job has been to find out why some proverbs pass from common usage. The moral lesson may not seem as significant as it once did or may have lost some of its symbolic force. An English proverb of Elizabethan times, "The blind man eats many a fly," is not heard today, but certainly said something about 16th Century culinary problems.

54

Mieder, who is a likable fanatic when it comes to proverbs, has few problems turning up new candidates for study. "I spent hours today looking for the derivation of 'good things come in small packages'," he said recently. "Some camera firm was using it in their advertising. It is obviously proverbial. Any American would consider it so, yet it is not to be found in any of the proverb collections I reviewed ... One fellow finished an essay on a proverb once by saying that he wished someone could help him. Every time he read something, he started picking out the proverbial expressions, making more work for himself. It's the same with me. When I read something proverbial, a bell rings." And then the chase is on.

Out of diversity

Common ideas appear often in the folk wisdom of diverse peoples. In his efforts to classify proverbs, Matti Kuusi has tried to identify some common proverbial types, particularly among proverbs of number, those dealing with relationships between the one and the many, part of a group and the whole. Among some of the types:

One component spoils the whole:
One rotten peach spoils a hundred peaches. (*Japanese*)
One hen that bursts makes the whole pen stink. (*Thai*)
The totem-eater may be alone, but he causes the whole dan to be cursed. (*Luganda*)
An ill-won penny will cast down a pound. (*English*)

When one member of a group suffers, the others suffer:
One finger gashed–all the fingers are covered with blood. (*Nkundu*)
No ease for the mouth when one tooth is aching. (*Chinese*)
If the children drink spoiled milk, the parents get the stomach ache. (*Albanian*)
If the son's little finger hurts, tine mother's heart hurts. (*White Russian*)

Two or many endeavors at once are too much:
The rider of two horses splits asunder. (*Swahili*)
No man can do two things at once. (*English*)
Two pieces of meat confuse the fly's mind. (*Hausa*)
He who chases two rabbits won't catch either. (*Czech*)

One can't hold water in one's mouth and blow fire at the same time. (*Portuguese*)

It is good to do things together:
A pair shortens the road. (*Irish*)
It takes the clap of two hands to make a sound. (*Korean*)
Do not five men walk a mile in a little while? (*Finnish*)
One elephant does not raise a cloud of dust. (*Ovambo*)
One finger does not kill a louse. (*Kikuyu*)

Heal thyself
A sampler of medical proverbs:
He who eats on a full stomach digs his grave with his teeth. (*Russian*)
Eat well or poorly, but drink as much as you can. (*Spanish*)
There is no remedy for death. (*Arabian*)
If you can't become a king, become a doctor. (*Indian*)
If you can't be good, be careful. (*Spanish*)
God heals, yet the physician pockets the fee. (*English*)
Illness comes on horseback and leaves on foot. (*French*)
Keep your feet dry, keep your neck warm, eat like a donkey, drink like an ox. (*Italian*)
Give green fruit and unshaven men a wide berth. (*Spanish*)
Cleanliness is godliness. (*Lebanese*)
Today feasting, tomorrow reclining in the coffin. (*French*)
He who eats only one dish rarely needs the physician. (*English*)
He who puts himself in the power of the doctor has only himself to blame. (*Italian*)

Newsday (June 27, 1975), part II, pp. 4A-5A. Reprinted numerous times with different titles, for example as "In the Proverbial Stew," *Boston Globe* (July 6, 1975), p. 1B; "Probing Perennial Proverbs," *The Montreal Star* (July 19, 1975), p. 1C; and "Hot on the Trail of a Proverb," *San Francisco Sunday Examiner and Chronicle* (August 10, 1975), p. 5.

It's a Long March That Has No Turning –
Rethinking Some Famous Thoughts (1975)

John Jensen

Name the famous politician who said:

(a) Where there's a will there's a way.
(b) Never put off until tomorrow what you can do today. A stitch in time saves nine.
(c) There's no point in shutting the stable door after the horse has bolted.
(d) "Pack up your troubles in your old kit bag and smile, smile, smile." It's being cheerful what keeps you going.

There is a sturdy British ring, a cosy familiarity about these platitudes which suggest home-grown authorship, but the suggestion is misleading. According to A. Doak Barnett (writing, in 1967, while Professor of Political Science at Columbia University) the volume in which these homilies appear has become "the sacred scripture for one-fifth of mankind". By no stretch of statistics could any British politician claim 700,000,000 devotees. Only a foreigner, only the Head of the Chinese People's Republic, only Chairman Mao Tse-Tung can do that.

Mao's political testament, *Quotations from Chairman Mao Tse-Tung* (Bantam Books 35p), more commonly remembered as the 'Little Red Book', has been called the most powerful – and challenging – document of the century. The jacket blurb reveals the secret of its success: "Here, in words of a terrible simplicity ... is a book that is all too easy to understand". For corroboration let's run through the sayings once more, this time in the Chinese Leader's own words:

(a) *Nothing in the world is difficult for one who sets his mind to it.*
(b) *Don't wait until problems pile up and cause a lot of trouble before trying to solve them.*
(c) *As for criticism, do it in good time, don't get into the habit of criticizing only after the event.*
(d) *In times of difficulty we must not lose sight of our achievements, must see the bright future and must pluck up our courage.*

In order to achieve his "terrible simplicity" it is my belief that Mao deliberately plundered Britain's heritage of clichés, proverbs and folk-sayings. He did so with such cunning, expertise and subtlety that, until now, no-one has twigged. How did he manage it without visiting our shores? The answer is a matter of conjecture but the Chinese Leader's early years provide a vital clue.

Mao Tse-Tung was born in Shaoshan, Hunan, in 1893. His education was completed at Hunan Province No. 1 Normal School, for which we should all be grateful (the alternative to Normal School does not bear thinking about). At 18 he was accepted as Assistant Librarian at Peking University where, it seems fair to assume, he would have had access to the library's Foreign Section and its stock of British books and publications. Charles Dickens in his leather-bound entirety must have been there, rubbing bindings, I shouldn't wonder, with a large, haphazard selection of Victorian children's books, the familiar kind filled with cautionary tales and hectoring nursery rhymes. It was through the pages of these latter, lesser English works that Mao probably found the seeds from which his later thoughts were to blossom. The blossoming was profuse enough to disguise the original notion without in any way detracting from its essential simplicity. For example:

The way these comrades look at problems is wrong. They do not look at the essential or main aspects but emphasise the non-essential or minor ones. It should be pointed out that these non-essential or minor aspects must not be overlooked and must be dealt with one by one. But they should not be taken as the essential or main aspects, or we will lose our bearings.

Comrades, as we might say, should learn to tell the wood from the trees.

Mao seems to have taken a lesson from us. Can we now return the compliment? Or, rather, can we learn from ourselves? With the aid of British platitudes – some of which, admittedly, have been borrowed from non-British sources – the Chinese Leader has managed to elevate his country to the status of Great Powerdom. Britain, if she is to survive and succeed should, and must, make use of her vast natural reserves of truisms and crass banalities. We need our own "Little Red Book". If Mao's thoughts could, as has been claimed, "shake the world" surely the Prime Minister can produce a slim volume which will shake the Nation? Already I'm trembling at the thought.

Our "Little Red Book", or "Little Pink Book", or "Little Blue Book" is still merely a dream. Until it becomes a reality can we find aid and comfort in the published offerings of Mao Tse-Tung? Yes, indeed. Everyone agrees the Nation has its problems. How should they be tackled?

Mao suggests:

(i) *We should look at problems from different aspects, not just one.*

(ii) *To investigate a problem is, indeed, to solve it.*

However,

(iii) *Anyone who sees only the bright side but not the difficulties cannot fight effectively for the accomplishment of the ... tasks.*

Those who do appreciate the difficulties will,

(iv) *Fight, fail, fight again, fail again, fight again ... till ... victory.*

To recapitulate in English:

(i) *There are two sides to every coin. Truth is many-sided.*

(ii) *Seek and ye shall find.*

(iii) *Look before you leap. Only fools rush in where angels fear to tread.*

(iv) *If at first you don't succeed, try, try, try again.*

Don't you feel better already? More heartened? If we don't make mountains out of molehills, if we do one thing at a time and do it well, if we remember that more haste makes for less speed (slow and steady wins the race) we should ultimately win through. The Chairman of the People's Republic of China has divined these truths and has given us the recipe for success:

What we need is an enthusiastic but calm state of mind and intense but orderly work.

What *I* need is a large Scotch.

Punch (July 16, 1975), pp. 97-98.

New Saying: Anything Worth Doing Is Worth Doing Badly (1979)

June Bingham

Though some proverbs still hold true – "look before you leap" or your "miss" will be "as good as a mile" – others have become obsolete, even counter-productive. The one I most want to see buried is "Anything worth doing is worth doing well."

Particularly is it out of date for women. In today's world where women are trying simultaneously to have a career, a marriage, and a child or children, the word should be, "Anything worth doing is worth doing badly."

Not "badly" in the sense of catastrophe; but badly as opposed to perfectly.

In the old days the things a woman occupied herself with could be done to perfection, like the roast in the oven, the flowers in the vase, the sampler on the wall. But today's women's roles have expanded both in quality and quantity. As a result some standards need to be lowered. In place of permanent excellence there should be an option of mere competence for a designated period.

This distinction between excellence and competence might also be considered by men who are taking on more than the single traditional breadwinner role – and also by employers who do not like to watch their employees collapsing from exhaustion, or fleeing the job forever.

Excellence is the gear that people want to attain at the beginning of their job. Presumably they want to know – and to show – what their capabilities are. But after that demonstration, the person would not need to stay in "excellence gear" on a permanent basis.

Instead, if their marriage was new, or their children were small, they might ask for a period of pass-fail rather than marks, as far as eventual promotion was concerned. Just as the football player who catches the punt can signal "fair catch" and no one will tackle him, so the employee could signal "competence gear" and no one would expect the kind of extra effort that excellence often entails.

Employers might remind themselves that most salaries cover only "competence gear." The employees who eat and sleep their job, who engage in shop-talk during leisure hours, who stay late or take work home, are, in a sense, engaging in a volunteer activity.

Within the workplace, too, people could take turns as to who gets to be in which gear, when. Employers may need to invite more employee participation in work-planning than had been the case.

A person should not have to be superhuman to fulfill the roles she or he most wants in life. The old comment, "Good enough," used to sound condescending. Perhaps today it can take on the implication of: "I respect you for including other roles than this one in your life."

In less developed countries there has been "a revolution of rising expectations." In our own, perhaps over-developed, country we might have a "revolution of lowered expectations," in Lincoln's language, "for some of the people, some of the time," while they do the things well worth doing – but not ALL worth doing "well."

The Burlington Free Press (September 30, 1979), p. 1D.

Wisdom of the Tribe –
Why Proverbs Are Better Than Aphorisms (1983)

Hugh Kenner

At Oxford University Press, where *the best things in life* (1927) are priced at $16.95 *.and up, they also find work for idle hands to do* (1715), making Oxford Books and Dictionaries of ... of the English Language, of Quotations, of Proverbs, of Saints, of Aphorisms. (An *Oxford Book of Death* has been announced; I've not seen it.) *Waste not, want not* (1800) being another of their principles, not to mention *keep a thing seven years and you'll always find a use for it* (1816), they next make Concise Oxford Books out of big Oxford Books. Hence [John A. Simpson's] *The Concise Oxford Dictionary of Proverbs* [1982; $16.95]. *A librarian and his budget are soon parted* (1587, rev. 1983). But *give credit where credit is due* (1834), since *knowledge is power* (1597), even if *what you don't know can't hurt you* (1576).

You've read all those before? But their fascination is precisely this, that a few of them, and their whole genre, descend to us from a prehistory when nobody had read anything before because there was no reading or writing at all. Our links with preliterate man are few and cherishable.

They include Boston baked beans, a variant on what warmed miserable Roman legionaries in the dank of the British north seventeen centuries ago. For millennia people were cooking without cookbooks, passing on by example a skill that local necessity could vary. In oats country use oats for your pottage (and call it porridge), in bean country use beans. (We're on the verge of the proverb.) If a pig is handy, add pork. Pottage was monotonous, and someone made a bitter rhyme about

> ... *Pease porridge in the pot*
> *Nine days old.*

but adown the centuries pottage was filling, hot, and cheap, so the art of a broth made with local cereals and chunks of meat crossed with the colonists to Massachusetts. Bean pottage, in fact, pork and beans; as fortifying in New England as it had been near Hadrian's Wall.

What gets passed along like that is any set of skills, mental or physical, for dealing with unchanging circumstance. Proverbs were never "literature": like kitchen procedures, they are brief guides to action. They have survived, with so much else of the human enterprise, because a race beset with adversities–hunger, wear and tear, noncooperation–will cherish anything that seems to work. Here a browse in Elisabeth Ayrton's wonderful *English Provincial Cooking* [1983; $16.95], the culinary counterpart to an Oxford book, will do wonders for any head drugged by the literariness with which all Oxford enterprises infect reality.

She records incredible folk tenacity: meals served in A.D. 1300 that Roman officers of A.D. 70 would have recognized, being in fact the very cuisine Roman chefs had introduced to the town life of the raw new province: "different meats and birds, finely chopped, highly spiced and seasoned, moistened with rosewater or milk of almonds, and with mushrooms, truffles, artichoke bottoms, cockscombs and ox palates, sweetbreads and lambs' tongues added." On that wet northern island! You can see why they cherished the procedures for centuries.

Being recipes for managing our affairs, proverbs have been cherished likewise. The Oxford proverb book exhibits "There is the proverb, the more cooks the worse potage [*sic*]," as recorded in those words (1575) by a man who was writing a life of the poet Thos. Carew. Here Oxford is doing what Oxford has done best ever since the great Dictionary: catching the first written instance. The saying was not coined in 1575; note that in 1575 it was already a proverb. It could have been coined in North Britain, at Hadrian's Wall, near the garrison's great iron pot: someone wanting to put in gobbets of a hare just caught, someone else crying no, these onions, another insisting on oats; fisticuffs; and that night's pottage, in a cold, wet, comfortless place, turning out perfectly awful. There were too many cooks entirely, said someone in Latin: *too many cooks spoil the broth*, as we say now.

We say it now because it had seemed worth saying again and again, descending father to son, mother to daughter, mouth to mouth for centuries before J. Hooker chanced to put it in print. It was useful because it touched on a general truth, not confined to cooking. Too many steersmen wreck the ship. Too many coaches zilch the team. Too many programmers make garbage of the program. Likewise, *a stitch in time saves nine*, a mender's platitude, is still consulted as they make the space shuttle ready.

Proverbs ground themselves in such skills as cooking and sewing, skills that get passed on intact. They use the experience people gain in those skills to project what we're always wanting, some general guide for action. They did this for millennia before we'd acquired, the habit of seeking guidance from something written. They were short and memorable and self-explanatory. When you heard about the bird that fouls its own nest, or the need to catch your hare before you could cook it, you remembered both the words and a principle. Proverbs are our oldest poetry, even our oldest rhymes. *Ean me patheis, ou me matheis*, said pre-literate Greeks who meant to impress on their young that if you don't suffer, you don't learn. It does lose in translation.

But such was'not the opinion of Aristotle, who quaintly called proverbs "the remnants of an ancient philosophy that has perished through large-scale human destruction." Penman Aristotle, like most literates, could not conceive that wise men had ever existed who could not write. Since written wisdom (as every *Times* reader knows) is continuous and systematic and nearly unstoppable, these odds and ends had to be fragments left over from catastrophe.

If at Oxford they're not quite as innocent as Aristotle, they're still a trifle casual about the impingement of media. "Even as late as the seventeenth century," they tell us, "proverbs often had the status of universal truths." A more illuminating sentence would be, "As late as the seventeenth century little was in print to read, and few could read it." If, on the evidence of the *Concise Oxford*, a lot of proverbs seem to date from the seventeenth century, that's because a lot of what everybody said was just then getting into print.

Once in print and freed from the tenacity of folk memory, proverbs commence an odd kind of alteration. Initially reflections on the hazards of existence, they soon turned their faces toward the computer age, claiming to sketch input-output linkages: "If *this* is so, *that* will happen." Thus in 1390 Chaucer had called idleness "the minister and nurse unto vices," suggesting by "minister and nurse" no more than a predisposing ambience. But in 1874 we find a Trollope character saying, "Two and two make four; *idleness is the root of all evil*." That seems to say, if Johnny is idle, by iron law he'll be wicked.

So with "Keep a thing seven years. ..." In 1663 the folk wisdom was practical: keep it that long and if it's still no use throw it out. But by 1816 Sir Walter Scott is equipping "seven years"

64

with a guarantee: "They say, *keep a thing seven years, an' ye'll aye find a use for't.*"

Waste not, want not implies a guarantee likewise. But not in the earliest instance the Oxford book records: the evangelist John Wesley, remarking of some frugal soul, "He will waste nothing; but he must want nothing" (1772). Commending a piece of good management, Wesley offered no special hint that a general law was displayed. But the sense of how the world works was changing fast, and within a quarter century we encounter the bleak *waste not, want not*, with its savage corollary, "In want? Behold a wastrel!" (That's open to objection: "I *never* waste anything. But I'm *always* in want." The look of not seeming to deliver has helped give proverbs a bad name. The quarter goes in the slot, the Baby Ruth [candy bar] doesn't come out.)

They were expressions of a communal sense of things. They became nickel-plated formulae. In 1605 a man named Sandys mentioned "honestie" as being thought "the best policie," but judged such a conception "grosse." Honor had better credentials than just efficacy. No longer: witness a 1980 citation from one J. Gash: "When a crisis comes to the crunch I'm full of this alert feeling. I think it's a sort of realization that *honesty's the best policy.*" The Gash barbarity falls into the rhythm of a thousand commencement speeches, meant to fill their auditors full of this alert feeling, a sort of realization yes indeed, and a boiled watch never pots and two thwacks don't make a blight, make that two flacks, and you know it's a sort of realization, I think.

The *Concise Oxford* quotes Gash by way of establishing one proverb's continuing currency, without comment on a shifted meaning. Elsewhere it alerts us that something has radically slipped. What could get spoiled for a ha'porth of tar was a sheep, whose sores a little tar would protect from flies. There are parts of England where "sheep" sounds like "ship," so what was getting written down by the mid-nineteenth century was a now familiar phrase that makes little sense. What goes wrong with a *ship* that a dab of tar might fix?

And as for the exception proving the rule, it was once a law maxim, *exceptio probat regulam in casibus non exceptis.* There *probat* means "confirms," and a 1640 translator had an English version just right: "Exception strengthens the force of a Law in Cases not excepted." Expanded out of legalese, that maxim says, "Each time we define an exception we reaffirm the norm."

("You may do it this once" restates that it isn't done.) English took over *probat* as "proves," and proceeded to muddle "proof" as in "proof of the pudding" with "proof" as in Euclid. Eventually people were saying *the exception proves the rule*, having let its sense decline into sheer gibberish the way strait jackets have gone "straight."

The only thing an exception could possibly "prove" is that the rule is faulty, and you wonder sometimes if people pay attention to a single word they say. They've covered that base too: *what everybody says must be true* (1400).

So repetition coarsens sayings into gibberish? Never fear. Quill in hand, alert at the escritoire, many a writer will pass hours contriving something with the look of a proverb, but new and tamper-proof. If *The Concise Oxford Dictionary of Proverbs* contains chiefly the authenticated texts of things we've heard before, [John Gross's] *The Oxford Book of Aphorisms* [1983; $19.95] harvests one-liners of calculated novelty. "A nice man is a man of nasty ideas"–Swift, *Thoughts on Various Subjects*, 1711. On a facing page, Cesare Pavese is reflecting that "Perfect behaviour is born of complete indifference," and nearby Christopher Ricks is inverting a French proverb: in his version, "*Qui s'accuse s'excuse.*" It was T. S. Eliot who wrote in a Ricksian spirit, "The spirit killeth, but the letter giveth life." That works because 1) we've heard St. Paul's version overmuch, and 2) the unrigorous give "spirit" a bad name. You can reverse nearly any proverb and get a kind of sense: "Honesty is the worst policy"; "Better never than late"; "Invention is the mother of necessity."

"A great deal of learning can be packed into an empty head"–Karl Kraus, 1909–and much glitter can likewise glint from an empty phrase. "God will often say to us: 'You are not in Heaven for fun!'"–Jules Renard, 1906–I don't know what that means. Likewise, "That all men should be brothers is the dream of people who have no brothers." Or, "One does what one is; one becomes what one does." It's easy, as Oscar Wilde often demonstrated, to be arrestingly vacuous ("One's real life is so often the life that one does not lead").

Not at all folk wisdom, the aphorisms flaunt this or that author's solitary ingenuity, a flicker to arrest some solitary reader, hinting dissent from the authority of proverbs. Their appeal can show us how very much alone literate man, *Homo litteratus*, can feel. Unimpressed by communal "knowledge" a free press has compacted into cubical platitude, repelled by old wives' saws fast rotting into toothless cliché, assailed by words that pelt faster than anyone could *speak* them–Homer never withstood words at such a rate–the reader–yes, you, now–longs for something new, something to halt the quick scan of practiced eyes, to provoke an Oho or Aha or even a Golly. And what's this? "It is easier to keep a dozen lovers guessing than to keep one lover after he has stopped guessing"–Helen Rowland, *Reflections of a Bachelor Girl*, 1903. If no great truth, it will last as long as ten minutes.

What the aphorisms lack is the proverb's ability to generalize. They have the air of brittle special cases: how special indeed my life is! How exceptional! Such bait their consumers swallow. The names of sages mustered in this book's index can come to seem like pseudonyms for Dorothy Parker.

If we're to go by the Oxford book's samplings, some of the most gullible producers and consumers, from Montaigne's time to now, have been French. The clean, straightforward syntax of French, the etched contours of its terms, make it a language in which, Faulkner's French translator once complained, it is difficult to be obscure. Its tritest remarks will crystallize into proverbs, sentences whose pith and balance seem as inevitable as the algebra at NASA. A Frenchman's head aches, we may guess, with the pressure of the obvious, and much French ingenuity has gone into unobvious remarks like "Of all sexual aberrations, chastity is the strangest" (Anatole France); or "A great man does enough for us when he refrains from doing us harm" (Beaumarchais); even "Great minds tend toward banality" (Gide, a banal mind?).

"Remarks are not literature," remarked Gertrude Stein, having lived some decades in France.

Literacy is dismayed by the cliché, cliché meaning something it's met twice before. Moon/June? Cliché! "Thou shall not kill"? Cliché! Literacy flattens these into arrangements of twenty-six letters, and we've seen *that* arrangement. Passed mouth to ear, *a stitch in time saves nine* said more than the letters say: it conveyed, in a form in which anybody could use it, a substantial portion of a philosophy of life.

Nor is the genre dead. *If anything can go wrong, it will*, "Commonly known as *Murphy's Law*," is "said to have been invented by George Nichols in 1949 ... developed from a remark made by a colleague, Captain E. Murphy, of the Wright Field-Aircraft Laboratory." We're invited to compare *the bread never falls but on its buttered side,* first acknowledged by A. D. Richardson (*Beyond Mississippi,* 1867), and may come to think we discern in these two sayings a dark underside of the famous American optimism.

To do that would be to underrate the insight of Edward A. Murphy, a reliability engineer for Hughes Helicopters, Inc., who surfaced in a recent issue of *Science 83* to deplore a universal misquotation. What Murphy said was, "If there is a wrong way to do something, then someone will do it." He said it on an ascertainable date, when a costly and dangerous experiment had gone blooey after some drone methodically installed each of sixteen sensors backward.

Edward Murphy was talking about human inattention, not cosmic malevolence, so by heeding his law you can forestall much trouble. No shoulder-shrug, it's practical, like all proverbs: a caution against thoughtlessness.

But it's the thoughtless who have snatched his ball and run with it, and the misquoted form is the one Oxford authenticates. Heed that, and you'll soon be doing nothing at all, because what's the use? And your do-nothing world will have no need for proverbs. It will turn instead wholly to aphorisms, for the savor of their relentless cynicism.

Harper's (May 1983), pp. 84-86.

Proverbs or Aphorisms? (1983)

Stefan Kanfer

There are two classes of people in the world, observed Robert Benchley, "those who constantly divide the people of the world into two classes, and those who do not."

Half of those who divide quote Benchley and his fellow- aphorists. The other half prefer proverbs. And why not? The aphorism is a personal observation inflated into a universal truth, a private posing as a general. A proverb is anonymous human history compressed to the size of a seed. "Whom the gods love die young" implies a greater tragedy than anything from Euripides: old people weeping at the grave site of their children. "Love is blind" echoes of gossip in the marketplace, giggling students and clucking counselors: an Elizabethan comedy flowering from three words.

"A proverb," said Cervantes, "is a short sentence based on long experience," and to prove it he had Sancho and his *paisanos* fling those sentences around like pesetas. "There's no sauce in the world like hunger"; "Never look for birds of this year in the nests of the last"; "Patience, and shuffle the cards." His English contemporary was of two minds about folklore, as he was about everything. Hamlet disdains it: "The proverb is something musty." Yet the plays overflow with musty somethings: "Men are April when they woo: December when they wed"; "A little pot and soon hot"; "The fashion wears out more apparel than the man": and, more to the point, "Patch grief with proverbs."

Like Sancho and Shakespeare, those who praise proverbs favor nature over artifice and peasantry over peerage. Benjamin Franklin always preferred "a drop of reason to a flood of words" and filled *Poor Richard's Almanac* with colonial one-liners: "Three may keep a secret, if two of them are dead"; "The used key is always bright." Emerson thought proverbs "the sanctuary of the intuitions." Tolstoy's knowledge of common tradition led him to an encyclopedia of wisdom. Eastern European sayings have always assumed the clarity and force of vodka: "Where the needle goes, the thread follows"; "The devil pours honey into other men's wives"; "The Russian has three strong principles: *perhaps, somehow* and *never mind.*" In the epoch of the Romanoffs, wisdom was the only thing that was shared equally. Cossacks who conducted pogroms and victims in the shtetls flavored their remarks with the same sour salt. Russian: "The rich would have to eat money, but luckily the poor provide food." Yiddish: "If the rich could hire others to die for them, the poor could make a nice living."

No culture is without proverbs, but many are poor in aphorisms, a fact that leads Critic Hugh Kenner to hail the ancient phrases as something "worth saying again and again, descending father to son, mother to daughter, mouth to mouth." Gazing at *The Concise Oxford Dictionary of Proverbs*, he lauds the short and simple annals of the poor. But he holds *The Oxford Book of Aphorisms* at the proverbial arm's length: "What the aphorisms lack is the proverb's ability to generalize. They have the air of brittle special cases: How special indeed my life is! How exceptional!"

But that very air is the oxygen of the epigram. W.H. Auden, who collected and concocted them, readily admitted that "aphorisms are essentially an aristocratic genre. Implicit is a conviction that [the writer] is wiser than his readers." François de La Rochefoucauld was a duke; elbowed out of prominence in Louis XIV's court, he retreated to an estate to polish his words until nobility could see its face in the surface: "We all have strength enough to endure the misfortunes of others"; "In jealousy there is more self-love than love"; "Hypocrisy is the homage that vice pays to virtue"; "Lovers never get tired of each other, because they are always talking about themselves."

George Savile, first Marquis of Halifax, was alternately in and out of favor with the house of Stuart; his observations were worn smooth by disappointment: "Ambition is either on all fours or on tiptoes"; "The enquiry into a dream is another dream"; "Love is presently out of breath when it is to go uphill, from the children to the parents." By the time aphorisms became the property of the people, commoners had learned to speak like counts. The humbly born Sebastian Chamfort decided that "whoever is not a misanthrope at 40 can never have loved mankind." Nietzsche's phrases bore a strychnine smile: "The thought of suicide is a great consolation; with the help of it one has got through many a bad night"; "Wit closes the coffin on an emotion."

By the mid-19th century, the aphorism had become a favorite of the English. Oscar Wilde exposed the flip side of bromides; "Punctuality is the thief of time"; "Old enough to know worse."

But he could be as pontifical as the next prince: "A thing is not necessarily true because a man dies for it"; "One's real life is often the life that one does not lead." George Bernard Shaw saw the aphorism as the new home for political slogans: "All great truths begin as blasphemies." His contemporary G.K. Chesterton was the last master of the paradox: "Silence is the unbearable repartee"; "A figure of speech can often get into a crack too small for a definition"; "Tradition is the democracy of the dead."

That democracy remains in office; the custom of the sharpened axiom continues. Elizabeth Bowen's "Memory is the editor of one's sense of life" is a Shakespearean perception; Peter De Vries' "Gluttony is an emotional escape, a sign that something is eating us" belongs with the best of the Edwardians. Hannah Arendt's observation compresses the century down to a sentence: "Power and violence are opposites: where one rules absolutely, the other is absent."

Yet the aphorists do not enjoy the last frown. Even now, proverb makers are at work. Traditions have to begin somewhere; today folk sayings arise from economics: "There is no such thing as a free lunch"; from the comics: "Keep on truckin'", and even from computers: "Garbage in, garbage out."

Which, then, has more application to modern life, the people's phrases or the aristocrats'? Not aphorisms, says the proverb: "Fine words butter no parsnips." Not proverbs, insists Alfred North Whitehead's terse dictum: "Seek simplicity and I distrust it." Still, both categories are noted not only for their concision but their consolation. Collectors of aphorisms may yet find support from the biblical proverb "Knowledge increaseth strength." As for the partisans of folk sayings, they can for once side with the fastidious William Wordsworth:

Wisdom is ofttimes nearer when we stoop
Than when we soar.

Time (July 11, 1983), p. 74.

Don't Go to Pear Tree For An Axiom –
Out of the Ozarks (1984)

William Childress

Many an Ozarkian has grown up with axioms ringing in his ears, and I'm no exception. Axioms are those pithy little sayings that will have you nodding wisely and saying, "Yes, there's a lot of truth in that," whether there is or not. Axioms sound true by their very nature. After all, they come from a Greek root meaning "worthy."

Some axioms, of course, are instant teachers and never need repeating. They are epitomized wisdom, and if your mind is right you never question them more than once. Such maxims are "Once burned, twice learned" and – a personal favorite of mine – "Never pick up a live skunk by its tail." It Is the painful proverbs that make the most lasting impression.

But some sayings are simply silly. They will not hold up under hard examination. Take the one I always thought Ben Franklin was responsible for, but which is at least 2,000 years old. No telling how many would-be sewers were frustrated by "A stitch in time saves nine."

The heck it does. Not long ago, my favorite pair of Big Smith overalls, barely 10 years old, developed a slight tear along the main outside leg seam.

Digging out my old U.S. Army sewing kit, I threaded a needle and took the stitch mandated by Ovid and others. Exactly one washing later, the stitch was an unraveled mess – and several inches more had come loose along the outside seam. Far from saving nine, the stitch I took made it necessary for me to take nine – or more.

Another familiar maxim is attributed to Franklin a lot but isn't his. It may belong to some ad-man with an apple-growers co-op, though, because it surely sold a lot of apples. "An apple a day keeps the doctor away" was the way I heard it – and it didn't take me long to prove that was a lot of malarkey, too.

We used to have an orchard on one of the old sharecrop farms I lived on as a kid. In this orchard, apple and peach trees rubbed branches with plum and pear trees. Mostly, these were fruits grown to be canned, and were greener than the bitable kinds found in markets today.

On more than one occasion, I gave religion to a balky mule by zinging a half-pound green pear into the space between his eyes. Normally, a mule will look up only if an anvil lands there – but these pears could hit like howitzer shells. On our ornery days, especially if cousins had come visiting, we'd have "green fruit fights" – and the only welts that raised any higher were the ones we got from our old man's belt for wasting food.

We kids, being cursed with hollow legs, were always hungry – or thought we were. So we rarely waited for the always-green apples to get less green, but fell to raiding the orchards as soon as they reached walnut size. We'd rub the sour slices with a chunk of cow lick salt and make them almost palatable. But our stomachs soon told us the truth, and many's the green-apple bellyache our family doctors had to "purge" us of. They usually gave us an atrocity that is pronounced "slack lime" but is spelled "slaked lime." This stuff was mixed in water and shaken – which is what you also were after you'd taken it and vomited.

Who knows, if we'd stuck to just one apple, maybe it would have kept the doctor away. It didn't matter anyway, because calling a doctor was just an excuse for our folks to study his techniques, so they could practice them on us and save a 50-cent fee in any future emergencies.

"Time is of the essence" is another axiom I never could understand. I thought I understood it, and indeed, I approached it from every side and angle, looking it over with genuine interest – before finally giving a sigh of defeat and admitting that its translation was up to better heads than mine. Time was of the essence, huh? Essence of what? Turpentine? Peppermint? It was obviously not an axiom at all, but a sentence waiting to be completed.

I once had a teacher who was crazy about ancient Rome, and knew the history of every brick and author in it. Her favorite axiomist was Publilius Syrus, who lived a century before Christ. His maxims were toast and marmalade to her, and she consumed them at a great rate, the better to spew them back at us. Being rural, I preferred Aesop's Fables, which dealt with natural critters like grasshoppers, ants and wolves. But Miz Hay loved the sonorous, not the simple.

"Billy," she would gravely ask me out of nowhere (we could be in a hallway, or at recess – no place was safe from her axioms), "what is left when honor is lost?"

A flash of inspiration, and I replied: "A passing grade?" Miz Hay scowled at me every morning after that. But we did not always lack communication. Another of her favorite Syrusian maxims was, "You should go to a pear tree for pears, not to an elm."

I gave that one considerable thought. But no matter how I looked it over, I always came to the same conclusion: If this was intelligence, I was Jefferson Davis. My cousins and I had gone to pear trees for pears many a time. And just about as often, our parents had stripped a branch off an elm tree and walloped us for doing so.

St.Louis Post-Dispatch (October 28, 1984), p. 2D.

Russia's Book of Proverbs –
Must Reading for Arms Negotiators (1985)

James Reston

In planning for next month's nuclear talks with the Russians in Geneva, U.S. officials here have been reading *Pravda*, which in English means "truth," but in official Russian means anything but the truth.

They have also gathered together a shelf of position papers on Soviet history as long and complicated as the Pentagon, but for some reason, they always forget to include my skinny little book of Russian proverbs.

The Soviet negotiators know these proverbs as well as they know the multiplication tables, and quote them whenever they are in trouble. *Kak izvestno* (as is well known), they always say, there's an old Russian proverb: Keep feet in mud, and not in stars.

But in the hands of U.S. negotiators, these Russian proverbs, like the Bible, can be interpreted in many different ways.

For example, said the old Russians:

Wag your tongue as much as you please, but don't wave
   your gun.
Fear has big eyes.
Before a fight, two men are boasters; afterwards, only
   one.
The future is his who knows how to wait.
Better turn back than lose your way.
Don't drive your horse with a whip – use the oat bag.
All that trembles doesn't fall.
We are related: the same sun dries our rags.
The slower you drive, the farther you get.
A bad compromise is better than a good battle.
Be friends with the wolf, but keep one hand on your ax.
In this world, not everyone with a long knife is a cook.
Even the doorstep of the rich finds itself embarrassed by
   the poor.
The cow may be black, but the milk comes out white.
All the brave men are in prison.
Once a word is out of your mouth you can't swallow it
   again.

You can't drive straight on a twisting lane.

The Russian has three principles: perhaps, somehow, and never mind.

Make yourself into a sheep, and you'll meet a wolf nearby.

The Russian is clever, but it comes slowly – all the way from the back of his head.

In Moscow they ring the bells often but not for dinner.

Learn good things – the bad will teach you by themselves.

He has been sent to Siberia to count the birches.

Life is unbearable, but death is not so pleasant either.

What good is honor on an empty stomach?

If you're a rooster, crow; if you're a hen, shut up and lay eggs.

Noblemen make promises, and peasants have to keep them.

In this country you can't even pick a mushroom without bowing.

If you tickle yourself, you can laugh when you please.

The little one is too small; the big one is too big; the medium one is just right – but I can't get it.

Wash a pig as much as you like, it goes right back to the mud.

Russians do not fear the cross, but they fear the club.

When you live close to the graveyard, you can't weep for everybody.

Live a hundred years, learn a hundred years – still you die a fool.

Honor is on top of his tongue and a knife is under it.

Great is Holy Russia, but the sun shines elsewhere, too.

The church is near but the road is all ice; the tavern is far but I'll walk very carefully.

If we knew beforehand where we were going to fall, we could lay down a carpet.

The shortage will be divided among the peasants.

Fools shoot and God directs the bullet.

You'll never get a hangover from other people's vodka.

Live and scratch – when you're dead the itching will stop.

Marriage is like sneezing: even when you feel it coming
   on, you can't stop.
If you're tired of a friend, lend him money.
Better the first quarrel than the last.
The bullet is no respecter of uniforms.
Pray to God but keep rowing to the shore.
When the sheath is broken, you cannot hide the sword.

Here endeth the book of Russian Proverbs. In Geneva they
could be useful, if anybody remembers.

The New York Times (February 17, 1985), p. E19.

Age-Old Proverbs That Ring a Bell –
And Some That We Don't Recall So Well (1985)

Paul Bannister

"Practice makes perfect" is the most popular proverb of them all–and the saying that most easily will evoke a mental image is, "When the cat's away, the mice will play."

That's the finding of memory expert Kenneth L. Higbee, a psychology professor at Brigham Young University, who did a research project on proverbs.

In his study, Dr. Higbee asked 50 students to arrange a lengthy list of proverbs in order of familiarity. He had another 50 students rate the proverbs in order of how easily they aroused mental pictures.

Here are the 12 most familiar proverbs:

Practice makes perfect.
Better late than never.
If at first you don't succeed, try, try again,
Like father, like son.
A place for everything and everything in its place.
Two wrongs don't make a right.
Two's company, three's a crowd.
Don't count your chickens before they're hatched.
All's well that ends well.
Easier said than done.
Practice what you preach.
An apple a day keeps the doctor away.

The five least-known proverbs are: One swallow does not make a summer; little pitchers have big ears; it's better to be right than President; vows made in storms are forgotten in calms, and it's an ill wind that blows nobody any good.

The five best proverbs for evoking a mental image, in order, are: When the cat's away, the mice will play; the early bird catches the worm; like father, like son; don't count your chickens before they're hatched; kill two birds with one stone.

And the five most difficult proverbs for people to picture in their minds are: Brevity is the soul of wit; the exception proves the rule; there's many a slip twixt cup and lip; one swallow does not make a summer, and a little learning can be a dangerous thing.

National Enquirer (March 12, 1985), p. 36.

Better Safe Than Sorry When It Comes to Sayings (1985)

Charles Osgood

I have decided not to live by the wise old sayings anymore. It's not that the wise old sayings don't have a lot of truth and distilled experience in them, it's just that they never quite seem to fit a given situation.

Look before you leap is sound advice, all right. You can get into lots of trouble by leaping before looking.

But if you do too much pre-leap looking, you violate another and completely contradictory wise old saying:

He who hesitates is lost.

It's certainly not going to do you much good looking before leaping, if, in the process, you end up lost because of the inherent hesitating.

Conversely, if in order to avoid loss due to hesitation, you leap before you look, it will be clear to everybody that you are a fool:

Fools rush in where angels fear to tread, as you may know.

Some wise old sayings leave you not quite sure what you are supposed to do:

For example, *A rolling stone gathers no moss.*

Does this mean you are supposed to be like a rolling stone so that you won't gather any moss? Or does it mean that you are not supposed to be a rolling stone, so that you will gather some moss? It all depends on whether you want to gather moss, I suppose.

Why anybody would want to gather moss is certainly beyond me, but *Everyone to his own taste*, as the wise old saying says.

If you ask me, a maxim only gets to be a maxim when it isn't true anymore:

The best offense is a good defense.

Everybody in football knows that, but they also know it isn't true. That's why winning teams always have a good offense and a good defense. The best offense is a good offense ... and the best defense is a good defense.

The same people who would have you believe that *The best offense is a good defense*, probably would tell you that *The best defense is a good offense.*

A bird in the hand is not worth two in the bush, either. I would rather have two birds in a bush than one in my hand any day. If there were a bird in my hand, I would not know what to do with it, to tell you the truth. I do not want a bird in my hand. Anybody with a bird in his hand will soon find out that he was better off when it was in the bush with that other bird.

Take care of the pennies and the dollars will take care of themselves.

This is a great saying if you have pennies but no dollars. If you have dollars and pennies and take care of the pennies on the theory that the dollars will take care of themselves, you are making a big mistake.

The thing to do is to take care of the dollars and let the pennies take care of themselves. If people go around taking care of their pennies and letting their dollars take care of themselves, it's no wonder that:

A fool and his money are soon parted.

USA Weekend (December 6-8, 1985), p. 22.

Clichés – Words of Wisdom on Sayings Like "Raining Cats and Dogs" (1987)

Gregg Levoy

Nowhere does the saying "Imitation is the highest form of flattery" more readily apply than to the cliché.

For centuries people have been using and abusing clichés, with nary a trace of boredom or fatigue – familiarity does not always breed contempt – and with nary a footnote given to their originators.

Perhaps that is because we have forgotten who those literary forefathers (and mothers) were.

In an attempt to remedy this situation, then, here is a compendium of the origins of some of our most noble platitudes.

Acid test: In 1918 Woodrow Wilson said, "The acid test of their good will," meaning a sternly critical exam designed to reveal the slightest flaw. The term comes from the use of nitric acid to test gold for impurities. Inferior metals will decompose – gold won't.

Barking up the wrong tree: Raccoon hunting, usually done at night, relies on dogs to force raccoons up trees and then stand there barking until hunters arrive. Often a dog will bark up the wrong tree, wasting his and the hunter's time and energy. Hence, attention ill-directed.

Beat around the bush: This term, meaning to approach something indirectly, goes back a few centuries. Hunters hired beaters to beat bushes to arouse game birds for the shooting. So, beaters stirred up the action, but hunters got to the point.

The bigger they are, the harder they fall: This one comes from prizefighting. In 1902 "Ruby Roberts" Fitzsimmons, one-time heavyweight champion of the world, said this at a fight with James J. Jeffries, a much bigger man. By the way, clichés aren't always true. Jeffries won.

Cloud nine: It means to be euphoric, and it is actual U.S. Weather Bureau terminology. Clouds are divided into classes, each of which is also divided into nine types. Cloud nine is the cumulo-nimbus cloud that builds up on hot summer afternoons, and may reach heights of 30,000 to 40,000 feet. If one is really high, one is said to be on cloud nine.

Don't look a gift horse in the mouth: One of the oldest proverbs, this goes back to 420 A.D. Traditionally the age of a horse could be determined by examining the condition of his teeth. It was considered poor manners to do that, however, with a horse that was given to you. By extension, don't inquire too closely into the value of a gift.

Living high on the hog: It means living prosperously, and it is quite an accurate description, since you have to go pretty high on the hog to get the tender, and expensive, cuts of loin and roast.

Getting up on the wrong side of the bed: From a late 18th-century superstition that right is right and left is wrong. If you got out of bed on the left side, or with your left leg first, or made the error of putting your left shoe on first, it was considered bad luck. And if your day was thus stricken, the rest of your day promised to be no better.

Leave no stone unturned: This goes back to the wars between the Persians (led by general Mardonius) and the Thebians (led by general Polycrates) in 471 B.C. Mardonius was supposed to have hidden a great treasure under his tent, but when he was defeated, Polycrates couldn't find it. When he consulted the Oracle at Delphi, he was told to return and leave no stone unturned, and he found the treasure.

A corollary to this tells of a young man standing by the seashore, throwing stone after stone at a flock of birds at the water's edge. When his grandfather reprimanded him for his cruelty, the young man remarked that he was only trying to fulfill his lifelong ambition to leave no tern unstoned.

Paint the town red: This term for a wild spree probably originated on the frontier. In the 19th century that section of town hosting brothels and saloons was, and still is, known as the red-light district. So a group of lusty cowboys out for a night on the town might very well decide to make the whole town red.

Raining cats and dogs: This comes from the Dark Ages when cats were thought to cause rain, and dogs wind and storms.

Just to show that expressions don't become clichés only as a function of their great longevity, there are quite a few modern ones that have become "user friendly." The "bottom line" is that clichés will "keep on truckin'."

The Minneapolis Star Tribune (Sept. 9, 1987), p. 1C and p. 7C.

82

You Know What They Say ...
Are Proverbs Nuggets of Truth or Fool's Gold? (1988)

Alfie Kohn

Proverbs are heirlooms, treasured and passed on from generation to generation. These pithy, unforgettable phrases seem to sum up timeless wisdom about human nature. But are the truisms really true? Stacked up against the results of psychological research, they're pretty hit-and-miss: Some home-grown adages hit; some maxims miss.

[Laugh and the World Laughs With You;] Cry and you cry alone.

Misery may love company (depressed people are more likely to seek emotional support than are people who are not depressed), but company clearly does not love misery. In 1976, psychologist James C. Coyne, while at Miami University, asked 45 female college students to talk on the phone for 20 minutes with other women, some of whom were depressed–although the students weren't told that. Later, the students indicated they had much less interest in spending time with the depressed women than with the others.

Such reactions are part of a vicious circle that is all too common among unhappy people: Their behavior drives away the very people whose support and acceptance they need, thereby worsening their depression and intensifying their need for support. These findings are also important because they suggest that when depressed people say others view them negatively, they may well be right.

Spare the rod and spoil the child.

Few proverbs have been so thoroughly disproved–or have caused so much harm–as this one. Nearly 40 years of research have shown conclusively that the "rod" produces children who are more aggressive than their peers. "Physical punishment teaches that the way to solve problems is to beat up others," says Leonard Eron, a research psychologist at the University of Illinois at Chicago. He and others explain that having children focus on what they did wrong and why it was wrong encourages them to internalize control of their own actions. But physical punishment, while suppressing misbehavior in the short run, ultimately promotes nothing more than a determination to avoid getting caught.

83

In 1960 Eron and his colleagues studied 870 8-year-olds in rural New York and found a clear-cut relationship between the severity of the physical punishment they received–ranging from none at all to slaps and spankings–and how aggressive other children judged them to be. Twenty-two years later, the researchers tracked down some of these same people and found that the aggressive kids were now aggressive adults. And those adults now had aggressive children of their own.

The squeaky wheel gets the grease.

Obviously we don't get everything we ask for, but many people get more than others just by demanding it. Salaries are a case in point. Psychologist Brenda Major and her colleagues at the State University of New York at Buffalo asked management students, most of whom had real-world work experience under their belts, to play the role of a personnel supervisor at a department store. Folders from mock applicants indicated what salary levels were expected–some of them below, some at and some above the range advertised.

The result? Pay expectations didn't affect who was offered a job. But of the applicants who were hired, those who squeaked louder got more grease–in their palms. "Although applicants did not receive exactly what they asked for," the researchers say, "the more pay an applicant requested, the more pay he or she was offered."

Actions speak louder than words.

Common sense suggests that our impressions of people are shaped more by how they act than by what they say about themselves. But Brandeis University psychologist Teresa M. Amabile and her student Loren G. Kabat tested this idea by videotaping women while they deliberately acted either introverted or extroverted in conversations and while they described themselves as having one or the other personality trait.

Then, 160 students watched the videotapes and evaluated how "outgoing," "friendly," "shy" or "withdrawn" the women were. When the women's self-descriptions and actual behavior conflicted, the students usually gave more credence to behavior. In general, the students' judgments were influenced about 20 times more strongly by what the women did than by what they said about themselves.

Actions speak louder than words not only when we judge the character of adults but when we try to shape the character of children. Adults who want to encourage children to be generous should practice what they preach, according to psychologists James H. Bryan and Nancy Hodges Walbek of Northwestern University. These researchers awarded gift certificates to fourth-graders for playing a miniature bowling game and offered them a chance to put some of their winnings in a box "for the poor children" if they chose. The children had previously seen adults who either donated or didn't and who preached either generosity or selfishness. When the adults' actions didn't match their advice, the researchers found, the children were more likely to pay attention to the deeds than to the words.

Beauty is only skin deep.

Psychologists Karen Dion, Ellen Berscheid and Elaine Hatfield found in 1972 that when people are good-looking, we assume many other good things about them. These researchers asked 60 students to describe people's character solely on the basis of their photographs. The more attractive people were rated as more socially desirable and likely to have more prestigious jobs and happier marriages than those who were less attractive. This study, entitled "What is Beautiful is Good," unleashed a torrent of social psychological studies on attractiveness. Scores of researchers since then have uncovered a major self-fulfilling prophecy: Because attractive people are treated as if they have more to offer, they live up to our positive expectations. Sadly, those less pleasing to look at live down to our negative expectations.

In studies looking at the relationship between attractiveness and personality, good-looking people turn out to have higher self-esteem and to be happier, less neurotic and more resistant to peer pressure than those who are less attractive. The list goes on. Those blessed with good looks also have more influence on others, get higher salaries, receive more lenient decisions in court, are thought by their students to be superior teachers and are more valued as friends, colleagues and lovers. The general pattern is true of both men and women.

One of the most distressing findings is that attractiveness is related to the perception–and perhaps even the reality–of serious mental disorders. Psychologist Warren H. Jones and his colleagues at the University of Tulsa found that it was assumed that ugly people were more likely to be psychologically disturbed than were good-looking ones. Even when Jones and his coworkers made a point of telling people to disregard attractiveness, they still rated the unattractive people as more troubled.

When Kevin O'Grady, a psychologist at the University of New Mexico, stopped people on the street and asked them to fill out a questionnaire assessing their chances of ever developing psychological disorders, he found that the better-looking people were, the more remote seemed their chances of becoming mentally ill.

The trouble is, these predictions may be right. A study by psychologist Amerigo Farina and colleagues at the University of Connecticut showed that female psychiatric patients were relatively unattractive compared with other women–and not simply because their troubles had spoiled their looks. A study of a similar group of female patients showed that, judging by yearbook photographs, they were less attractive than their peers even back in high school, before they were hospitalized.

"The way we treat attractive versus unattractive people shapes the way they think about themselves," says University of Hawaii psychologist Hatfield, "and, as a consequence, the kind of people they become." Beauty in our culture is clearly more than a superficial matter.

Beauty is as beauty does.
The central finding of the research on attractiveness is that what is beautiful is indeed good. But psychologist Alan E. Gross and colleague Christine Crofton of the University of Missouri at St. Louis wondered whether the reverse is also true: Is what is good beautiful? In other words, do our judgments of people's attractiveness rest partly on how we view their character?

Gross and Crofton sorted photos of women by their attractiveness and attached them to invented personality descriptions. Some were presented as good students, friendly, energetic and so on; others as average; and a third group as losers. People were asked to evaluate how attractive they found these people. It turned out that the more favorably described they were, the better-looking they were judged to be, regardless of how physically attractive they really were. (Other researchers have found that character descriptions affect how women's attractiveness is judged but not men's.)

Marry in haste, repent at leisure.

Any way you look at it, this proverb is true. If "marrying in haste" means marrying young, then many studies support the adage. People who wed as teenagers are twice as likely to get divorced as those who wed in their 20s.

If "haste" means a whirlwind romance before marriage–at whatever age–that, too, can lead to marital problems. A large-scale British study from the 1970s revealed that 20 percent of those who were divorced–as opposed to only 8 percent of those still married–had known their partner for less than a year before tying the knot.

Familiarity breeds contempt.

Yes, intimate knowledge can lead to passionate hatred, but familiarity is usually more likely to breed liking than contempt. In a classic series of studies, psychologist Robert Zajonc of the University of Michigan showed people a set of seven-letter Turkish words. They didn't know what the words meant, but the more often people saw certain words, the more likely they were to say they meant something good. Likewise, after being shown yearbook photographs of men they didn't know, people said they liked the men whose photos they had seen more often. If you already have reason to dislike something or someone strongly, greater exposure probably won't change your feelings. But most of us seem to find things and people more likable as we get used to them–at least up to a point. David J. Hargreaves, a psychologist at the University of Leicester, in England, believes that after enough exposure to a piece of music, say, or a work of art, a person will find it less pleasant. Too much familiarity, Hargreaves contends, can leave us wanting less.

He who lives by the sword, dies by the sword.

If the contemporary "sword" is a handgun, then this maxim seems to be true. A study of more than 700 gunshot deaths in the Seattle area from 1978 to 1983 showed that most of them had occurred in homes where a gun was kept. Moreover, the guns were far more likely to kill a resident than an intruder. In only two cases was a stranger killed; the rest were accidental deaths, suicides or homicides in which the victim was either a friend of the gun owner or a member of the family.

Many proverbs, like muscles and expert witnesses, come in opposing pairs. For every adage counseling caution, such as

"Look before you leap," there is one exhorting us to throw caution to the winds, such as, "He who hesitates is lost." We are told that "Too many cooks spoil the broth" but also advised that "Many hands make light work." People tell us that "Variety is the spice of life," but they also say that "Old shoes are easiest."

Intrigued by the way we react to such conflicting advice, psychologist Karl Halvor Teigen of the University of Bergen, Norway, devised a clever experiment in 1986. He transformed 24 proverbs into their opposites. Thus, for example, "Fear is stronger than love" became "Love is stronger than fear," and "Truth needs no colors" became "Truth needs colors."

Teigen gave his students lists that contained some authentic sayings and some that he had just reversed, asking them to rate how original and true the proverbs were. The result: no significant difference between the wisdom of the ages and Teigen's newly minted counterfeits.

When proverbs conflict, which ones should we believe? You can pick the one that suits the moment, or you can lean on the psychological experts. Here's how three pairs of proverbs stack up against the research:

You're never too old to learn vs. You can't teach an old dog new tricks.

People learn new things their whole lives through, but aging does make the process somewhat harder. As a rule, older adults have more difficulties with intellectual functioning than do younger adults. For example, some studies suggest that beyond age 60, people find it more difficult to remember texts they read or hear and have trouble distinguishing between more- and less-important ideas in the text. But since there is considerable variation among people of any given age, there are a good number of elderly exceptions to the rule.

Psychologists Warner Schaie and Christopher Hertzog of Pennsylvania State University have been testing a group of 162 people at seven-year intervals since 1956 to see how their intelligence changes. A number of measures have shown a decline in ability that becomes evident after age 60. But Schaie and other researchers have found that, up to a point, older people can be taught skills that will compensate for or reverse this decline.

Many types of training seem to help in the short run, although the effects don't always last. Psychologist Paul Baltes and his colleagues at the Max Planck Institute in Berlin, for example, put more than 200 older people through a training program that helped them to identify rules and concepts useful in solving problems on intelligence tests. The people's scores did improve. Although they had begun to fall back after six months, they were still ahead of where they were before the training began.

In a study conducted by Schaie and psychologist Sherry L. Willis, a group of people whose average age was over 72 were given five one-hour training sessions similar to those used by Baltes, then tested and compared with their own levels of cognitive ability of 14 years earlier. The training brought 40 percent back to their previous mark and helped many others to a less dramatic extent.

A "substantial proportion" of older people, Schaie and Willis conclude, were victims of the "use it or lose it" rule: Their intellectual abilities probably declined due to disuse. But those abilities are not really lost, they say. They can be regained, at least in part, through "relatively simple and inexpensive educational training techniques."

Absence makes the heart grow fonder vs. Out of sight, out of mind.

The effect of absence depends on how you felt to begin with. If a lover is absent (assuming you aren't distracted by someone new), separation is likely to intensify whatever you felt before you were torn apart. If you felt positively, absence will allow you to cling to an idealized version of your beloved that can't be contradicted by real-life imperfections.

That's the conclusion of Abraham Tesser, a psychologist at the University of Georgia, based on more than a decade of work with attitudes toward everything from people to paintings. "Absence has the potential for making the heart grow fonder," he says, but if your feelings start out negative, "absence will make the heart grow colder."

Psychologist Phillip Shaver and his colleagues at the University of Denver came up with a similar conclusion. They asked 400 college freshmen what they felt about the people they left back home. It turned out that their relationships with family members had improved, but high school romances tended to disintegrate with distance. High school loves weren't necessarily forgotten; they just weren't remembered as being all that great after all.

Birds of a feather flock together vs. Opposites attract.

People are more like birds than magnets. After lots of research, the idea that opposites attract still has gained little experimental support, according to psychologist Richard W. Lewak of the Del Mar Psychiatric Clinic and his co-workers in California. Many studies have shown that people who share the same racial, religious and economic backgrounds usually flock together, as do those with similar political views. And when it comes to attraction powerful enough to draw people into wedlock, "Marriage partners tend to be more alike than different," the researchers say. Lewak's own work shows that we tend to marry people whose IQ's are more or less similar to our own. And, as psychologist Bernard Murstein of Connecticut College and other researchers have found, despite our fantasies of marrying the most magnificent-looking person possible, we're likely to wind up with someone about as attractive as we are. According to University of Michigan psychologist David M. Buss, the principle that people are attracted to those similar to themselves is "one of the most well established replicable findings in the psychology and biology of human mating."

Psychology Today, 22, no. 4 (April 1988), pp. 36-41.

Too Many Cooks Mix a Metaphor –
As My Mom Never Said (1988)

Joe Queenan

A Boston chef pummels a soup tureen, telling his employer: "Spare the rod, spoil the broth." A nine-year-old San Diego girl is hospitalized with second-degree burns after her mother tells her: "You've cooked your goose, now lie in it." A St. Louis zookeeper declares, "Monkey do, but you can't make him drink it."

All across the nation a disturbing new phenomenon is manifesting itself: chronic misquotation of society's most revered maxims, usually resulting from the hybridization of totally unrelated pieces of hackneyed advice. According to Dr. Stanley "The Greek" Aston-Foucault, co-chairman of the President's Commission on Banality and author of *What Johnny Don't Know*, "The epidemic of maxim-mangling that has erupted in this country is quite literally rocking the linguistic foundations of our society, making communication all but impossible.

"Although almost universally maligned," Aston-Foucault contends, "sententious phrases such as 'The grass is always greener on the other side' are actually repositories of society's deepest convictions about itself. Americans, as a people, truly believe that sunny sides should be kept up and that shoes that fit ought to be worn. Today, however, these archetypal kernels of savvy lingo are being undermined as never before."

Critics almost universally agree that the blame for this situation lies with the public schools. "Miseducated by a generation of unqualified teachers, our children are getting the short end of the stick," fumes Millicent Terkel, chairperson of Watchdog on Banality, a non-profit organization sponsoring sententiousness at the state and municipal levels. "In a recent study of our high school graduates, 76 percent said that it was impossible to see the forest while the cat was away, 86 percent believed that blood was thicker than the milk of human kindness, and an astonishing 96 percent agreed with the statement: 'You don't miss your water till the sun shines, Nellie.'"

Yet certain critics are less ready to assign blame to teachers. In *What About Those Chicano SAT Scores?*, ethnolinguist Trish-Medusa Radcliffe cites three separate cases in which major publishing houses headed by bigots deliberately included misquoted maxims in Spanish-English textbooks in the hopes of confusing young Hispanics and preventing them from improving their own economic well-being. Alluding to Dunceman and Dinkel's sabotaged grammar school primer, *Let's Have Fun, Maybe*, Radcliffe says: "When a young Latino shows up at a job interview and tells the interviewer that he's ready to roll up his nose, put his mouth to the grindstone, keep his elbows clean and his big sleeves shut, and then expects to be told he's got good feet on his shoulders, he's not likely to get many middle-management jobs."

Lothar O'Grady, deputy cryptoethnolinguist at the Hoke Foundation, concedes that semiliterate teachers and racist conspiracies are a major part of the problem, but points out that some modified maxims may be a "reflection of society's wholly justified rethinking of its position on certain enduring realities." "Last week I read that three major New York restaurants were closed by the Board of Health because employees were sleeping in the meat locker. So maybe kids are right when they say that 'too many cooks lie down with the lamb.' "

Aston-Foucault grudgingly agrees that some of the misquoted adages may reflect a more accurate grasp of emerging political, social, and economic realities. "I'm willing to admit that a penny saved is worth two in the bush," he says. "I'm even willing to admit that an empty barrel will keep the doctor away. But does anyone seriously believe that he who hesitates is the mother of invention?"

Terkel takes a similar position. "For some time we have been living in a country whose men no longer want a girl just like the girl that married dear old dad, in a country whose women would not bake a cake even if they knew you were coming. But now we find ourselves surrounded by people who honestly believe that if you can't beat them, skin a cat, that there's more than one way for every dog to do as the Romans do, and that what goes up, the merrier. I'm not sure this is a good place to be raising kids."

The New Republic (May 2, 1988), pp. 13-14.

It's a Wise Horse that Doesn't Chew a Hose: The Wisdom of the Ages Is All Very Good – Provided You Can Make Any Sense Out of It (1988)

Judith Stone

Strange to think that an actual, unsung person must once have sat down and hammered out a masterpiece of pith like "The early bird catches the worm." But someone had to, sometime. Men and women in medieval cloisters probably toiled for weeks on a single proverb: "Yo! Brother Acidophilus! Check this out: 'He who hesitates is viscous!' It doesn't sing? Okay. How about, 'He who hesitates is fat'? No? Let me work on it." An adage doesn't just happen, you know.

As long ago as 2350 B.C. an Egyptian vizier wrote "The Maxims of Ptahhotep," among which is this gem: "Good speech is more hidden than malachite, yet it is found in the possession of women slaves at the millstones." (Probably it was punchier in the original ancient Egyptian, which read roughly, "Beetle, beetle, squiggly line, moon, King Tut-style hat, asp." Proverbs that sound terribly wise in languages you don't understand often seem to translate as something like, "Better to tap-dance with a crustacean than play Yahtzee with the devil.")

Such folk wisdom is without doubt metaphorically helpful, I recently mused, but is it scientifically sound? Does the early bird indeed catch the worm, and is there some evolutionary advantage to avian punctuality? If you lead a horse to water, can you make him drink? Can you make him do drugs? I decided to ask the experts. And, in general, their answers increased my admiration for the anonymous aphorists of the ages.

Apparently, for example, a sailor's delight really is a red sky at night, although you'd expect it to be a red light somewhat less celestial. But meteorologist David Smith of the U.S. Naval Academy Department of Oceanography insists it's a red sky, and some sort of honor code prohibits him from lying about what turns on a mariner.

"There's wisdom in the adage," he says, "but it's useful only when the sun is behind you. In middle latitudes, weather tends to move from west to east. At night the sun is to the west. The reddish tint is sunlight being bent by clouds to the east, which means that the weather systems have already passed you, and you can expect a clearing trend. In the morning the sun is to the

east. Red means light's being refracted by clouds to the west –
bad weather is approaching. 'Red sky at morning, sailors take
warning.'" A more helpful adage might be, Red sky at morning,
sailors take Dramamine.

Another popular saying would require only minor alterations
to be 100 percent scientifically correct, though its rhythm would
be ruined: You can lead a horse to water, but you probably can't
make him drink unless you shove a tube down his nose. "It's
very, very difficult to get a horse to drink if he doesn't want to,"
says Jack Algeo, head of the animal sciences department at California Polytechnic State University in San Luis Obispo. "I've
seen horses hauled from far away refuse to drink water they're
not used to. They'll look at it and put their noses in it, but they
won't drink."

The tricks used to induce human beverage intake – salty bar
snacks, little paper umbrellas, wet T-shirt contests – just aren't
going to work on Mr. Ed. "You might add a few drops of flavor-
ing to the water – horses like molasses, or Jell-O flavors like
strawberry or raspberry," Algeo suggests. "If you absolutely had
to get fluids into a horse – though I've never seen one that dehy-
drated – you could run a tube through the nasal passage and into
the esophagus. If you try to pass a tube orally, he'll chew on it. A
horse can chew a hose in half." Waiting's the best ploy, Algeo
says. Within a few hours even the most intransigent neighsayer
is usually slurping up a storm.

Next I learned the correct thing to mutter when your boss's
idiot nephew gets another promotion: "Blood is ten to thirty percent thicker than water!" According to hematologist Daniel
Weisdorf of the University of Minnesota, the thickness of blood
can be determined through a procedure called viscometry, which
measures how long a certain amount of blood takes to drip
through a thin glass tube. "If you run equal amounts of blood and
water through identical tubes," Weisdorf says, "you'll see that
the blood takes longer to drip out than the water does."

Geologists I spoke to were adamant that a rolling stone gathers no moss. "If indeed the particle is rolling, it would be
abraded, or worn down, not accreted, or added to," says Karl
Koenig of Texas A&M. "Anything accreted to it would be
scraped away as soon as it impinged on another surface." But I
felt it was important to get the moss's side of the story, so I went
to William Buck, curator of bryophytes at the New York Botani-

94

cal Garden. "I don't see how a rock can pick up anything," he says, "be it moss or a date for Saturday night." And that's the last word on moss transit.

The whole bird-worm thing doesn't tie up quite so neatly. "Those birds, such as robins, that eat worms are more likely to catch them in the morning, because worms come to the surface when the ground is moist and cool and disappear in the heat of the day," says Mike Cunningham, associate curator of birds at the Los Angeles Zoo. But because their metabolic rate is so high, he adds, most birds feed in the morning and the evening. So presumably a late bird could also get a worm? "A worm-eating bird," says Cunningham, "looks for worms whenever it can get them."

Maybe you're not interested in catching worms but in catching flies – specifically, whether you can catch more with honey than with vinegar. "There happens to be a kind of fly called the vinegar fly," says entomologist Al Grigarick of the University of California at Davis, "which is attracted to fermenting odors. If you want to attract the greatest variety of flies, however, honey is probably your best bet. But neither will catch any flies unless it's used as bait in a trap; the flies won't land in it, but beside it." The best way to use sweets as bait, Grigarick says, is to soak string in sugar solution and insecticide. "Houseflies seem to be attracted to stringlike objects," he explains. "They have sensory receptors that allow them to taste with their feet as well as their mouthparts, and they pick up the insecticide that way." I think the moral here is, Don't eat with your feet.

Or maybe don't eat at all, if you're sneezing: I'd heard somewhere that the expression "Feed a cold, starve a fever" originated perhaps 1,000 years ago and employed the Old English word *steorfan*, "to die." Its true meaning then, according to this theory, was, "Feed a cold and you will die of a fever." I ran this by George H. Brown, professor of English at Stanford. *Steorfan* – and subsequently the Middle English word *sterven* – did once mean to die, he confirmed. But by the nineteenth century, when the expression first appears in the literature (and colds and fevers were epidemic in England), starve had been in use in its modern sense for at least 300 years. Nineteenth-century physicians shared with common folk the belief that a cold, thought to be caused by a chill, could be cured by heating up the body, with food as fuel. A fever required cooling, achieved by fasting. This belief was probably based on the writings of Hippocrates: "As the soil is, to trees, so is the stomach to animals. It nourishes, it warms, it cools; as it empties it cools, as it fills it warms."

A satisfying explanation, but medically beside the point. "A cold is caused by a virus; it's self-limiting," says internist Joel Curtis of Beth Israel Medical Center in New York. What or how much you eat has no bearing on the length or severity of the illness.

But Ogden Nash, purveyor of pedigreed doggerel, was right on the money when he maintained in his poem "Reflections on Ice-Breaking" that "Candy / Is dandy / But liquor / Is quicker."

"Alcohol begins its absorption directly across the stomach," says Curtis Wright, a researcher in behavioral pharmacology at Johns Hopkins School of Medicine. "Blood alcohol begins to rise almost immediately after ingestion. In general, sugar can't be absorbed until it moves from the stomach to the small intestine. Most candy contains sucrose, a disaccharide that has to be split into glucose and fructose before it can be absorbed."

And that's why alcohol is so much more efficacious than Milk Duds as a social lubricant.

If you read last month's column, you know why eating candy creates a feeling of well being. Ingesting any carbohydrate triggers an insulin surge, starting a chain reaction that ultimately increases the level of endorphins, the brain's feel-good chemical. How does alcohol work its magic?

"You could stir up a lively debate, among scientists as to what exactly is involved in intoxication," Wright says. "Some people believe that alcohol actually produces a narcoticlike substance in the brain, but that theory hasn't held up too well recently. There's also a hypothesis that alcohol produces a swelling of all the membranes of the body. That swelling distorts certain chemical receptors in the brain that are very closely related to the barbiturates and benzodiazapines – Valium-like drugs that are generally thought to be euphorigenic. These distorted chemical receptors then fire abnormally, as if a drug were there."

Talk about a swell party.

One intriguing, highly specialized subset of folk wisdom is parental guidance: "Your face is going to freeze in that horrible expression!" Where do moms and dads pick up this stuff? It must be genetic, or maybe hormonal, because once otherwise sane and admirable people such as ourselves reproduce, we are possessed by devils – Ma and Pazuzu – who make us say things like, "Will you be happy when you break it?" and "Sure it's fun, until someone loses an eye."

Speaking of which, a favorite in the parent's admonition derby is "Don't read in that light, you'll ruin your eyes." Wrong. "People falsely equate illumination with vision," says ophthalmologist Hampton Roy of the University of Arkansas Medical Center. "Sometimes people over forty who suffer from presbyopia [an inability of the lens to change shape in order to focus up close] can see better when their pupils contract in brighter light. Perhaps because some mothers see better in brighter light, they think their children will see better in brighter light. But as long as you can see the page, you're fine." In fact, intense ultraviolet light, both natural and artificial, is bad for your eyes. Ophthalmologist Sidney Lerman of Emory University, who's been studying the long-term effects of ultraviolet light, says that it causes at least 10 percent of the cataracts in this country. He hastens to add that testing can reveal those individuals who are vulnerable and that with proper protection, such cataracts can be prevented.

Maybe when your mother told you not to read in that light, you'd whine, "But Lumpy's mother lets him." That really fried your mom's hide, didn't it? "And if Lumpy told you to jump off a cliff," she'd ask acidly, "would you do it?" The scientific answer to your mother's question is, "Probably not." According to child psychiatrist Charles Binger of the University of California at San Francisco, although acceptance by peers is terribly important to young people, most adolescents won't abandon family values in the face of peer pressure. "Studies of normal kids show that, contrary to popular belief, they go through adolescence without being particularly rebellious. The better the home life, the less likely the child is to flee to peers, and the more likely he or she is to choose peers wisely."

Finally, I wanted to learn the truth behind a popular rhetorical device used when the reply to a question is obviously affirmative. We might call it the theological-ursine-scatological-sylvan interrogative series: Is the pope Catholic? Does a bear – let's say sit – in the woods? The first statement is indisputable. But what's the straight poop on the second? "If you want to get picky," says Penny Kalk, collections manager of the mammal department at the Bronx Zoo, "it would depend upon the bear." Polar bears, she points out, sometimes drift for days on ice floes; they may answer the call of nature there, or in the water. "But the American black bear, the animal most people have in mind when they think 'bear,' lives in the woods; that's where they eat, and what goes in must come out."

I still have much to investigate. Are scientists absolutely positive, for example, that not the tiniest quantum of benefit can be wrung from crying over spilled milk? This project will take a while. Has it been worth the trouble so far? Does it make the universe a more explicable, comfortable place to live? Is the pope Catholic? Is good speech more hidden than malachite?

Discover (October 1988), pp. 76-78.

Words of Wisdom (1989)

Perry W. Buffington

Is it true that birds of a feather flock together? Do our actions speak louder than words? What about beauty–is it more than skin deep? Does absence make the heart grow fonder? And if the rod is spared, is the child really spoiled? Some of these adages may be right on the mark, but others miss the point altogether. Yet proverbs are used frequently and are often regarded as gospel. Whether they are actually nuggets of truth is only of secondary importance; the simple proverb's beauty is much more than skin deep.

The proverb is an heirloom which connects one generation with another. These pithy phrases represent ageless wisdom about human existence. Although they have been studied psychologically for only 15 years, they have been around forever and are found in every spoken language with remarkable similarity of meaning.

The proverb, "A bird in the hand is worth two in the bush," originated in medieval Latin, and variants of it are found in Romanian, Italian, Spanish, German, Icelandic, and other languages. One can find the equivalent of the biblical proverb (which, like many, has a parallel in ancient Greek), "An eye for an eye, a tooth for a tooth," in many languages. For instance, in East Africa the same proverb reads: "A goat's hide buys a goat's hide and a gourd a gourd."

Proverbs seem to have never-ending lives of their own. Once created, they tend to be valued, collected, and passed on by societies. Ancient Egyptian proverb collections date back to as early as 2500 BC. Proverbs were used in ancient China to provide ethical instruction, and those found in the Vedic writings of India were used to promote philosophical ideas. Used in monasteries, proverbs taught novices Latin and were incorporated into sermons, homilies, and scholarly works. As a result, they were preserved in manuscripts.

The first English collection was the *Proverbs of Alfred*, published in the early 12th Century. Based on the timbre of that time, these contained religious and moral precepts. British playwright John Heywood's dialogue of 1546 helped proverbs in literature and oratory to reach new heights in England during the 16th and 17th centuries. Following suit, North America discovered proverbs via Benjamin Franklin's *Poor Richard's Almanac*, published annually from 1732-1757. Franklin took traditional European proverbs and reworked them from the American perspective.

Due to a resurgence of interest in folklore, the proverb is now receiving due attention. Even in psychology, the simple proverb has found new meaning. Dr. Richard Honeck, professor of psychology at The University of Cincinnati, has been studying proverb retention for over 15 years. As one of a handful of researchers, his love of the proverb has grown out of his desire to better understand how an individual processes and ultimately understands language. The proverb is unique, however, because its comprehension requires extra mental manipulation.

According to Honeck, the expert in proverb comprehension, "When people hear a proverb, they must go beyond surface meaning and come up with a figurative understanding." The simple proverb goes through a four-step, mental transformation process before it is completely processed.

The first step is recognition. Honeck explains, "By this [recognition] I mean, people realize that at a purely literal level, the proverb does *not* fit. Imagine the child whose bike has a flat tire. The parent walks up, and instead of saying, 'I told you so!' says, 'A stitch in time saves nine.' The kid must recognize that the bike has nothing to do with stitches. There is some other meaning involved here."

How this insight comes about is not known. Likewise, how one moves from recognition to the second step, "literal transformation stage," is not understood by any psycholinguistic researcher. According to Honeck, "Somehow, the child in the example realizes that the information cannot be used in a literal way. But how that child takes a flat tire and transforms it into 'stitches in time' is not known to anyone. But it happens." Now, the deceptively simple proverb is mentally transformed and linked with the problem event, and the third stage emerges.

Honeck explains: "The third step, figurative-meaning stage, is the point which most researchers have found interesting. This stage has to do with abstract meaning. When a person remembers a proverb, they also remember a figurative meaning, an abstract meaning of some kind. When they get to this stage, it is relatively and permanently represented in memory–long-term memory–so that it is available when it comes up again." Now the child understands that had he put air in his bike tire all along (a stitch in time), he would have avoided the work of repairing a flat, damaged tire (saves nine stitches). The literal and figurative meanings together with stage-two insight, are one.

Finally, Honeck explains, application is possible. He refers to the last stage as "instantiation." As he puts it, "This word basically means example or illustration. Now that the person, the child in our example, understands what the proverb means, he or she can recognize all sorts of examples. Theoretically, the child can, in a totally new context, recognize other instances where somebody could validly say, 'A stitch in time saves nine.'" Now, not only can a person recognize a proverb, but he or she can also use it abstractly and effectively.

It is this abstract quality that separates the proverb from the maxim, adage, fable (actually an extended proverb), aphorism, and metaphor. The proverb is,as Honeck puts it, "more abstract, and has a wider variety of situations which can illustrate it. It has a wider range of applications." Additionally, the proverb is written in the present tense and has a figurative meaning "designed to make a pragmatic point."

What does the proverb do? According to Honeck, "Proverbs are essentially complex names for categories." They allow a person to pigeon-hole or compartmentalize a whole bunch of different situations under one umbrella. They make complex situations seem simple, and are explanatory, used to make points without saying, "I told you so." They are nonconfrontational.

Proverbs also promote a special type of thinking. Numerous research articles have extolled the value of proverbs as a means of teaching abstract thinking, an ability associated with brighter individuals and demonstrated to be essential in problem-solving, creativity, and general intelligence. In fact, there is even a psychological test that measures one's ability to understand proverbs. As Honeck stresses, "Proverbs are a way for individuals to see that language can be understood and used at a variety of levels for a variety of functions." The same skills used in proverb comprehension are utilized when a person mentally moves from a literal, concrete, situation-specific understanding of things to an abstract, figurative level. This is considered to be the mark of higher intelligence. Proverbs teach the ability to understand without requiring that person be shown specific situations. It may be said that abstract thinking allows a person to think beyond the present.

Proverbs also tie one generation to the next. There is no gap here, in that grandmother's proverbial wisdom is assumed applicable today.

But do proverbs promote the truth? Are they nuggets of wisdom? The answer is yes and no. Honeck states, "Proverbs are not really designed to be all-time, in-perpetuity carriers of truth. They are actually half-truths. The proverb makes a point about the specific situation in which it is used; in that sense, it is a truth that the parent [teacher, friend] wants to get across." The proverb standing alone, without a situation to support it, may be a proverbial lie.

For instance, you've heard that birds of a feather flock together. This proverb has some basis in fact. It's well known that people with similar interests, religious views, political opinions, and economic backgrounds tend to associate regularly. Individuals who seek to marry each other tend to be more alike than different. Simply put, people are attracted to those who are similar to themselves.

What about actions? Do they speak louder than words? Absolutely. Social psychologists have demonstrated that our first and later impressions are based on how people act. Studies were conducted where participants were given a list of adjectives said to describe a person and were then allowed to observe that individual. When the descriptive adjectives did not match the observed behavior, participants gave more credence to the actions than to the words.

However, concerning beauty, people may pay lip-service to the fact that it is only skin deep, but our culture sends out a different message. Human actions suggest that no one really thinks beauty is skin deep. The "pretty people" of our society are treated more favorably than any other group. As a result, a type of self-fulfilling prophecy emerges. Attractive people tend to accomplish more than their average-looking peers. The comely have higher salaries and greater self-esteem. They are less susceptible to peer pressure, tend to receive more lenient court verdicts, and are less likely to be diagnosed as mentally disturbed. Overall, pretty people are valued, and ugly ones are pushed aside. When someone uses this proverb to assuage your worries about appearance, it may not hold.

The next example is really a half-truth. In some situations, absence does make the heart grow fonder. However, it is possible for the heart to grow colder. When someone you care about is removed from your sight, the feelings you had for them will intensify. If you genuinely adored them, then this fondness will increase. If you had some unresolved negative feelings about the person lurking in your mind, chances are you will find someone new.

And does sparing the rod spoil the child? This is one proverb that is unequivocally wrong. A half-century of research and data have shown that corporal punishment produces children who are more aggressive than those who are punished by other means. The more accurate proverb should read, "Spare the rod, use behavior mod [modification]."

Proverbs are a colorful part of any culture, and they unite one generation with the next. They represent a common-sense psychology which helps to explain almost every situation. But remember, not all glittering proverbs are golden truths. In fact, some are fool's gold. So, make sure the proverb fits the situation, and then always provide advice on how to solve the real problem at hand.

References:
Honeck, R.P., & Kibler, C.T. (November 1984). The role of imagery, analogy, and instantiation in proverb comprehension. *Journal of PsycholinguisticResearch*, 13, 393-414.
Kohn, A. (April 1988). You know what they say. *Psychology Today*, 22, 36-41.

Sky (February 1989), pp. 78-80, 82.

Love Proverbs Are Universal, Says an Expert – and Like Love Itself, They Can Bite (1989)

Anonymous

Proverbs, says Prof. Wolfgang Mieder (at home in Vermont), show "different cultures have the same experiences."

"I've always enjoyed Valentine's Day," says Prof. Wolfgang Mieder. He means that professionally as well as personally. An internationally known paremiologist, or scholar of proverbs, Mieder not only sends Valentines ("all my female colleagues get one ... my wife too"), he also studies them as keys to the state of proverbial wisdom. "Proverbs spread faster than ever," he says. "What used to take generations can now reach currency almost overnight." (For example, "Different strokes for different folks.")

Starting with his doctoral thesis at Michigan State, Mieder, 44, has written more than 100 articles and 30 scholarly books on the origin and evolution of proverbs, which he defines as "a concise statement of an apparent truth which has currency among the people." This month the University of Vermont professor will publish his third popular book, *Love: Proverbs of the Heart*, a collection of 500 timeless maxims from around the world. "Proverbs are not high philosophy," he says, and quotes an old English proverb. "They are the children of experience."

What is striking is how universal that experience is. Variations on "Love is blind," for instance, can be found in French, Spanish, Italian, German, Russian, Japanese and the original Latin ("Amor caecus"). No one knows how many proverbs exist in the world, but the number, says Mieder, must be phenomenal. "The Finnish Literary Society has identified way over a million, and that's just for Finland," he says. Moreover, the number grows daily. Mieder found one of his favorites in a feminist T-shirt ad in 1977: "A woman without a man is like a fish without a bicycle." The irony struck him as true to the form. "Proverbs are not saccharine," he says. "If you want romance, read lyric poetry."

> Curse not your wife in the evening, or you will have to
>   sleep alone.
>   (Chinese)
> Love and fear cannot be hidden.
>   (Russian)

Love is like butter, it's good with bread.
  (Yiddish)
A cunning person's kiss is like that of a mosquito.
  (Rumanian)
Love is like dew that falls on both nettles and lilies.
  (Swedish)
When the heart is full of lust, the mouth is full of lies.
  (Scottish)
A man chases a woman until she catches him.
  (American)
When husband and wife agree with each other, they can
  dry up the ocean with buckets.
  (Vietnamese)
If the wife sins, the husband is not innocent.
  (Italian)
Kisses are keys.
  (English)
He who flatters the mother will hug the daughter.
  (Estonian)
The woman cries before the wedding and the man after.
  (Polish)
No hate is ever as strong as that which stems from love.
  (German)
The quarrels of married couples and the west wind stop
  at evening.
  (Japanese)
A deaf husband and a blind wife are always a happy
  couple.
  (French)
To those we love best, we say the least.
  (Philippine)
That which is loved is always beautiful.
  (Norwegian)

People (February 20, 1989), pp. 112-113.

So They Say ...
Finding a Grain of Truth in Old Wives' Tales (1991)

Malinda Reinke and Dannika Simpson

You know what they say ...

Where there's smoke, there's fire. Birds of a feather flock together. You can lead a horse to water, but you can't make him drink.

Words to live by.

Or are they?

We've been throwing old proverbs around for so long hardly anyone remembers where they came from.

For example: "The way to a man's heart is through his stomach."

Who said that?

Writer Fanny Fern said it back in the mid 1800s. And before her, the poet Lord Byron said it. And before him, an Englishwoman named Hester Lynch Thrale planted the seed for the proverb in her published memoirs about her dear friend, the English author (and apparent food lover) Samuel Johnson. That was in 1786, two years after Johnson's death.

But is the maxim true today? In this era of physical fitness, maybe not.

Still, we use it freely.

The fact is, before we can say "truth is stranger than fiction," some adage is out of our mouth with little regard to whether there's much fact to back it up.

So just for fun, we decided to pick a few favorite sayings, track their origins – this was harder than finding a needle in a haystack – and ask experts if the proverbs hold true today.

Findings were mixed.

The proof of that is in the pudding.

Too many cooks spoil the broth.

Origin: Too many cooks spoil the broth. Sir Balthazar Gerbier, "Principles of Building," 1662.

Findings: Alas. True.

"Absolutely. Most likely, 99.9 percent of the time the broth will spoil."

So says Chef Frederic Sonnenschmidt, certified master chef and culinary dean at the Culinary Institute of America in Hyde Park, N.Y.

"It doesn't matter how many people you have to do something," Sonnenschmidt says. "Without a leader, they can't function."

You can have 20 people in the kitchen – each with ideas about how to make the meal taste better.

"But if there are too many cooks but no chef, the broth will spoil by the time they make a decision," he says.

A penny saved is a penny earned.

Origin: A penny saved is a penny got. William Somerville, "The Sweet-Scented Miser," 1727.

Findings: Not true.

Not really.

Not anymore.

"I'm not sure that's so these days," says Claire S. Longden, CPF, of Rhinebeck, N.Y., – one of the top financial planners nationwide, according to Money magazine.

"You go out and you earn your penny. Then you put it in a savings account at 5 percent interest. But inflation, they say, is 4 percent and last year it was 5 percent – and if you shop at all you realize it's a hell of a lot more than that. So your savings doesn't make you much. In fact, if inflation kept going up you would eventually lose money."

You can catch more flies with honey than you can with vinegar.

Origin: More flies are taken with a drop of honey than a ton of vinegar. Thomas Fuller (1654-1734), "Gnomologia."

Findings: True.

Sally Love of the Insect Zoo at the Smithsonian Institution in Washington, D.C, says this is no big secret.

"The sweetness will attract them more than something acidic," she says with a chuckle.

You can't teach an old dog new tricks.

Origin: "An old dog will learn no new tricks." Thomas B'Urfey. (No year.)

Findings: False. False. False.

"Oh, for heaven's sake, I wouldn't be in business if that were true," says Barbara Whan who operates The Educated Dog in Rhinebeck, N.Y., and New York City.

"As the person who taught me how to teach dogs 11 years ago said: 'If a dog knows how to learn, it can learn at any age.'"

The Burlington Free Press (August 11, 1991), p. 1D.

107

The Proverbial Collector
For Decades, the University of Vermont's Wolfgang Mieder
Has Been Tracking the Origins of Thousands of Common
American Proverbs (1992)

Alvin P. Sanoff in conversation with Wolfgang Mieder

Do most proverbs contain fundamental truths?
Proverbs are concise statements–usually no more than seven to eight words–of an apparent truth that has currency. Notice I said *apparent*. Proverbs do not provide universal truths. After all, when compared, some are absolutely contradictory, such as "Absence makes the heart grow fonder" and "Out of sight, out of mind."

Proverbs also tend to be misogynist. In almost every culture, you find such invectives as "Women are the devil's nets" or "Tell a woman and you tell the world." We say that "A diamond is a girl's best friend," yet "A dog is a man's best friend." The further back in history we go, the worse proverbs are for women, probably because many proverbs originated in patriarchal societies.

How common are proverbs that contain an egalitarian message?
My favorite proverb of all is "Different strokes for different folks." Most proverbs are prescriptive, but this is a truly liberating proverb that expresses an American world view. It comes from the Afro-American population in the South and probably originated in the 1950s. It later became very popular through the television show "Diffrent Strokes." It has been used a lot in advertisements. My favorite advertising variation is "Different Volks for Different Folks."

Some of my other favorites come from Yiddish and are rich in contrasting imagery and metaphor. I have in mind such proverbs as "Pride lies on the dunghill" and "A fool grows without rain." Every immigrant group settling in America has brought proverbs with it, enriching the language. "The apple doesn't fall far from the tree," for example, comes from Germany. The first recorded reference was in a letter written by Ralph Waldo Emerson in 1839. Emerson knew German and learned the proverb through that language.

Is Benjamin Franklin the most widely quoted of all the proverb writers in American history?

Probably, though I am sorry to say that Franklin copied many proverbs from other collections. He didn't, for example, coin "Early to bed and early to rise makes a man healthy, wealthy and wise." That proverb dates back to 1496, and Franklin most likely got it out of a proverb collection from 1656. At best, he coined perhaps 20 proverbs on his own. These probably include: "Laziness travels so slowly that poverty soon overtakes him"; "There will be sleeping enough in the grave," and, finally, "Three removes are as bad as a fire," which means that if you change your location three times, that is almost as bad as losing everything.

Who then is the best maker of proverbs?

That is almost impossible to answer because we don't know the original authors of most proverbs. Shakespeare's plays contain the earliest written documentation of many popular proverbs, but that does not prove that he coined them, since he had a good ear for folk speech. I can say, however, that he was among the heaviest users of proverbs, as was Geoffrey Chaucer in the Middle Ages and, more recently, Charles Dickens, George Bernard Shaw, Carl Sandburg and Robert Frost. But Frost's phrase "Good fences make good neighbors" in the poem "Mending Wall" was not his invention. I found it in an 1850 almanac, and it was an almanac not from New Hampshire but from South Carolina.

In the political arena, Nikita Khrushchev liked to use proverbs. In fact, when he came to the United Nations, translators Scotch-taped Russian proverbs in their booths so they would be ready. Lenin also used them quite a bit, as did Hitler. There are invectives everywhere in proverbial speech, and it is painful to see how the Nazis used them. In 1942, they actually published a 300-page collection of antisemitic proverbs. In American political life, Ronald Reagan, Harry Truman and Abraham Lincoln were all heavy proverb users. But some of the proverbs we associate with Lincoln, such as "Don't swap horses in midstream," were not his creations.

Are there many proverbs whose sources can be clearly established by digging through archives?

Tracing the history of proverbs is a constant adventure, and sometimes one can unearth the original source. "A picture is worth a thousand words," for example, was coined in 1921 by Fred Barnard, an advertising executive. He used it in a two-page advertisement in the magazine *Printers' Ink* to persuade advertisers to start using pictures. By the way, this new book is very different in its approach to proverb research. Unlike most such collections, it is not based on written sources; it is based on gathering oral proverbs over some 40 years. We started out by collecting 250,000 items. We eliminated duplication and eventually narrowed the book to close to 20,000 proverbs that are really in use in the United States today.

[The conversation was centered around Wolfgang Mieder, Stewart A. Kingsbury, and Kelsie B. Harder (eds.), *A Dictionary of American Proverbs*. New York: Oxford University Press, 1992.]

U.S. News & World Report (January 13, 1992), p. 57.

Dueling Proverbs –
Can a Young Dog Learn Old Tricks? (1992)

Roger L. Welsch

My father is German, and he does some German things, and I can say so, because I'm a German. So don't send me letters about how the Germans invented cream-filled pastries, designed the first autobahn, and used to have great singing contests. I know all that. Being German, my father speaks in proverbs. To him, proverbs are little nuggets of traditional wisdom that speak to every issue and question. "Why can't I have a car of my own?" I would ask, and Dad would answer, "The apple doesn't fall far from the tree."

"Huh?" I would say.

Or maybe he would tell me to mow the lawn and I would explain that I couldn't because ... because ... because I had to study for a woodworking shop exam the next day. He would say, "Strain at a gnat and swallow a camel." I would say, "Huh?" And he would say, "Mow the lawn." And I would think, "Germans!"

Now that I think of it, that was the reasonable side of Dad. If I took a stand and clearly had logic, justice, and maybe Mom on my side, he would, without a pause, say something like, "Augen-flaugen bracht magen Platz."

"What does that mean, Dad?" I'd ask, even though I knew better.

"That means, 'Don't slander your neighbor until you have walked six miles in his moccasins.'"

"After that it's okay to slander him?" I asked, realizing at once that I would have done better by asking him which of those words was German for "moccasins."

"Flanzen bogen distel sichen Universitaet – Honor thy father or lose driving privileges until you graduate from college," he explained.

When I did go off to college, one of the first things I did was take a course in German to see if Dad was really speaking German. As it turned out, he was, sort of. But the real advantage of what eventually became my graduate degree in German was that I came to understand his proverbs and learned enough more, thanks to his tuition payments, to argue effectively with him, using an arsenal of my own proverbs.

In graduate folklore school at Indiana University I learned that in many cultures, proverbs are correctly considered to be collective wisdom and can be introduced in court as common law. Never mind that there are contradictory proverbs: contradictory legal opinions clash in American courts every day.

My old man hadn't been using conventional debate and logic, perhaps, but he was exercising some skills that constitute a legitimate alternative for many peoples of the world. Okay, two can play that game. Armed with two degrees, two published books, and a few more years of experience, I returned home, ready to deal with Dad.

"I wonder if you'd loan me enough to buy a new car, Dad. After all, 'As the twig is bent, so grows the tree.'"

"Champagne thirst, beer budget," he responded.

"Well, maybe, but 'the Lord helps him who helps himself.' 'Nothing ventured, nothing gained,'" I said, firing both barrels at once.

"Wer nicht hoert, muss fuehl."

"Well, I'm ready to take my own lumps but, Pop, 'a burned child fears the fire.'"

"Eigenlob stinkt," he said over the top of his newspaper. "Vanity stinks." End of conversation. *Schluss.* I was left proverbless. Hmmm. Apparently I hadn't learned enough proverbs. Education or not, I was still outclassed when it came to dueling proverbs.

On one particularly memorable occasion, I thought I had him cornered. We were arguing about what keeps airplanes up. He said no one really understands. I talked aerodynamics and noted that I learned all this stuff in Air ROTC when I was in school. I explained that air passing at high speed over the airfoil generates low pressure on the top. I did end runs around his "The proof of the pudding is in the eating" and "A man convinced against his will is of the same opinion still." I dismissed "For every pot there's a lid" as irrelevant and countered "Look before you leap" with "He who hesitates is lost."

Thrust and parry, lunge and retreat, slash and burn. Then I abandoned his game and tried to get the momentum going my way. I turned to science. I explained venturi tubes, drag, speed, lift, all those things. Finally I turned to the television set where Bobby Rahal was explaining the ground-effects race car. He talked about venturi tubes, airfoils, drag, speed, lift, all those things. Rahal, a brainy guy as well as a top-notch car driver, used a diagram board and drew precisely the same ideas I had been trying to explain to Dad. For me, it was like a gift from heaven. I had independent, expert verification for my position, right there in front of us, with no possibility of Dad blowing it all away with some proverb.

In triumph I crowed and pointed to the television set. "There you have it, Dad. Irrefutable evidence that I am right."

"The exception proves the rule," he smiled.

I'm now fifty-five years old and he's seventy-eight and I don't even try anymore. "There's more than one way to skin a cat."

Natural History, no. 4 (April 1992), p. 68.

Homogeneity Is Good for Linguistic Color (1992)

Pieter Sijpkes

High trees catch a lot of wind.
A ship on the beach is a beacon in the sea.
The way the clock ticks at home, it ticks nowhere.
Don't haul dead cows out of the ditch.
You can't pick feathers off a frog.

Since I arrived in Canada, quite a while ago, I have amused (and, I guess, occasionally annoyed) my friends and colleagues with an endless stream of translated Dutch sayings, like those above. It seems that linguistic patterns are hard to break; the habit of expressing something in an idiomatic rather then a merely descriptive way defies the language barrier.

It puzzled me initially that Canadian English was not spiced by the same wealth of proverbs, sayings, aphorisms and expressions that I was accustomed to in my native Holland. The English I heard spoken in Montreal was efficient, but plain. I was delighted, on the other hand, to find that the French spoken here was very rich in expressions; understanding advertising slogans or the text of editorial cartoons was (and is) a challenge.

Why would Dutch and Quebec French use phrases and expressions so freely, while the Canadian English that I hear daily seems almost devoid of them? The answer must lie in the homogeneity of a population as well as the length and continuity of its history. Composite expressions can, over time, greatly enrich a language, fleshing out its bare-bones structure. But the subtlety of such sayings will inevitably elude a new arrival in Canada, who, speaking English as a second or third language, will soon enough learn how to rent an apartment or communicate with an employer, but will actually sniff when told to "smell the roses."

As a result, old-stock English-speaking Canadians feel restrained in using sayings. A continuous cycle of simplification remains at work.

(On a smaller scale, most families have homemade expressions that require lengthy explanations to non-family members; becoming part of the family, as an in-law for instance, means getting to know at least some of these treasured expressions.)

Another aspect of language that is equally influenced by cultural homogeneity and history is humor. Jokes are often based on wordplay, double entendres or expressions used out of context. In order to "get it," one has to, instantaneously, see the relationship between the straight and the oblique meanings of what a message presents. Watching Ding et Dong, two Québécois comedians who regularly perform on Radio-Canada, is as frustrating as it is funny, because their performance is often permeated by expressions impossible for the uninitiated to appreciate.

Airfarce, the CBC's weekly comedy show, on the other hand, relies almost exclusively on slapstick interpretations of the utterings of public figures; reading a newspaper is sufficient preparation for the newcomer to laugh at the right time.

In addition to the formation of expressions by particular groups over time, there exists the deliberate creation of sub-languages rich in expressions. "Argot" was originally an idiomatic language created and meant to be understood only by thieves, but is now used as a label for the specialized language used by any subgroup: sociologists' argot, for example. Black society in the U.S. to this day uses a language that differs from mainstream American English, partly the result of a heritage that required a concealed language for survival.

In more recent history, sexual minorities have developed a jargon that can only be deciphered by the use of recently published dictionaries. Finally, young people continuously create new expressions, from "valley talk" to rock language.

While language was developed to communicate, sayings, expressions and proverbs act on contradictory levels: they increase the complexity and richness of language as they often, simultaneously, obfuscate.

With a much more mobile population and with the universal access to electronic media, are linguistic idiosyncrasies like composite expressions doomed? Will we in the future all speak a bland world-language, devoid of local color?

I don't think so. Marshall McLuhan's prediction of a global village has come true in the world-wide use of credit cards, telephones, Coca-Cola and "read my lips," but, maybe on the rebound of this overwhelming globalism, nationalism and regionalism are much more prominent now then they were even a few decades ago. Increased economic scale, such as the EC in Europe and NAFTA in North America, appear to foster smaller cultural units; the Flemish and the Walloons in Belgium are more distinctive now than they were before the advent of the EC, which raises intriguing questions with regard to NAFTA, Quebec and Canada.

Maybe there will always be action and counteraction – outgoingness balanced by inward-lookingness. As they say in Dutch: "If it doesn't come out of the length, it'll come out of the width."

The Montreal Gazette (August 22, 1992), p. J2.

A Proverb Each Day Keeps this Scholar at Play:
Ranging through History and Across Cultures, the University
of Vermont's Wolfgang Mieder Mines Maxims for Their Wit
and Wisdom (1992)

Richard Wolkomir

Wolfgang Mieder, the world's top proverb expert, is smitten with "Different strokes for different folks." It heads his all-time personal proverb hit parade because it is so American. "It doesn't tell you what to do!" he says.

Not being told what to do drew Mieder to the United States as a teenager. Ever since emigrating here from Germany at age 16, he has devoted himself to leaving no proverbial stone un-turned. Besides teaching about proverbs at the University of Vermont, where he chairs the Department of German and Rus-sian, he has published more than 50 books (so far) on his favorite subject, including the massive new Oxford University Press *Dictionary of American Proverbs*. He edits Proverbium, the annual compendium of scholarly articles on proverbs, and churns out barrages of proverb studies.

"Different strokes for different folks," for instance, got his attention in 1968, when it hit the big time in the song "Everyday People," by Sly and the Family Stone. Mieder later found its parallel in a 1732 English proverb, "Different sores must have different salves," but he concluded that the "sores" proverb never made it in the United States, probably because "not many people now know what salves are anymore." He spotted a version of "different strokes" in an African-American folklore dissertation. Then he worked his way through folklore archives at the University of California at Berkeley, and pondered studies of inner-city and black slang. Finally he traced "different strokes" to Southern blacks in the 1950s. It even appeared in a series of 1970s Volks-wagen ads: "Different Volks for Different Folks." Another per-mutation was the television sitcom *Diff'rent Strokes*.

Usually, Mieder's proverb probes go further back. Many "American" proverbs originated in ancient Greece and Rome and in medieval Europe, spreading from country to country in Latin texts. For example, "Big fish eat little fish" goes back nearly 3,000 years, to the Greek poet Hesiod, in the eighth century B.C. Mieder suspects it originated in Sumer, which produced the first proverb collections–on cuneiform tablets.

Mieder also monitors ongoing proverb research, from proverb-based schizophrenia tests to efforts to reduce the world's millions of proverbs to just a few linguistic types. And he is working out America's "proverbial minimum," a list of proverbs you must know to be able to chug along in the society.

Colleagues accuse Mieder of workaholism. "The hardest work is to do nothing," he counters in his Schleswig-Holstein accent. "An idle man is the devil's playfellow," he says. "The sleepy fox catches no chickens! Hard work never hurt anybody! He that rises late must trot all day!" He works until midnight and rises with the robins. Vacations? He looks appalled. A doctor once cured Mieder's migraine headaches by telling him, "In your case, don't even try taking it easy."

Mieder follows the doctor's orders. He is slight, under 5 foot 5, with a gingery mustache and the air of a hummingbird who drank too much coffee. Even sitting at his computer he seems to dart about, the result of mental turbocharging.

New mutants of old proverbs

His office in his Vermont hillside home contains the world's most extensive private proverb library, 5,000 books, dissertations, monographs and articles. It also houses an 8,000-slide archive of proverbs in art, advertising and everything else, including dish towels.

"You name it," says Mieder. "You could ask me, 'Are there any ads by the Ford Motor Company that use proverbs?' And I could look in the archive and say, 'Yes–"One Drive is Worth A Thousand Words,"' which was for the 1984 T-bird." That slogan is a mutant version of "One picture is worth a thousand words." And Mieder can tell you the origins of that proverb, too. Its structure, he says, is one of the universal types: "One of something is worth vast numbers of something else." He can spin off examples, such as "One good head is better than a hundred strong hands" (English), "A friend is better than a thousand silver pieces" (Greek), "A moment is worth a thousand gold pieces" (Korean), "A single penny fairly got is worth a thousand that are not" (German), and "Silence is worth a thousand pieces of silver" (Burmese).

The structure of "One picture is worth a thousand words" may derive from a familiar type, but the actual proverb was dreamed up in 1921 by Fred R. Barnard of the Street Railways Advertising Company. He used it in a piece he wrote for the advertising journal *Printers' Ink*, advocating pictures in advertisements.

"One picture" hit on something about how the mind works–at least, the American mind in the nascent media age–and became part of the national psychic genome. That is one way to look at proverbs: as bits of mental DNA passed on from generation to generation. Some persist, others mutate and evolve. Some disappear. But proverbs are slippery things, and defining them precisely has eluded proverb scholars, or paroemiologists.

"Proverbs are crystallized bits of wisdom," says Mieder, adding that they average seven words, tend to have several levels of meaning and apply to various situations. That is why they are not necessarily true. If "Absence makes the heart grow fonder," why do we say "Out of sight, out of mind"? And if "He who hesitates is lost," how come you have to "Look before you leap"? Mix and match, says Mieder. "We pick the proverb that fits the situation." He has his own favorite definition: "A proverb is a concise statement of an apparent truth that has currency."

Besides currency, a proverb has bite, and that can be dangerous. Poetic devices like rhyme and ellipsis, the omission of unneeded words, make proverbs condensed and powerful. They *sound* true. But they are really prepackaged thoughts, and–humans being what we are–those thoughts are not always healthy.

"Thousands of proverbs are slurs," says Mieder. For example, Europe has many anti-Semitic proverbs. "Hitler exploited proverbs, and twisted them," Mieder says, adding that one of his most touching moments came after he discussed the Nazi misuse of proverbs at a meeting of the American Folklore Society. An auditorium full of people gave him a standing ovation. He has just finished writing a paper on "The only good Indian is a dead Indian," which he has traced to Gen. Philip Sheridan, in January 1869, at Fort Cobb in Indian Territory. "Right after the Civil War, all those troops had nothing better to do than to hunt down Indians in the name of Manifest Destiny," he says. "It's terrible invective, one of the sadder American proverbs."

Meanwhile, thousands of proverbs are about women, and most of them are misogynistic. "Women are as wavering as the wind," Mieder recites. "A woman is the weaker vessel"; "A woman's tongue wags like a lamb's tail." On the other hand, on Mieder's office wall at the university hangs a hand-lettered proverb: "Before you meet the handsome prince, you really have to kiss a lot of TOADS." It is an example of the modern "anti- proverb"–an old-fashioned proverb given a twist–a phenomenon that fascinates Mieder. "A woman's place is in the House ... and the Senate!" he says, reciting another favorite. Or "A man's home is his castle; let him clean it." In the media age, we like our proverbs ironic, with attitude.

Recently, Mieder gave a guest lecture on anti-proverbs at Smith College, in Massachusetts. His audience was a roomful of distinguished professors. He arrived at this gathering with a special mission: to blow the lid off Ben Franklin. Most of us think Franklin was a big-time coiner of proverbs. But of the 1,044 proverbs in *Poor Richard's Almanac*, Mieder said, only a smattering were Franklin's own. "Laziness travels so slowly that poverty soon overtakes it" was one. "There will be sleeping enough in the grave" was another. A good many of the rest, Franklin snitched.

Mieder cited "Early to bed, early to rise, makes a man healthy, wealthy, and wise" from *Poor Richard's* of 1735. It must have been one of Franklin's favorites because he called for it to be inscribed on copper coins. "But a variant of 'Early to bed, early to rise' was recorded in English for the first time in 1496, which was 210 years before Franklin was born," Mieder said.

Ben did make an attempt to come clean. In his preface to *Poor Richard's* of 1758, he admitted that when people quoted "his" proverbs, his vanity was "wonderfully delighted." But, he confessed, "I was conscious that not a tenth part of the wisdom was my own." The proverbs, he acknowledged, were "the gleanings that I made of the sense of all ages and nations."

By now, Mieder was darting about the room in full Energizer rabbit mode, showing how "Early to bed" had quickly burrowed into the American psyche. It even appeared in *Moby-Dick*, where Herman Melville blended it with "The early bird catches the worm," another favorite proverb, to describe a harpooner: "Generally he's an early bird–airley to bed and airley to rise–yes, he's the bird that catches the worm." But "Early to bed" piqued Mark Twain, who said rising early made him look "blue, and pulpy, and swelled, like a drowned man." Twain charged that Franklin's maxim was "full of animosity toward boys." "And that boy," he added, "is hounded to death and robbed of his natural rest."

Groucho Marx also objected to the proverb, on the grounds that wealthy people he knew "will fire the help if they are disturbed before 3 in the afternoon." And James Thurber noted that "Early to rise and early to bed makes a male healthy and wealthy and dead."

"Proverb literacy" is down, Mieder said. More and more young people know fewer and fewer of the old ones, which is too bad because proverbs are part of the country's social glue. On the other hand, he said, new proverbs spring up, like the computer age's "Garbage in, garbage out." And popular music serves as a kind of proverb bank. "There was Bob Dylan's 'Like a Rolling Stone,'" Mieder enthusiastically told the distinguished professors. "And Cher did 'Apples Don't Fall Far From the Tree.' "

The "Apples" proverb came to this country from Germany, as did Mieder, on his own. His father was the purchasing agent for the old Hanseatic port of Lübeck; his mother, a secretary for the city. As a high school student in the 1950s, Mieder was an enthusiastic member of the rowing team–"I still row in my dry dock upstairs," he says. But he was no scholar: "I felt stifled in the German schools of that time." He had no plans for college, but he wanted to be a forest ranger. His other enthusiasm was America.

"America meant freedom, liberation from traditional authority, a certain rebellion," Mieder says. Nights, after he was supposed to be asleep, young Wolfgang would hide under the covers with a flashlight, reading forbidden American comic books while listening on his headset to Radio Luxembourg, the "Station of the Stars." "I liked Harry Belafonte–'Banana Boat' was really good–and I was a big fan of the Everly Brothers and especially Buddy Holly." He went on to be a Beatles fan and a "real Bob Dylan fan" and also a fan of Ray Charles, the Supremes ...

He was crazy about American cars, too, especially the kind with big tail-fins, or sporty jobs. "Once in a while you'd see a Corvette, or maybe a Thunderbird," he recalls.

When Mieder was 16, he learned that his poor vision disqualified him as a forest ranger. Impulsively, he wrote to a Detroit newspaper photographer he had once met when the journalist had visited relatives in Germany. Would it be possible, he asked, to put a notice in the paper asking if anyone would temporarily take in "a little German boy"? Not long after, he received a letter saying that 12 families were lined up and school began in two weeks. "I hadn't told my parents that I'd written–that was my little surprise," he says.

Amazingly, his parents said he could go for a year. But his father wrote out a contract, which they both signed, requiring Wolfgang to write a letter every Sunday. And shortly afterward, in August of 1960, the little German boy boarded a Manhattan-bound liner crammed with hundreds of U.S. college students sailing home from a summer in Europe. Mieder became the ship's pet.

"I was the youngest on the boat, in my lederhosen," he says. "I learned all the colloquial English you can dream of, including curses, and I was drinking Heineken beer. By the time we saw the Statue of Liberty, which was one of my life's most moving moments, I was an educated young man!"

A teacher he'd met on the ship helped him navigate the honking streets to the Port Authority Bus Terminal. The bus was full, so he had to wait six hours for the next one, unable to let his Detroit hosts know he was delayed–"I didn't know how to make a telephone call." Later, when the bus made a rest stop, he didn't know how to work the soda machine.

As Mieder had expected, Detroit was heaven. First he stayed with a 26-year-old fireman and his wife. "The three of us would drive in their white 1959 Chevrolet–with the big fins–to the drive-in, and we'd sit in that huge car munching popcorn and watching John Wayne," says Mieder.

He was in the capital of Motown music and cars. "I'd go to car dealers and collect those booklets, showing those beautiful cars, and I'd send them to my father, who didn't have a car," he says. In the U.S. high schools, Mieder flowered. Teachers amazed him by taking an interest. "I suddenly realized I wasn't so stupid after all!" He shot to the head of his class and even quit track because it interfered with his studies.

Meanwhile, he moved in with another family. They proved equally hospitable, but they did point out that " 'Wolfgang' just doesn't make it as an American name." He was offered three choices by his host family: Joe, Leo or Pete. Mieder chose Pete. "I began signing my letters to my family 'Pete.' " After a while, the weekly letters coming to him from Lübeck began, "Dear Pete."

122

Pete wrote home to ask if he could stay one more year. On his birthday, he received a telegram: *"Du darfst bleiben,"* "You may stay."

As it turned out, he was to stay far beyond another year. He went to live with a Ford executive who had teenage children. "All of my intellectual interests really blossomed in that family," he says. His record was so exceptional that he won a scholarship to Olivet College, in Michigan, where he earned straight A's. He planned to be a chemist but decided that, as a scientist, he was unoriginal. "Mainly I had Sitzfleisch, which means 'sitting meat,' or endurance for hard work," he explains. He toyed with majoring in French, then opted for Germanùand became "Wolf-gang" again.

As Olivet's top graduate, he went on to the University of Michigan. Next he worked his way through the PhD program at Michigan State as a teaching assistant. There he met his future wife, Barbara, also earning a doctorate in German. And, in a seminar on German folklore, Mieder discovered proverbs.

"It just kind of clicked with me," he says. "How they work, how they're constructed, their history, and how they're every-where–from Carl Sandburg's poetry to art, psychology, politics, and advertisements for cars and cameras." Proverbs, he believes, show us something about how we think. "My interest in proverbs actually is a fascination with how we are ruled by traditional atti-tudes, and anti-proverbs show how we try to break out."

By studying proverbs, he found, he had discovered a window on any number of human societies. In some African tribes, for instance, lawsuits are decided in terms of proverb battles, the winner being the litigant judged to produce the most apt proverbs.

In our own society, people's sanity or IQ may be determined by how they explain proverbs. Such proverb tests have been used since the early 1900s, in the belief that people with certain men-tal disorders, particularly schizophrenia, cannot comprehend a proverb's abstract meanings. Similarly, some psychologists be-lieve the ability to understand proverb abstractions is a measure of intelligence.

But folklorists like Mieder, backed by some recent studies, question the value of proverbs for psychological testing. They note that proverbs' meanings depend on the situations in which they are used. And many proverbs do not fit our changed society. A city youth who has never met a Rhode Island Red might have trouble deciphering "Never cackle unless you lay." Nationality also can affect interpretations. The Scots, for instance, tend to read "A rolling stone gathers no moss" as extolling the virtues of action as opposed to the more sedentary life. The English, however, tend to equate it with the beautiful growth of moss on a stone in a stream, a metaphor for tradition and stability.

These examples suggest that proverbs reveal "national character." But paroemiologists following that road have hit a dead end. "I could put together a bunch of proverbs that show Americans are materialistic, and I could put together another collection showing that Americans really value friendship and love," says Mieder. "If I know the 300 most common American proverbs, the ones we really use, then *maybe* I can say something."

In fact, that is one of Mieder's current projects, although aimed at a different goal than determining national character. The idea of establishing a country's "proverbial minimum" began in Russia in the 1970s, when scholars developed a questionnaire and identified about 300 proverbs that every Russian knows. In the former Soviet Union, people of many nationalities often found themselves struggling to learn Russian, a proverb-rich language, and mastering the proverbial minimum was vital. Now efforts are under way to establish proverbial minimums for other nations, too.

Mieder is pushing the project in the United States: "I've already done statistical analyses, figuring out which proverbs are particularly frequent in 20th-century U.S. writing." Some proverbs that show up often are: "A bird in the hand is worth two in the bush," "The early bird catches the worm," "Chickens come home to roost," "Charity begins at home," "Easy come, easy go" and "Business before pleasure." Mieder cautions, however, "we would have to distribute about 10,000 questionnaires around the United States to see what proverbs people actually use." Establishing a U.S. proverbial minimum will ease the path for immigrants learning English, he adds.

Meanwhile, linguists are taking a whack at the world's millions of extant proverbs, trying to reduce them to a small number of basic structures. On one level, they reduce proverbs to simple formulas, like "Where there's X, there's Y." But on a deeper level, where they use symbolic logic, their results are pages full of pluses, minuses, equal signs and does-not-equal signs.

124

"I'm not in the pure linguist school because it's too dry for me," says Mieder. "My specialty is historical, interdisciplinary and comparative studies–my problem is I like it all!"

To each his own. Or, as that quintessentially American proverb puts it: "Different strokes for different folks!"

Smithsonian (September 1992), pp. 110-112, 114, 116, and 118.

A condensed version of this article with the new title "'One Proverb Is Worth a Thousand Words': This Expert Leaves no Stone Unturned" appeared in *Reader's Digest* (March 1993), pp. 153-154, 156, 158.

It Never Rains But It Pours!
Discovering English Proverbs (1992)

Ann Hislop

An hour before midnight is worth two after or so my mother used to tell me as I slunk down to breakfast, eyes propped open with matchsticks, after a particularly late night. But is it really true that sleep before 12 p.m. is twice as good for you as sleep after that hour? At the time, like most young people, I regarded this proverb as a nonsensical piece of folk wisdom, an old wives' tale with no relevance to my own life. I mean, an hour is an hour is an hour ... it's 60 minutes, a.m. or p.m. However, now older and wiser, I remember my mother's words as I scramble into bed at 11 o'clock. I am now a firm believer in the value of getting at least one hour's sleep before midnight!

Advice about how to live a healthy life is one example of the type of received wisdom which is condensed and passed on to the next generation in the form of proverbs. Proverbs also serve to express general truths in a short and colourful way, for example, *There's no smoke without fire*, meaning that there is generally some truth in even the wildest rumours.

Another type of proverb acts as a reminder of the correct way to behave, for example, *Don't wash your dirty linen in public*. This means don't discuss personal or family problems in front of strangers or in public. Other proverbs are offered to people as a means of comfort and consolation in times of trouble, for example, *It's no use crying over spilt milk*. This proverb advises that it really is a waste of time to weep over mistakes that have already been made. Instead, it is much better to *Make the best of a bad job* – to do your best whatever the situation.

Proverbs exist in most languages and are, in the words of John Simpson, author of *The Concise Oxford Dictionary of Proverbs*, "time capsules from the past which contain a wealth of human experience in a nutshell".

Some English proverbs are native to Britain, for example, *It never rains but it pours*, a reference to the joys of the British weather! This proverb means that when one thing goes wrong, many other things go wrong as well. Another home-grown proverb is *Every dog is allowed one bite*. This proverb is based on an old English law dating back to the 17th century. The law said that the first time a dog bit somebody, its owner did not have to pay

126

compensation to the victim because one bite did not prove that the dog was vicious. Hence the idea carried in the proverb, that everyone should be allowed to make a mistake without being punished for it.

Other proverbs have come into the language from Latin or Greek, through the classical authors, or from the French in the years following the conquest of England by the Normans in 1066. Lucretius, a classical Roman author, created the proverb *One man's meat is another man's poison*, meaning that what is good for one person can be harmful to another. And the proverb *Let sleeping dogs lie*, meaning don't cause trouble when it can be avoided, came into English from the French in the 14th century.

As Britain came into contact with other countries and cultures, English became enriched with the words and wisdom of different languages. From the Chinese, we borrowed the colourful proverb *He who rides a tiger is afraid to dismount*, meaning that if you start on a dangerous enterprise, it is often easier to carry it through to the end than to stop halfway. Much more commonly used, *Don't change horses in midstream* carries the same message. *Dogs bark but the caravan goes on* comes from Arabic and, of course, the caravan referred to is not a mobile home, but a group of people and camels moving through the desert. This proverb implies a rather fatalistic view of life. It conveys the idea that life moves steadily forwards despite minor distractions and obstacles – such as dogs barking.

Some proverbs have been in the language for 1000 years, for example, *A friend in need is a friend indeed*. The message here is that someone who stays with you and helps you in times of trouble, rather than turning their back, is a true friend. Other proverbs, however, are much more recent, and reflect changes in the way that we live.

From the United States come the following two pieces of new wisdom. *Garbage in – garbage out*, from the computer world, reminds people that computers are only as good as their programs. From big business we have *There's no such thing as a free lunch*, meaning nothing is free. If someone buys you lunch, they will expect a favour in return.

Some English people are reluctant to use proverbs in their everyday conversation because they see them as vehicles of rather trite, conventional wisdom. Nevertheless, proverbs are still quite common in both written and spoken English. They are used in popular fiction and as headlines in the tabloids, and continue to provide a homely commentary on life and a reminder that the wisdom of our ancestors may still be useful to us today.

BBC English for Language Learners, no. 70 (October 1992), pp. 12-13.

Words to Live by, or at Least Ponder (1992)

Mike Royko

A flattering invitation recently arrived. It was from Joseph Neely, an author in Michigan, who wrote:

"I am compiling a book which features the favorite saying of successful persons such as you. This book is intended to inspire people and to give them some insight into the philosophies which help certain people to accomplish significant tasks.

Essentially, I am looking for a saying which has given you comfort, kept you focused on your goals, or inspired you during your life. The saying can be one which you composed or it can be from some other source.

As of this date, I have received contributions for this book from a diverse group of persons, including former NATO commander and White House Chief of Staff Alexander Haig; minister and author Norman Vincent Peale; Dr. Deborah McGriff, the first African-American woman to serve as superintendent of a major urban school system; and Notre Dame's head football coach Lou Holtz, to name just a few."

That's an impressive group, and I'd like to be in it. But I've never had one favorite saying that inspired, comforted or focused me throughout my life. And I don't have any that would be likely to inspire someone else to lead a better life.

At different times, a variety of sayings have helped me in one way or another.

Like most young men of my generation, I believed in the saying our mothers passed on to us: "Always wear clean underwear, so if you get in an accident and go in the hospital, you won't be embarrassed." That's still a good idea, although I would add, "and no pastel colors."

As a lad, I abided by a saying in my neighborhood that went: "Don't go on the other side of Chicago Avenue, because the Italian kids there will always jump a Polack." The one time I became careless, a group of young men surrounded me and demanded my name. I said: "Rocko Rico Royko," which I thought was a clever ruse.

But they jumped me anyway.

That experience led me to believe in the saying that is familiar to many Cub fans: "You win some and you lose some, but mostly you lose some."

129

Then there was my grandfather's favorite saying: "Never trust a Russian." He said that long before the Cold War began. So I asked my grandmother what he meant by it, and she provided another saying: "Never trust your drunken grandfather."

Later, when I was in the military, I placed great faith in the popular saying: "Don't never volunteer for nothing." But it didn't make much difference, because if you didn't volunteer, they made you do it anyway.

Early in my newspaper career, a wise old reporter passed along a saying that helped me become thrifty. He said: "Always stash away some (deleted) money, so if you got a boss you hate, you can say, '(Deleted) you' and quit." I'm still saving.

And another mentor had a saying I tried to follow: "Be nice to the copy boy, even if he's a mope, because he might grow up to be your boss someday." And sure enough, several mopes did.

Some co-workers once tired of hearing me complain about not having anything to write about. So they put an inspirational plaque on my wall that showed a little sailboat with limp sails and a man pulling some oars. It bore the words: "When there's no wind, row."

But I've since taken it down and replaced it with a sign that says: "When there is no wind, book a cabin on a cruise ship, sit by the pool, order a cool drink, and look at the babes."

Several of my friends have had sayings that I like, although I'm not sure what they mean.

For example, Studs Terkel, the author and broadcaster, always ends his radio show by saying: "Take it easy, but take it." I once asked him if that was something he learned when he went to law school, but he denied it.

The late Marty O'Connor, a Chicago reporter, used to say: "Only suckers beef." He said it was an old South Side Irish expression. While it sounded manly, it wouldn't make sense today, when the most successful special-interest groups are those that beef the loudest and most often. Now the saying should be: "Only suckers don't form an organization, compile a list of unreasonable demands, and hold a crabby press conference."

I used to be impressed by the line John Wayne uttered in so many of his Western movies: "A man's got to do what a man's got to do." But when feminists heightened my social sensitivities, I realized it was a sexist saying. After all, the feminists pointed out, we could just as well say, "A woman's got to do what a woman's got to do." For that matter, a puppy's got to do what a puppy's got to do. That's life, which is a favorite saying of Frank Sinatra. Or maybe Mike Ditka.

So I guess I won't qualify for Mr. Neely's book of inspirational sayings. Unless he would consider using one of my friend Slats Grobnik's lines.

Slats has always tossed off this salutation when saying goodbye to friends: "Stay out of the trees, watch out for the wild goose, and take care of your hernia."

When I ask what it means, he shrugs and says: "Just do it; you won't go wrong."

He's right, but I'm not sure it's something to live by. Unless you have a hernia.

Anyway, I appreciate Mr. Neely's kind invitation. Although I haven't been able to contribute to his book, he did give me something to write about.

As I always say: "Another day, another dollar."

The Burlington Free Press (December 3, 1992), p. 10A.

131

The Proverbial Dilemma (1993)

Paul Dickson

Collect and Create New Proverbs, Rules and Aphorisms; Live by Them; Dump Those That Don't Work – "Always slow down for Dead Man's Curve."

This was the gist of a letter sent to me by a friend, Neal Wilgus, of New Mexico. He called it "Wilgus's Warning," and I immediately added it to my ever-growing list of personal rules to live by.

For this American male in his early 50's, the rule is a trenchant and much wittier reminder to diet, exercise and observe general mid-life moderation than, say, a long list of traditional do's and don'ts. I have posted Wilgus's Warning next to the closet where I keep my walking shoes. It will have other applications, too, but I'm not sure when or where. What I do know is that I will be faced with a choice, and my lips will move and I will utter Wilgus's Warning.

Here is another of the many I use:

You have to work quickly and find a niche.

This has hung above my desk there since I ripped it from the October 6, 1986, issue of *Forbes*. Originally used as a photo caption, it was not intended as any sort of revealed wisdom. It is a very personal reminder that bills have to be paid, that personal productivity counts and that it is fine to have a specialty (in my case, books about words and the English language).

Then there is this one:

Remember Hellmann's Principle.

I see this message every morning when I fire up my computer, which has been programmed to deliver it on the screen before I do anything else. The principle was given to me a few years ago by an artist named A. Peter Hollis who used it in the same way I do. He discovered it one day while looking at a jar of mayonnaise.

The principle?

"Keep cool but do not freeze."

Getting the Message

Messages such as these are displayed all around the spaces where I live and work. Others are tucked away in some fold of my brain. They are pointed and concise and pass for this individual's attempt to codify and use common sense – and not-so-common sense. Most are no longer than eight or nine words and are modern versions of ancient and traditional proverbs.

Wilgus's Warning and Hellmann's Principle are important to me, but so too is Agnes Allen's Law, which states that "Almost anything is easier to get into than out of." The "anything" applies to everything from arguments, to debt, to installment plans, to committees. It is most useful as a caution. I still serve on committees and other bodies, but I have chosen to do so selectively thanks to this law.

This is how it has been for centuries. We post around us warnings and aphorisms and rules – bits of common sense and conventional wisdom that serve as guideposts to help us through daily life. The only problem is that so much of the traditional advice does not work for people who find themselves trying to live in the last part of the twentieth century. We find ourselves searching for the ones that do work today.

Many of the proverbs and bits of cautionary advice we have grown up with make about as much sense today as a hearty, cholesterol-heavy breakfast to "keep you running and on top of the world" or cigarette smoking to "calm the nerves." These are not ancient notions, but they passed for sensible not too long ago. Some, such as "Handsome is as handsome does," are ambiguous. And "Feed a cold, starve a fever" (or is it "starve a cold, feed a fever"?) makes little sense. Does "haste make waste" during a fire?

We seem to be awash in inherited but wrongheaded "wisdom," flawed common sense and bad assumption – that fish is brain food, that nine out of 10 businesses fail in their first year, that Rome wasn't built in a day (who said it was?), that the road to hell is paved with good intentions, that you can't argue with the "facts."

Some of our most treasured traditional proverbs are directly contradicted by others. Is "out of sight out of mind" correct, or do we believe that "absence makes the heart grow fonder"?

In reviewing the *Oxford Dictionary of English Proverbs* for a British magazine in 1970, critic Richard Boston postulated a new semi-scientific law: "For every proverb that so confidently asserts its little bit of wisdom, there is usually an equal and opposite proverb that contradicts it." His examples were many, but one will suffice: "Though many hands make light work, too many cooks spoil the broth."

Writer and humorist Leo Rosten once reflected on the old proverb that "a picture was worth a thousand words," writing in rebuttal, "OK. Draw me a picture of the Gettysburg Address." Rosten also pointed out that two heads were not better than one if both were stupid.

Fact is, a lot of the commonest aphorisms and bits of conventional wisdom are in need of scrapping, or at least of serious revision.

The realization that many of the proverbs and platitudes embroidered on the cushions at our grandparents' homes are no longer relevant is the reason why a number of people are creating and borrowing their own sets of rules that make sense today. It has been said that life is a do-it-yourself project without a set of instructions. These new rules then become the instructions. Some of them help us cope, others instruct.

Word from the Center

The fact is that I have become a major collector of these rules and laws. To say that I have been fascinated by them would be understatement. Humorous, often exaggerated, sometimes cynical, they are also a serious attempt for us to get a handle on things ... to distill experience.

Where do all these items come from? A little background is in order.

It started simply. In 1976, this author created something called the Murphy Center for the Codification of Human and Organizational Law. He appointed himself its first director, and has been, since 1989, its self-appointed Director for Life. It originally amounted to a mere shoebox into which rules and laws were filed.

The Center was created in an effort to collect, test and make a few bucks from "revealed truth," which is often the by-product of what the Center likes to think of as O.F.F.M.&G.C., or Other Folk's Foibles, Misfortunes and General Confusion. It was mainly inspired by Murphy's Law ("If anything can go wrong it will") and influenced by the fact that we had put men on the moon but still seemed unable to create shoelaces that didn't break at inopportune moments.

The now esteemed and verging-on-venerable Murphy Center is alive and well and enjoying its perverse nature. This means that it thrives on a little turmoil, bad economic times and the widespread awareness that the universe is flawed. The Center has published three books of its findings and has now spread out into eight shoeboxes.

The Center pioneered research into some of the major givens of the twentieth century: that a wrong number will displace a body immersed in water; that a defective pay phone will find your last quarter; and that you, personally, will be sought out by a shopping cart with a defective wheel.

These are therefore good times for the Murphy Center, which has already outlived such temporary institutions as the World Football League, Communism, the Cold War, the Berlin Wall and a host of other institutions. The glory of the Center is, not a mail delivery day goes by without the arrival of something profound, thought-provoking or fascinating. Some are goofy, and others are as simple as this item from Wayne Dolan, 77, of Raytown, Mo.:

Dolan's Query. Did your wife ever get a permanent wave? Where is it now?

The plan is to keep the Center up, running and collecting new laws, rules and axioms from its worldwide network of research fellows until the year 2001, or until things get unsnarled.

Short Bursts Are Best

Meanwhile, the Center's collection has proved to be most useful to its custodian. Put directly, some of these witty and overstated rules, laws and maxims are useful in day-to-day life. The brevity and wit that caused them to be written, also render them useful.

Taped to the sunvisor of my car is this simple statement: "You're not late until you get there." It is there to remind me that if I am late for an appointment and 1 can do nothing about it, I had better relax and face the music when I reach my destination. Another helpful thought that comes into play when, say, you are late because of a flat tire. This is when one should invoke Burnham's Tenth Law: "If there's no alternative, there's no problem." (James Burnham, from the June 24, 1988, National Review) There is no alternative to changing the tire, so there is really no problem.

If I have been late for the dentist's office I then invoke another rule, really a caution. BEWARE: A LITTLE. It is an item of my own devising that stems from my personal belief that the scariest words in the language are "a little." For example, "a little problem" at the car repair shop, "a little turbulence" during a flight or in this case, "a little discomfort" in the dentist's chair.

I find that Burnham's Tenth is also most useful in meetings and while serving on committees where it can be brought to bear.

A recent acquisition useful in reporting and writing was sent along by Dr. Terry Smith, Northeast Missouri State University:

Smith's Rule. Discount by at least 90% the truth of any statement preceded by the phrase "Of course ..."

And from V. Richard Smith of LaGrange, Ill., comes this handy travel tip:

Smith's Law of Municipal Location. When in a strange city, the first person you ask directions of will also be from out of town.

What the Center's collection amounts to is the very things that others have created to help them cope and forge ahead. Under the letter H, for example, I now have three or four hundred items filed. Here are some of the most useful:

Harris's Law. Any philosophy that can be put "in a nutshell" belongs there. (Anon.)

Hendrickson's Law. If a problem causes too many meetings, the meetings become more important than the problem. (Anon.)

Hofstadter's Law. It always takes longer than you think it will take, even if you take into account Hofstadter's Law. (Douglas R. Hofstadter, *Scientific American*, January 1982)

Holberger's Rule. It doesn't matter how hard you work on something; what counts is finishing and having it work. (Tracy Kidder, *The Soul of a New Machine*)

Hovancik's Wait Till Tomorrow Principle. Today is the last day of the first part of your life. (John Hovancik, South Orange, N.J.)

And thanks to the household law collection, there is no contingency in the home that I cannot confront. A recent addition to the household collection is:

The Poorman Flaw. In any home improvement project, there will be one mistake so gross that the only solution is to incorporate it into the design. (Created by Paul A. Poorman, Stowe, Oh.)

There are few of us who don't rely on these ranging from just plain folks up to the President. Just before he was elected, Bill Clinton told a writer for *USA Today* of his rules, beginning with this truism:

Clinton's Conundrum. When you're starting to have a good time, you're supposed to be someplace else.

The late Sam Walton of Wal-Mart fame (and fortune) left a set of 10 rules for building a business in his book, *Sam Walton: Made in America, My Story*. Walton's rules are gems. For instance, there is Rule 6: "Celebrate your successes. Find some humor in your failures. Don't take yourself so seriously." The Waltonism that is hard to beat is Rule 10: "Swim upstream ... If everybody else is doing it one way, there's a good chance you can find your niche by going in exactly the opposite direction." Walton pointed out that prime example of swimming upstream in his life was going against the notion that a town of less than 50,000 cannot support a discount store for very long.

Snow and Swallows

Some of these rules are downright cynical and therefore are quite useful in certain occasions. Our frustrations become absorbed by a mock-scientific "law of nature."

While this little essay was being written, the Monster Blizzard of '93 hit the East Coast. Three days after the blizzard struck, the small Maryland town where I live was still socked in with snow and ice. I checked in with the person in charge of such things and was told that the town had a "big problem" which was that the man under contract to keep the streets clean was stretched out on the beach in Cancun, Mexico, and the man he left in charge did not know how to operate the snow plow. Some people would find this aggravating, but not those who are versed in:

Fetridge's Law. Important things that are supposed to happen do not happen, especially when people are looking.

Legend has it that this law was named for Claude Fetridge, a radio engineer who proposed to the NBC radio network in 1936 that he produce a live broadcast of the departure of the swallows from their famous roost at Mission San Juan Capistrano, which always takes place on St. John's Day, October 23. The network bought the premise and sent a large crew to broadcast the event. The swallows unexpectedly left a day ahead of schedule.

Old Saws Resharpened

The time is ripe for a recasting of traditional proverbs. Many of the old ones are simply worn out. Here are some proposed revisions form the files of the Murphy Center created by a number of people. Several are from Philip J. Frankenfeld of Chicago who is master of the art of the revised proverb.

A bird in the hand is superfluous.

Cast your bread on the waters and you get soggy bread.

Don't put off until tomorrow what you can get done sometime next week.

The early bird catches the worm, but on the other hand, the early worm gets eaten by the bird.

Early to bed gets the worm.

Early to bed, early to rise and your girl goes out with other guys. (From a guy named John who seemed to have learned this one the hard way.)

Exceptions disprove rules – a single exception to the law of gravity would be enough.

If at first you don't succeed, you're running about average.

If at first you don't succeed, redefine success.

A fool and his money are some party.

He who hesitates is bossed.

Many hands want light work.

Too many cooks use lard.

Never judge a book by its cover price.

A penny saved is a penny.

People who live in glass houses aren't very smart.

Practice does not make perfect.

(Golf, sex and child-rearing all prove this. No matter how many times we have done it, it is not easier to get up in the morning.)

A rolling stone angers his boss.

A rolling stone leaves broken objects in its wake.

As you sew, so shall you rip.

A watched pot is usually owned by someone without cable.

Living: The Magazine of Life (Summer 1993), pp. 21-25.

Mom's Old Sayings Still Remembered and Quoted (1993)

Jane Heitman

A word to the wise may or may not be sufficient, but those maxims must have been repeated because they had some validity. Our question this week has to do with that.

Can you think of any of those old sayings – ones that you may have benefited from – that you think are truly good advice for everyone in today's world?

We received lots of replies. Here are some of them:

My mother had a quote for every occasion. I had tight, long, curly hair and it was brushed each morning. In tune with my screaming, I heard, *"Beauty feeleth no pain!"* Oh, yeah?

As my brother and I were beating each other to a pulp, we heard, *"Birds in their nests agree!"* Ha! Ha! Ha!

Dorothy G. Dettman, Kirkwood

To my mother, Mattie Griffin: These things will always remain with me. As a mother of two and a grandmother of three, I have passed these on.

1. *No matter who you are or where you go, never forget where you came from – you may have to go back.*

2. *I cried because I had no shoes, until I saw a man with no feet.*

Darlene Bell, Moline Acres

Many years ago, while in a German prison camp (WWII), a chaplain told me, *"The more you complain, the longer God lets you live."*

The other lifetime maxim I learned from a fortune cookie: *In nature, there are neither rewards nor punishments; there are consequences.*

I'm sure all of us could benefit by keeping these two phrases in our hearts.

Bernard Eder, St. Louis

If you can't say anything nice, don't say anything at all.

These are words of wisdom that would greatly benefit some members of my own family, whose only pleasure in life is seeing someone exit a room so they can talk about them.

Judy Kohler, St. Louis

This is an old saying of my mother's: *A man on horseback will never notice it!*

K. Hard, Ballwin

Although my parents passed on 45 years ago, some of their wise words come to my mind at various intervals.

When I might be considering making a change, my mother might help with *"You know what you've got, but you don't know what you're gonna get."*

There were times when my father would caution, *"Those who won't listen must feel caution."* And at other times he might say, *"Forgive, forget; let bygones be bygones and make a fresh start."*

Elmer N. Stuetzer, Lemay

Our mother, Joan Penhorst, used to say to my sister and me that *"God never closes a door that He doesn't open another."*

This has helped me many times not to dwell on the ending of a special time in my life, but to eagerly anticipate the next experience or adventure God has in store for me.

Joan Barghann, Ferguson

I remember a number of sayings from my grandmother and my mother. We lived through the Great Depression that colored these sayings:

Willfully waste – woefully want.

Many hands make swift work.

Celeste P. Jolly, Ironton, Mo.

When I was a teen-ager, in moments of crisis or whenever my world had come crashing down around me, my mother would always say, *"Everything happens for the best."* My reaction to this was to groan to myself and think, "There she goes again with THAT!"

Another of my mother's favorites was *"You can always find someone else who is worse off than you are."*

Since I have become a senior citizen, I can identify better with the timelessness of these oft-repeated sayings, rather than with the teen-ager who was so bored to be on the receiving end of the good advice.

Eunice Wilkening, St. Louis

My dad told me years ago, *"Stop worrying; you can die from worrying."* Whenever I face a real problem, I think of that and it puts things into perspective!

Other pieces of advice, *"Haste makes waste"* and *"He shall conquer who is strong and has the will to wait,"* from my Home Teacher at Ben Bluett Jr. High in 1922 have helped me make decisions.

I think all these sayings are helpful in today's world. I thank my family and teachers for these words of wisdom.

Dorothy Walter, Ladue

My father used to say, *"Paper never refuses ink."* In other words, read critically.

Richard Y. Norrish, Edwardsville, Ill.

A very old proverb my husband's mother used frequently and I say often to my children: *"Eaten bread is soon forgotten."*

Catherine M. Smythe, Kirkwood

I have heard the following sayings from both my mother and grandmother. They have taught me to be nice even when I don't want to be, to work hard and know what real happiness is.

You can catch more flies with honey than with vinegar.
The greatest happiness comes in doing for others.
Work is a blessing!

Cherlyn Fuhrman, Caseyville, Ill.

When I was in my teens, I was very self-conscious. A very wise Sunday School teacher told me: *"You wouldn't worry so much about what people think of you if you knew how seldom they do."*

Mary Jo Owen, Kirkwood

I do not know where this old saying originated, but when I was in school, my best friend's mother used to recite it to us on occasion: *"When a job is once begun, never leave it till it's done. Be thy labor great or small, do it well or not at all."*

Naomi R. Weller, Litchfield, Ill.

A saying that I remember from years past that I think is important: *"Character is what you really are; reputation is what people think you are."*

Sister Jane Sweeney, St. Louis

St. Louis Post-Dispatch (September 13, 1993), p. 3D.

Dueling Proverbs:
A Stitch in Time ... Probably Doesn't Make Much Difference (1993)

Rod L. Evans and Irwin M. Berent

Many popular sayings are correct, even insightful, when applied to life's circumstances. But when proverbs are viewed without qualification, they can cancel each other out. For instance, while it's often true that "too many cooks spoil the broth," there are times when "two heads are better than one." Read on, because ...

He who hesitates is lost.
BUT
Look before you leap.

Birds of a feather flock together.
BUT
Opposites attract.

You're never too old to learn.
BUT
You can't teach an old dog new tricks.

Ask no questions and hear no lies.
BUT
Ask and you shall receive.

Variety is the spice of life.
BUT
Don't change horses in midstream.

Doubt is the beginning, not the end, of wisdom.
BUT
Faith will move mountains.

The pen is mightier than the sword.
BUT
Actions speak louder than words.

Don't cross the bridge till you come to it.
BUT
Forewarned is forearmed.

Silence is golden.
BUT
The squeaky wheel gets the grease.

Clothes make the man.
BUT
Never judge a book by its cover.

The best things come in small packages.
BUT
The bigger, the better.

A miss is as good as a mile.
BUT
Half a loaf is better than none.

An old fox is not easily snared.
BUT
There's no fool like an old fool.

A good beginning makes a good ending.
BUT
It's not over till it's over.

Blood is thicker than water.
BUT
Many kinfolk, few friends.

Practice makes perfect.
BUT
All work and no play makes Jack a dull boy.

If you lie down with dogs, you'll get up with fleas.
BUT
If you can't beat 'em, join 'em.

A bird in the hand is worth two in the bush.
BUT
A man's reach should exceed his grasp.

There's safety in numbers.
BUT
Better be alone than in bad company.

If at first you don't succeed, try, try again.
BUT
Don't beat a dead horse.

And finally:

Hold fast to the words of your ancestors.
BUT
Wise men make proverbs and fools repeat them.

Reader's Digest October 1993), pp. 107-108.

Down with Slogans (1994)

Charles Curran

We have come up with some slogans and metaphors about libraries. We actually use these sayings, sometimes where it matters, in libraries – but also where it doesn't, in the literature, in the classroom, and in meetings of the cognoscenti. So we've got: "The library is the heart of (fill in the blank)." "Support staff are the backbone of the library." "Service is our highest calling." "*Access* has replaced *ownership.*"

"The library is the heart of the *whatever*" is our favorite metaphor, despite massive empirical evidence that the library is more like the liver and considerable suspicion that it sometimes behaves like the appendix.

Discomfort

Fascination with comparing ourselves to body parts has also inspired us to scatter skeletal references among the organs; hence, the support-staff-as-backbone metaphor. In the army, noncommissioned officers are called the backbones. Of course, as a private-first-class infantry grunt, I selected a part directly south of the backbone to describe my bosses. This accounts for my discomfort with slogans that etch our profession into public consciousness through comparison with fleshy gristle or the spiny things we use to filter poisons, maintain posture, sit on, or, in the case of the appendix, don't use at all.

The real crime in the support staff/ backbone deal is that we say support staff are crucial, frontline ambassadors, but we pay them minimum wage plus carfare, exclude them from participation in decision-making, contradict and embarrass them in the presence of clients, and ridicule them with a lower-caste term: *nonprofessional.*

As for "Service is our highest calling," sheep don't even bleat at this one. Service is an essential component of what we offer. But any librarian, who looks at the technological revolution, our competition, the imperative that we invent and provide value-added products, and the state of our information illiteracy and who still insists on intoning the "service-above-all" slogan needs serious employment counseling. Service is for tennis and maitre d's.

I learned firsthand about the foolishness of the "Access has replaced ownership" cuteism. I made the mistake of announcing this in a meeting at which the organization's information czar, collection-development staff, chair of the library committee, and frontline librarians were in attendance.

I explained the concept to them: You see, inflation and the information explosion conspire to make it impossible for any given library to have everything people want from it. So interlibrary loan was created to operationalize access. Translation: Prey upon larger collections, and thereby relieve the party of the first part from having to own what its clients request. This is in all the articles and textbooks, so I felt pretty safe in repeating the slogan.

Wrong! First, I'll translate the looks I got from the librarians: "Naiveté, thy name is Curran." "This is what happens when you let those people out of their ivory-tower cages." "We gotta start checking ID at the front door again." "Someone adjust that poor man's slobber cup."

Second, let me caution you against ever mouthing the slogans, platitudes, and mindless maxims that substitute for thought and common sense. At the very least, don't suggest to harried interloan personnel that they will *ever* convince impatient clients that "access has replaced ownership." In a pig's eye (speaking of organs).

Slogans are odious because they are one-dimensional and simplistic. They serve us for a second, then leave a nasty residue. And they have opposites – contradictory maxims. "Look before you leap" was okay advice if nobody was shooting at you and there were crocodiles in the castle moat. But subsequent to the invention of the crossbow, "He who hesitates is lost."

Proverb, Schmahverb

Ironically, slogans can elect, then topple, leaders of the free world. So read my lips: It isn't that slogans aren't powerful; it's just that they can't get the real job done. "Access has replaced ownership" is a supply-sider's axiom, not a client's. It is an abstraction that pleases Bibliographic Controlvenators; but in superimposing its doctrine of managerial convenience, it ignores the clarion call for libraries to be demand-driven, not supply-driven. Worse, it lures us into polemics when we should be concentrating on providing value-added packages, not musing over some bibliographic conundrum. What's next: "Neither a borrower nor a lender be"?

Admonitions alone won't feed the bulldog, however, so I am including some wise sayings you can memorize and repeat to help you keep from speaking in slogans: Repeat a platitude, expect an attitude. Declare a dictum, reside in hickdom. Mouth a cliché, you're passé. Proverb, schmahverb.

The Education Digest, 59, no. 8 (April 1994), pp. 72-73.

Why Old Proverbs Don't Apply Anymore (1994)

Michael Bixby Dudley

Proverbs have served as common sense guidance for millennia. However, as every student of history knows, there are times when logic flees in the face of hysteria, and the world seems topsy-turvy. The '90s are such a time.

A man's home is his castle. Aside from the fact that the word "man" is sexist, this used to be true. Not anymore. The Comprehensive Crime Act of 1984 (a good year for its enactment, don't you think?) has put this old-fashioned notion behind us. The Act allows your house to be seized and confiscated based on "probable cause" you may have engaged in an "illegal activity." No conviction is necessary for this confiscation. Since modern law is so comprehensive and complex, many Americans unknowingly undertake "illegal activities" every day. Remember, ignorance of the law is no excuse. In order to get your castle back, you must hire a lawyer and file suit to prove it was never the scene of (or "used to facilitate") any "illegal activity," whatever that means.

Sticks and stones may break my bones, but names will never hurt me. This outdated adage is no longer applicable, because, as one New Age "philosopher" has decreed, "words are the same as bullets." Therefore, speaking ill of people is now the moral equivalent of shooting them. So-called "speech codes," such as that being considered by the American Bar Association, provide for severe punishment for prohibited speech.

Two wrongs don't make a right. Modern jurisprudence and legal practice have shown it to be an anachronism. Affirmative action, which mandates present discrimination against one racial (or other) group as a "just remedy" for past discrimination by a different racial (or other) group, is now the law of the land. The fact that the alleged discriminator is long deceased does not enter into the equation. Clearly, under the law, past discrimination is the "fault" of the living.

Don't cry over spilt milk. This ancient proverb does not apply if you are a modern dairy farmer. Much milk has been spilt lately because it is "contaminated" with an artificial hormone which is the exact chemical equivalent of the natural hormone which makes cows produce milk for their offspring. Groups with names like "Save Our Children" have poured out (for the TV

147

cameras) hundreds of gallons of milk that don't contain bovine growth hormone, and dairy farmers, are, indeed, crying over it.

An ounce of prevention is worth a pound of cure. Zealous reformers have obviously discarded this shopworn homily. Several billion pounds of cure are seemingly required to ensure "health care security" for all Americans. Forget the ounce of prevention – it is no longer sufficient.

A stitch in time saves nine. Similar to "an ounce of prevention," and outdated as well.

Charity begins at home. Clearly archaic, as much of the support for "charitable" organizations comes from taxpayer dollars. According to the Urban Institute, "federal support to the nonprofit sector alone amounted to $40.4 billion in 1980." Charities now have huge budgets. In the Atlanta area, for example, nonprofit budgets are "four times larger than the city budget," according to Foundation News. These days, charity begins in walnut-paneled offices with deep plush carpeting and matching social agendas.

It's an ill wind that blows nobody good. There are no such ill winds anymore. Look at Hurricane Andrew. First, the residents of Florida got clobbered by the winds themselves. On top of that, the residents of Oshkosh and Peoria got clobbered with higher taxes to pay for the damages caused by those same ill winds. Indeed.

You can't cheat an honest man. Of course you can. Just make each and every law, rule, and regulation so obscure that even those who draft and interpret them haven't the faintest idea what they mean. That way everyone can be cheated at the same time, and no one will be the wiser.

Take care of the pennies and the pounds will take care of themselves. While you were watching your pennies, some folks in Washington started looking over your shoulder. They imposed a new retroactive tax, which relieved your hard-earned pounds of several "windfall" pence.

Do unto others as you would have them do unto you. Not true if you are Congress. If you are in government, it is your duty to exempt yourself from all laws which affect everyone else. Feel free to remove yourself from the encircling tentacles of OSHA, CERCLA, Equal Opportunity Laws, Fair Employment Acts, Social Security, and so forth. If you actually write laws, be sure to include the phrase, "This law shall not apply to the state or any political subdivision thereof." This way, you don't have to worry about what others would do unto you – you are exempt by law.

If at first you don't succeed, try, try again. This prescription for success was obviously written in the Dark Ages. Modern times demand a totally different strategy. First, see above: have a law passed to exempt yourself from even having to try in the first place. If that doesn't work, proclaim yourself a "victim" and demand compensation for your lack of success.

A rolling stone gathers no moss. No one has ever been able to figure out what this one means, so let's pass a law against its use!

The Freeman, 44, no. 8 (1994), pp. 445-446.

Teachers Aim to Clean up Clichés (1994)

Anonymous

Keeping up with political correctness is no longer an "uphill battle."

It's now "next to impossible."

At least it will be if the North York Women Teachers' Association has its way. The association has distributed a pamphlet that promotes alternatives to what it terms violent and militaristic language.

"More than one way to skin a cat", for example, is replaced in the pamphlet by "different ways to solve a problem."

"Kill two birds with one stone" should become "get two for the price of one."

Students should be encouraged to "go for it" rather than to "take a stab at it." The pamphlet suggests "shoot yourself in the foot" can be better expressed by "undermine your own position."

The booklet, distributed in schools in the Toronto suburb, says seemingly inoffensive expressions may invoke violence. So try to say "press" or "tap" a computer key – not "hit it."

The pamphlet advises its readers to challenge themselves to develop "catchy non-violent alternatives."

St. John's Evening Telegram (Newfoundland) (November 20, 1994), p. 7.

Happy New Year, from Poor Richard's Almanack (1995)

Thomas V. DiBacco

All right, the Republicans are back in power in Congress. No more liberal schmaltz in terms of New Year adages. It's back to basics. And nobody could be more basic than Benjamin Franklin's Poor Richard's Almanack, which first made its appearance in 1732.

On New Year's in early America, colonists often would read passages from two basic volumes – the Bible and Poor Richard – as a means of starting off the calendar on the right moral foot. And, of course, colonists had enormous respect for editor Franklin, whose conservatism, exemplified in business success and civic leadership, was enhanced with each passing year until his death in 1790.

"Poor Richard" was replete with New Year's resolutions in the form of maxims on everyday living that concentrated on such stabilizing virtues as thrift, industry, love and marriage – and patience. Although Franklin devised only a few of the numerous adages found in "Poor Richard," he was ingenious in his selections and in refining the thoughts of other authors.

Here are some examples:

"Industry pays debts, despair increases them."
"Pardoning the bad is injuring the good."
"Teach your child to hold his tongue, he'll learn fast
    enough to speak."
"Discontented minds, and fevers of the body, are not to
    be cured by changing beds or business."
"Creditors have better memories than debtors."
"There are no ugly loves, nor handsome prisons."
"Love, cough and a smoke, can't be well hid."
"Keep your eyes wide open before marriage, half shut
    afterwards."
"A ship under sail and a big-bellied woman are the hand-
    somest two things that can be seen common."
"At 20 years of age the will reigns; at 30 the wit; at 40
    the judgment."
"Three may keep a secret, if two of them are dead."
"If your head is wax, don't walk in the sun."

"Glass, china and reputation are easily cracked, and never well mended."

"Let thy child's first lesson be obedience, and the second will be what thou wilt."

"Mankind are very odd creatures: One half censure what they practice, the other half practice what they censure; the rest always say and do as they ought."

"To err is human, to repent divine, to persist devilish."

"Lawyers, preachers and tomtit's eggs, there are more of them hatched than come to perfection."

"There's a time to wink as well as to see."

"God heals and the doctor takes the fee."

"Love your neighbor, yet don't pull down your hedge."

"Fish and visitors stink in three days."

"The excellence of hogs is fatness; of men virtue."

"Write injuries in dust, benefits in marble."

"Be at war with your vices, at peace with your neighbors, and let every New Year find you a better man."

The Burlington Free Press (January 1, 1995), P. 2A.

Chewing the Rag – Vermonters Say It Right (1995)

Molly Walsh

Have you ever been so hungry you'd eat the north end of a southbound skunk? Ever met someone as stubborn as a pig on ice? Ever headed "downstreet" to do some shopping? Vermonters are known for speaking their minds in a unique way. Last month, *The Burlington Free Press* published an article about the Vermont dialect. With it, we invited readers to send in some of the expressions – current and old time – that they associate with Vermont.

Now the mail bag is full, with more than 200 words and sayings. Many contain references to farming, the land, animals and Vermont's cheapest form of entertainment – the weather. Vermonters also have developed many ways to say a person is stupid or lacking in virtue.

Many readers also shared memories of hearing a friend or relative in Vermont use a particular phrase, underscoring the fact that language is an important element of character. The list of sayings here does not include the good dozen off-color submissions that were not fit to be published in a family newspaper.

From Joseph W. Boulanger, Newport:
Dooryard
Broad shelf (counter)
Drier than a covered bridge
Darker than a pocket
Downstreet (downtown)

From Alice Peabody, Middlebury:
Least said, soonest mended
As independent as a hog on ice

From Kit Andrews, Burlington:
I may be a fool, but I'm not a damned fool.
"I remember as a small child hearing my parents say this to each other," Andrews writes. "Sometimes in kidding disagreements, sometimes remarking about current events. Then as a teen I gave my mother plenty of opportunities to drum this phrase into me as I tried to talk her into schemes or sneak around her rules."

From Carole Lucia, Enosburg Falls:
> Well, I'll be a son-of-a: Who cut your hair with a buck-
> saw and made it turn out curly.
> I can't remember two times 'round a broomstick (some-
> what forgetful)
> That man's not worth a peanut shuck

From Arlene M. Wimett, Salisbury:
> Higher than a woodpecker's hole
> Too much for the pump
> Clothespress
> He doesn't need that any more than a frog needs sideburns

From Carolyn Siccama, Burlington:
> A couple-three (two or three)

From Craig Reynolds, Charlotte:
> So dry the trees are following the dogs around
> My back is stiffer than a wedding drink
> The wind blows so hard, so often, that it quit one day
> last week and everyone fell down.
> Hotter than a little tin bell with a cover
> Stubborn as a pig on ice

From Judy Cleary and other staff members at Johnson State College:
> Slower than molasses running uphill in January
> It rained enough to wrinkle the spinach
> There'll be frost on the pumpkin tonight
> Snow deeper than a tall Swede
> Scarcer than hen's teeth
> Side by each
> Slicker than snot on a doorknob
> So noisy it could wake the living dead
> I'm so hungry I could eat the north end out of a
> southbound skunk
> I'm so sick that I'd have to get well to die
> I'm so broke that I can't even pay attention

Anonymous, Middlebury:
> Dumber than a stone.
> Handy as a hog winding a watch.
> Hotter than the hubs of hell.

154

From Philip M. Pierce, Franklin:
Tighter than the bark on a tree (stingy).
It's a matter of horse sense.
Cats granny! (an exclamation of surprise or disgust).
He thinks he's top turd on the wheelbarrow.

From N. Houston, Wolcott:
Pret-near (almost).
A chewing match (an argument).
Right out straight (busy).
Thicker than hair on a dog (close).
So homely his face hurts.
Fog goes up the mountain a-hoppin', rain comes down a
    droppin'.
Rain before seven, done by eleven.

From Robert E. Field, Bridport:
Wouldn't run uphill after it.
Two clapboards below zero.
Tougher than boiled owl.
A frog-hair more (a bit more).
Poor man's got two dogs; damn poor man's got four.
Cut cross-lots (take a short-cut).
Doesn't know enough to suck alum and drool.

From Gary Irish, Jericho:
Doesn't know enough to pound sand in a rat hole.
He'd never lay out for lack of a handle to drag him in by.
    (He's got a big nose.)
By gory.
Sugar snow (big flakes that fall during sugaring season).
I feel like I've been drug through a knothole (all tuck-
    ered out).
Irish also remembers that as a child, if he walked into the
house and did not shut the door behind him someone was sure to
ask him, "Were you brought up in a sawmill?" – a reference to
the fact that sawmills have no doors.

From Jerry Highter, Shoreham:
Dryer than a popcorn fart.
Pretty rough sleddin'.
He/she's quite a riggin' (an outlandish character, but
    likeable).

A hell-a-tee-ding-dong (going fast down a hill).

From Lucille West:
God all fishhooks!
Down-country (any state south of Vermont).
Poorer than Job's turkey.
There'll be white blackbirds by the time he gets done.

Anonymous:
Early to bed and early to rise makes a man father of a
large family.
If he had half a brain, it would be lonesome.
Too lazy to shake the dead flies off.
So lazy he married a pregnant woman.
Rollin' around like a sow on an apple barrel.
He hasn't got a pot to cook in, or a window to look
through.
Disgusting enough to make a minister swear.
Colder than the south side of a light pole.

From Glenn W. Skiff, South Burlington:
Worth about as much as a hole in the snow.
That coffee's colder than Billy-be-damned.
Them heifers took of in forty-'leven different directions.
Uglier than a hedge fence.
I don't read music enough to spoil my playing!
If you ain't never done it before, do it by guess and by
gosh.
It's plumb some, but not plumb plumb (almost perfect).

From Marylin Melendy, South Starksboro:
Yes, sir, Mr. Dooley!
Colder than a witch's brass broomstick.
Lazier than a peach orchard bull.
Tighter than a boar's rear end in fly time.
Hard telling not knowing.

From Marjorie S. Timbers, Essex Junction:
Drier than a cork leg.
Down cellar behind the axe (Two meanings: busy or hid-
ing).
Like cold potatoes, better-warmed up.
Get your hair cut pompadour (Get it cut very short).

From Robert L. Coon, St. Albans:
Chewing the rag (Light conversation).
The silent hog eats all the swill.
Built close to the ground (A short person).
An educated fool.
Can't blame a fool for what he doesn't know.
Homely in the cradle, pretty at the table.

From Richard E. Robinson of South Burlington:
So don't I (So do I).
Robinson has been hearing this expression since the 1970s when he moved here. He confesses it drives him crazy. "For years I have had to listen to Vermonters say 'so don't I,' when they really mean 'so do I.' "He "thanks God" that his son, a native Vermonter, never adopted this usage.

From Robert Lutz, Burlington:
"Bout as sprightly as a dead tree.
Snow butt-high to a tall cow.
The lord made her ugly; then he scared her.

Anonymous, Barre:
He was the meanest man that ever wore a pair of shoes.

From Gussie Levarn, Bristol:
The patient was on dizzytalis and trampilizers (Digitalis and tranquilizers).
Familiarity leads to conception.
As well as a June bride.
Doesn't amount to a fart in a whirlwind.

From Iola Atwood, Waterbury:
Happy as a toad lapping lightning.
Hen wet her apron! (A substitute for profanity).

From Peter Morris, Burlington:
Height the land.
Harder than Chinese algebra.
Well, snatch me bald-headed.
Well, that just eats my lunch.
Vermonster (What Vermonters call themselves but will not allow flatlanders to call them).

Outlanders, those from away, or dudes (Urban people who come to Vermont looking like L.L. Bean or Orvis centerfolds).

How many Vermonters does it take to change a light bulb? Three. One to change the bulb and two to sit around discussing how they liked the old one better.

Volvoful (of tourists).

He was so crooked, when they buried him, they had to screw him into the ground. And not only that, when they screwed him into the ground, they made sure it was head first, just in case he ever came back to life and tried to dig his way out he'd have to take the long way up.

From Julie C. Hogan:

Since Christ was a child (a very long time).

From Patricia and Edna Bean, Burlington:

Sweet Jerusalem on a bicycle!

Don't get your bowels in an uproar.

From Lou Dorwaldt Jr. of North Hero, who beard these from his good friend and neighbor, Gerald "Junior" Tudhope:

As free from brains as a frog from feathers.

Howling like the hounds of hell.

Goin' down to Canada.

From Georgia Christiano, Grand Isle:

Colder than your grandmother's preserves.

More nervous than a long-tailed cat in a room full of rocking chairs.

Straighter than a die.

Christiano writes: "My dad was an old-time Vermonter from 'Bah-ton' (Barton), and I used to love to listen to his stories, anecdotes, humor and accent." "

From Nona Flint, Brooklfield:

Flint writes: "My husband and I have lived in Vermont all our lives, as our parents did before us. We use an expression that I cannot find in any dictionary. It's "big and gombin'." I have no idea how it's spelled. It rhymes with bomb. It means big and clumsy – hard to maneuver because of its size and construction.

From Mary Elizabeth Koll, East Middlebury:

About as useless as a screen door on a submarine.

Got more brass than Carter's got liver pills.

As crooked as a lawyer.

It's enough to jar your mother's onions.

Rather have what he owes than what he owns.

One of those side-hill clodgers (A rather unrespectable person).

Skinny as a rail fence.

Mister, I tell you (or: mister, I'm a-tellin').

Homely enough to stop a freight train.

Jeezum-jee-hassafrats!

Have we missed any? If you have more Vermont expressions to add, send them to Molly Walsh, *The Free Press*, P.O. Box 10, Burlington, 05402.

The Burlington Free Press (April 2, 1995), p. 1D and p. 5D.

159

Fractured Epithets Abound (1995)

Debbie Salomon

A friend mentioned how a lot of old saws need sharpening – old saws being truisms, sayings, clichés, platitudes, epithets, words of wisdom or whatever your English teacher called them.

This idea stuck in my head as I listened to TV commentators mouth trite phrases like "all in a day's work," or "school of hard knocks" – which has many cheerleaders but no scholarships.

This is fun. Andy Rooney got rich doing it. Let's keep going:

A Rolling Stone gathers much cocaine.

One picture is worth a thousand faxes.

Home is where the coronary-bypass patient is.

A loaf of bread, a jug of wine cost 17 bucks at the gourmet food shop.

Children should be heard and not seen plastered to the TV.

Men and women work from sun to sun; then men watch "Seinfeld" while women do the laundry.

Physician, heal thyself because your colleagues can't afford malpractice insurance.

The shoemaker's children wear Nikes.

All the news that's fit to broadcast on C-Span.

A bird in hand is probably contaminated with salmonella.

We shook on it at the lawyer's office.

He's as good as his word processor.

A penny saved gets damn poor interest.

Imitation is the sincerest form of laziness.

Man's best friend is his ferret.

Kathy Ireland is man's breast friend.

A prenuptial agreement is a woman's best friend.

Like the pot calling the kettle African-American.

Sitting in the lap of the Japanese luxury car tariff.

Blondes have more hairdresser appointments.

Like taking child support from a baby.

Taxation with representation.

Teacher's pet files harassment charges.

An honest day's wages is something to hide from the welfare department.

Early to bed, early to rise means you like Limbaugh, not Letterman.

Water, water, everywhere – and most of it undrinkable.
Living off the fat-free land.
You can't make a silk purse out of polyester.
An apple a day equals one-fifth of the daily
    fruit/vegetable RDA.
It'll all come out in the Laundromat.
Build a better mousepad.
Mind your mannerisms.
One for the roadkill.
Watched pot never gets smoked.
To market, to market, to buy The Other White Meat.
As American as apple chutney.
Just say maybe.
Recycling caution to the winds.
"Give me liberty, or give me the death penalty!"
"Let 'em eat SnackWells!"
"Out, out damned DNA!"

Drats. Now I've got a headache. I'll just take two ibuprofen and call the doctor's voice mail in the morning.

The Burlington Free Press (June 3, 1995), p. 1C.

Speaking of Language –
Proverbs are Pithy Purveyors of Wisdom (1995)

Howard Richler

The Oxford English Dictionary (Second Edition) defines "proverb" as "a short pithy saying in common recognized use ... which is held to express some truth ascertained by experience or observation and familiar to all."

"The all" usually has a universal sense, but some times its meaning is restricted to particular societies and languages.

Take the Spanish, "En tierra de ciegos, el tuerto es rey" ("In the land of the blind, the one-eyed man is king"). An equivalent expression exists in French, but not in English or German, so it would appear we have hit upon a peculiarity among speakers of Romance languages. Not so. There is no equivalent expression in Italian, which, like English but unlike Spanish and French, does not possess a noun for "one-eyed man." One has to wonder if the condition of one-eyedness was epidemic at some point in France because the proverb is pluralized: "Au royaume des aveugles, les borgnes sont rois."

The same proverbs can be found in a multitude of languages, but they are very rarely direct translations. The English proverb, "A bird in the hand is worth two in the bush" in French isn't, "Un oiseau dans le main vaut deux dans le buisson" but "la haie," ("in the hedge"). This sentiment, however, is more likely to be expressed in French as, "Un tiens vaux mieux que deux tu l'auras."

In Italian, the equivalent proverb translates as "Better a finch in the hand than a thrush on a branch;" in German it becomes, "Better a sparrow in the hand than a dove on the roof." In Spanish it is, "A bird in the hand is worth more than a hundred flying."

English seems to be the only language that takes inventory of chickens as in, "Don't count your chickens before they're hatched." The definitive animal seems to be the bear. In French, the maxim states, "Il ne faut pas vendre la peau de l'ours avant de l'avoir tué." German, Russian and Spanish also feature the bear in their equivalent proverbs.

Place names are likely to change in proverbs and be given a local reference. In England one will "carry coals to Newcastle," whereas in Greece one "sends owls to Athens" and in Spain one transports "iron to Viscaysa."

Sometimes a foreign locale can be employed as in "Rome wasn't built in a day." Like English, German uses Rome, but other languages opt for their own cities as in, "Paris n'est pas fait en un jour." Russian chooses Moscow and Polish eschews its capital Warsaw in favor of Krakow. Spanish also ignores its capital in favor of the rhyming ancient Zamora; "No se gano Zamora en una hora." ("Zamora was not won in an hour.")

The "Zamora" proverb displays the popularity of rhyme and assonance in proverbs: "Birds of a feather, flock together," the highly unpoetic "When the cat's away, the mice will play," and "A stitch in time, saves nine."

David Crystal, in the Cambridge Encyclopedia of Language, states that many proverbs "can be divided into two parts that balance each other, often displaying parallel syntax and rhythm, and links of rhyme and alliteration." Two examples he lists are: Latin: "Praemonitus, praemunitus," ("forewarned is forearmed"), and Chinese "ai wu ji wu," ("if you love a house, love its crows").

A proverb is seen by many nowadays as no more than a cliché, in expressing trite, conventional wisdom. In the Concise Oxford Dictionary of Proverbs, author John Simpson points out that "in medieval times, and even as late as the 17th century, proverbs often had the status of universal truths and were used to confirm and refute an argument." By the 18th century, the esteemed position of proverbs had begun to wane and those who overused them were mocked. In Richardson's Clarissa Harlowe (1748), a character in a letter writes avuncularly, "It is a long lane that has no turning. Do not despise me for my proverbs."

This is not to say, however, that proverbs have lost their popularity worldwide. The book Refanero General Ideologoco Espanol, lists 65,000 commonly used Spanish proverbs.

There are some proverbs that seem to contradict each other. For example, the messages of "Look before you leap" – "He who hesitates is lost" and "Nothing ventured, nothing gained" – "Better safe than sorry" are diametrically opposed to each other.

Gazette readers are asked to supply commonly known proverbs whose messages are at odds with the following proverbs.

1. It's never too late to learn.
2. Clothes make the man.
3. If you want something done right, do it yourself.

163

4. Many hands make light work.
5. Absence makes the heart grow fonder.
6. It's the thought that counts.
7. Wisdom comes with age.
8. Use a carrot instead of a stick.

Solvers are invited to submit their answer to: *The Gazette*, Books Section, Proverbs for All Seasons, 250 St. Antoine St. W., H2Y 3R7. The first person with all the right answers plus one drawn at random with all the correct answers will both win a new book. No fax submissions please.

The Montreal Gazette (August 19, 1995), p. G2.

Dead Metaphor Society –
Colorful Phrases Linger; but Those Who Can Understand
Them Are Becoming Scarce as Hen's Teeth (1995)

Laurie Lucas

Try this next time you're chewing the rag with your teenager: "I'm not trying to be a wet blanket, but it's plain as a pikestaff that you must take the bull by the horns to improve your rotten grades. You're spending more time burning the candle at both ends and sowing your wild oats than burning the midnight oil. It's time to bite the bullet. If you come home three sheets in the wind again, I guarantee that you'll have no truck with your friends anymore, the whole kit and caboodle."

Ask 12-year-old Alexis Payne if she's ever carried the torch for a guy, and the question fires up confusion rather than giggles.

"Does that mean you're taking over what he's supposed to do?" wonders the seventh-grader at Shivela Middle School in Murrieta.

Her big sister, 17-year-old Jasmine Payne, perks on another puzzlement: Did she ever stew in her own juice? "Uh, revel in one's own glory?" ventures the senior at Murrieta Valley High School.

Besides yanking out the phone, the fastest way to hit a teenager's mute button is to sock him or her with a few pithy, centuries-old expressions.

Chances are, the kids won't know (or care) a fig about your quaint figures of speech. Or they may laugh up their sleeve like Jasmine, who admits she's clueless about that phrase. Instead, she chuckles out loud at your lingo. "I think it's hilarious," she declares.

According to Jules Levin, chairman of literatures and languages at the University of California, Riverside, these dead metaphors have a strong pulse when reincarnated as idioms.

From kings' courts to commoners' hovels, from churches to brothels, from farmers' fields to playgrounds, from the sea to the battlefield, thousands of clichés leapt into the lexicon as fresh turns of speech, then fossilized into idioms once the underlying imagery was forgotten.

Allan Metcalf, executive secretary of the American Dialect Society, says such phrases still breathe "because people in the past found good ways to say things." Today, he notes, such coinages pop out automatically, without our pondering their etymologies.

"They're picturesque speech," Levin explains. "The fact that people aren't clear about their meaning keeps them alive and a little mysterious."

Mysterious certainly sums up 13-year-old Genaro Gutierrez's response to several old saws.

After all, he and his classmates at Alessandro Middle School in Moreno Valley are too busy minting their own mots to worry much about mastering old maxims. When the phrase, "don't trip" trips off Genaro's tongue, it's teenspeak for "don't do something stupid."

And while "carrying coals to Newcastle" tripped up Jasmine Payne, her apology, "Oh my bad" (Oh, my mistake) makes perfect sense to her and cronies. And Jasmine knows a "hottie" (a good-looking guy) when she sees one and may likewise avoid someone who's "out there" (crazy).

Why do some expressions wilt from lack of nourishment while others take root and flourish? Metcalf, a professor of English at MacMurray College in Jacksonville, Ill., thinks still-popular anachronisms such as "dyed in the wool," "to eat crow" and "on the bandwagon" survived because of their concrete word pictures, even if the imagery is irrelevant today.

"I doubt that one person in 10,000 knows the origin of bandwagon, but it's still popular," says Metcalf.

So how about putting your IQ, or Idiom Quotient, to a trial by fire? Do you know the origin of the following commonly used, colorful phrases? All were culled from a book written by Charles Earle Funk in 1948 called "Hog on Ice & Other Curious Expressions."

To look a gift horse in the mouth: To show bad manners by criticizing a gift or favor.

The origin of this 14th-century proverb alludes to judging a horse's age by its teeth. Although the animal might appear young and frisky, the age and condition of its teeth might belie that.

On the bandwagon: Accepts or espouses a popular cause.

The expression dates from the presidential campaign in 1900 when William Jennings Bryan ran against William McKinley – though the band, the wagon and the practice were longtime features in American preelection politics. Parades honoring a political candidate were led by a loud band of musicians riding upon a large sturdy cart. As the band approached, some local leader would climb aboard the wagon and ride through the district, advertising his support of the candidate.

To stew in one's own juice: To suffer the consequences of one's own act.

Presumably, its precursor, "to fry in one's own grease," was originally literal. Having committed a crime, one was burned at the stake or fried in his own grease.

To ride on one's high horse: Affect arrogance or superiority, scorn those believed inferior.

In the 14th century, people of high rank in a royal pageant were mounted on "high" horses, meaning that they rode the "great horses," or heavy chargers used in battle or tournaments.

To carry the torch for someone: Refers to a burning passion or loyalty.

The torch has long been an emblem of enlightenment and of burning devotion. In 1775, Richard Sheridan used the expression, "The torch of love," in his epilogue to "The Rivals."

To read the riot act: Give a stern scolding or warning.

The allusion is to the actual Riot Act decreed in 1716 by George I of England. The punishment for rioting was penal servitude for life or at least three years of imprisonment with or without hard labor for two years.

Lock, stock and barrel: The whole works.

The expression probably dates at least to the American Revolution. The three essential components of a gun are the barrel, the stock, and the lock, or firing mechanism. In other words, the entire gun, the whole thing.

A dog in the manger: A person who keeps others from using something which he or she has but cannot or will not use. From Aesop's fable about the dog that kept the ox from eating the hay.

To wear one's heart on one's sleeve: An ostentatious display of limitless devotion.

During the Elizabethan period, a young man attached to his sleeve a gift from a young lady he loved, thus displaying his feelings. Shakespeare uses this in "Love's Labor's Lost," where Biron, speaking of Boyet, says, "This gallant pins the wenches on his sleeve," meaning that Boyet is openly devoted to all wenches.

A flash in the pan: A sudden, apparently brilliant effort that fails.

This expression dates to the late 17th century to the days of the flintlock musket. Sparks produced from a flint struck by a hammer ignited powder in a small depression, called a pan. This powder primed the explosion. When the charge fizzled, the powder simply emitted a flash.

Pull the wool over his eyes: To hoodwink or delude.

Probably wool referred to a wig pulled over a man's peepers in jest, or to temporarily blind him to steal his purse.

To laugh in or up one's sleeve: To be secretly amused, whether in derision or to avoid offense through open laughter.

The saying dates from the first half of the 16th century when the sleeves of a gentleman's costume were large enough to conceal his whole head, let alone his mouth.

To buy a pig in a poke: To buy something or accept an idea without having seen it or being certain of what it is.

The expression has hung around since the 14th century. The poke was a small sack, the pig was a young swine. The game was to sneak a cat in the poke and try to palm it off in the market as a pig. The trick was persuading the buyer that it would be best not to open the bag because the pig might escape. If the buyer insisted on seeing what he was getting and the seller opened the poke, he "let the cat out of the bag."

To run the gantlet (or gauntlet): To proceed while under attack from both sides, referring to criticism, gossip, or a series of unpleasantries.

During the Thirty Years' War (1618-1648) the British forces observed a form of punishment used by the Germans that originated among the Swedes. A soldier guilty of an offense was forced to strip to the waist and run between two rows of men who struck him with clubs, whips or rods. The Swedish term for the punishment, gatloppe, (literally, a running of the lane) was corrupted by the English into gantlope, then into gantlet, and finally, into gauntlet.

The Press-Enterprise [Riverside, California] (November 15, 1995), p. D1.

168

Let's Hear It for the Lowly Sound Bite!
In Which It Is Amply Demonstrated that the Sound Bite, Long a Pariah of Pundits and Pooh-bahs, Is Really a Help-meet to Man (1996)

Robert Wernick

In the year 1525, King Francis I of France led his troops into an indefensible position in some fruit orchards outside Pavia in Italy and, in the subsequent battle, lost his army and was himself taken prisoner. That night, in a long letter rambling through the tangled thickets of 16th-century prose, a disorderly jumble of subordinate clauses and dangling participles, the captive king wrote to his mother to explain how the unthinkable had happened, and pour out all his grief and rage and humiliation and unconquerable determination to survive. By the time his mother, her royal counselors and her ladies-in-waiting had read it and commented and gossiped about it, the message had been reduced to a single sentence: "All is lost but honor."

It was recognized at the time, and has been recognized ever since, as a perfect expression of the noble side of the brutal aristocratic culture that Francis personified, just as Leo Durocher's "Nice guys finish last" has been recognized as a perfect expression of the dark side of the individualist-competitive culture of the 20th century. Picayune scholars will go to any lengths to prove that deathless lapidary phrases like these were not actually said in precisely their reputed form by their reputed authors. They have asserted with footnotes that Richard III never said "My kingdom for a horse" any more than Yogi Berra said "It's déjà vu all over again." But the pedants miss the point. These phrases were what these people meant to say, and would have said if they had had more time and more verbal facility. You cannot expect a man like Francis I, covered with dust and blood, who has just seen his life crumble around him, his best friends screaming in agony, to produce a polished phrase following the rhetorical rules and devices fashionable at the moment. The phrase nevertheless belongs to the man who is said to have said it, and it is a part of living history.

Does it matter if Bishop Latimer, tied to the stake in Bloody Mary's England, said to his comrade in martyrdom, "Play the man, Master Ridley; we shall this day light such a candle, by God's grace, in England, as I trust shall never be put out," or if he only said something like it and the words were refashioned by the Protestant propagandist John Foxe? Those were the words that were learned and repeated and treasured by the people who turned England from a Catholic to a Protestant country in the years that followed. Honor, if not approval, has therefore been deservedly paid to Francis I and Durocher and Bishop Latimer and many others for having encapsulated or summarized whole eras, whole cultures, whole mass movements in a few memorable words. Just so, in more recent times, honor and approval (or disapproval) have been paid to Harry Truman for summing up his conception of the Presidency and of his own character with the words, "The buck stops here." And to Walt Kelly's Pogo when he reduced the philosophical uncertainties about degradation of the environment to the single compound sentence "We have met the enemy and he is us." Not to mention Nancy Reagan when she miniaturized the case for an individual-voluntaristic (as opposed to a macroeconomic-bureaucratic) approach to controlling substance abuse into three words, "Just say no"; and Walter Mondale when he skewered his political rivals with "Where's the beef?" a line lifted from the little old lady in the Wendy's ads. Calvin Coolidge, the most taciturn of our Presidents, is remembered for concentrating a thousand books of theology into his description of his preacher's Sunday morning sermon on sin: "He was agin it."

Honor will no longer be paid, however, if we listen to the TV commentators and newspaper editorialists who are daily shaping the minds of the new generation, Generation Z. According to these authorities, the old world of civilized rational discourse – in which Presidents wrote their own two-hour speeches in longhand, and ideas were exposed calmly and at length to the people – a leaky craft that in fact began taking water years ago, has now been sunk without a trace by a new form of torpedo called the sound bite.

Editorialists and commentators have taken this technical phrase from the radio and TV studios and turned it into a general term of abuse for any short statement they disagree with – a better term might be "unsound bite." It may be defined as a device used by wicked people to reduce complex issues to simple formulas in order to sway public opinion. Only take away the adjective "wicked" and you have a definition of one of the oldest and most honorable devices known to man.

170

In fact, it is hard to see how we could have made much progress at all without it. For civilized life, or any kind of life, demands a series of decisions, choices of roads taken and not taken. Ideally, you should take long and careful thought before any decision, and sound bites by themselves are no substitute for thought. But in the world of things as they are, it is impossible to think without them. The time available for careful thought that takes in all the variables and weighs every pro against every con is limited. We could not cross a street, much less fight a war or pass an omnibus appropriations bill, without having a mass of ready-made formulas available to summarize previous experience.

These formulas may be right or wrong, wise or foolish. They may be fiercely partisan or they may express universal beliefs. Every nation that goes to war produces sound bites to prove its cause is just, but not many can pass the test in the judgment of future historians. Everyone, however, accepts and acts upon the principle popularized in a sound bite by a U.S. Senator, William Learned Marcy, in 1832: "To the victor belong the spoils." Similarly, politicians and theologians can debate the merits and demerits of capitalism from here to doomsday, but the system itself runs on, merrily or not, following the principle reduced by Adam Smith to a commonsense sound bite: "It is not from the benevolence of the butcher, the brewer, or the baker, that we expect our dinner, but from their regard to their own interest."

You could spend years trying to achieve a precise calculation of the relative merits of Mr. Dole and Mr. Clinton, but you have to vote on November 5 of this year. Unless you are the kind of person who can analyze stacks of newspaper files and Congressional testimony, your decision will almost certainly be made on the basis of sound bites picked up from Dan Rather and C-SPAN and lectures in high school civics classes, and things you have heard in coffeeshops or bars, and tales your mother told you.

This was as true when America was full of wise founding fathers as it is today, when it is full of Don Imus and Howard Stern. Political speeches were longer in those days, and the voters may have vociferously enjoyed them, but that does not mean they were listening in the sense of following a closely reasoned argument. If audiences came away with anything at all permanently fixed in their minds, it was a sound bite, often the one that brought the speech to a triumphant close: Patrick Henry's "Give me liberty or give me death!"; Daniel Webster's "Liberty and Union, now and forever, one and inseparable"; Abraham Lincoln's "Government of the people, by the people, for the people, shall not perish from the earth"; William Jennings Bryan's "You shall not crucify mankind upon a cross of gold."

It has been the same in the 20th century: "The only thing we have to fear is fear itself"; "Ask not what your country can do for you, ask what you can do for your country"; "Free at last! Free at last! Thank God almighty, we are free at last!" Structurally, these famous phrases that once stirred multitudes to action in war and peace are no different from advertising slogans – from "You deserve a break today" to "Just do it" – that have also stirred multitudes, in their own way. They are short, they are forceful, they are resonant. If not, they do not linger in the memory of the people, they do not survive.

Julius Caesar understood this principle, when, after defeating Pharnaces II in Anatolia in 47 B.C., he sent back to Rome not an orderly exposition of his strategy and tactics but the three-word sound bite, *"Veni, vidi, vici"* – "I came, I saw, I conquered" – to convince the Roman public that he was a man who could get things done expeditiously with maximum panache and minimum cost, just the man they wanted to reclaim the vacant post of dictator.

Among the first sound bites with which most of us come into contact are the Ten Commandments. If Moses had come down from Sinai with a tablet saying, "Violent suppression by sharp or blunt instrument of the life of another human being is hereby prohibited except under conditions as specified hereunder in sections 76(c) to 348(d) of the penal code or as may hereinafter be amended by a two-thirds vote of the Sanhedrin operating under the bylaws of the tribe of Ephraim or by the Fourth Session of the Third Lateran Council, Section XVIII, folio xxiii, Paragraph 12," he would have lost his audience in short order. Instead he said, "Thou shalt not kill," and most of us ever since have been willing to accept it as an overriding law of our lives, even if we know that there are enough exceptions and interpretations and clarifications to fill whole libraries. (Only two chapters further on in Exodus we are told not to suffer a witch to live.)

In November, voters will probably make their calm and reasoned judgment as to which side's sound bites get closer to the bone. Voters, of course, can be deceived. Unscrupulous rabble-rousers have often used sound bites to lead whole populations astray. The voters of 1840 who voted with their feet to the rhythm of "Tippecanoe and Tyler Too" and ran Martin Van Buren out of the White House, did not have the slightest idea of what they were getting in his place. The Russian peasants who rallied around Lenin's sound bite "Peace, Land, Bread" in 1917 did not foresee that he was heading them toward years of civil war and the confiscation of all their land. The Louisiana voters of the 1930s who elected Huey Long on his promise to make "Every man a King" are still looking for their crowns. A political outsider, the late Prof. Timothy Leary had only to leer at the forlorn teenagers of California and tell them to "Turn on, tune in, drop out," and it was déjà vu all over again.

Sound bites, like any other form of human experience, must have values attached to them, and as with most other forms of human experience, the values are up for grabs. *"Ein Volk, Ein Reich, Ein Führer,"* which helped sweep Adolf Hitler into power, is in today's world everyone's idea of a repulsive and destructive sound bite. If Hitler had won the war, it would have been carved on our monuments and printed on our currency.

Woodrow Wilson won re-election to the Presidency of the United States by a very narrow margin in 1916, probably owing to the success of a single sound bite, "He kept us out of war," five months before he asked Congress to declare war on Germany. Whether his re-election was a good or a bad thing for America or the world, or whether it really made any difference at all, are questions historians will be debating with decreasing vigor for decades. Punchy, effective sound bites can come in any form you want. They can even be long (within reason). Take, for example, the unforgettable 35-word sentence ("We hold these truths to be self-evident, that all men are created equal, that they are endowed by their Creator with certain unalienable Rights, that among these are Life, Liberty and the pursuit of Happiness") in Thomas Jefferson's Declaration of Independence, an otherwise mostly unremembered document. Mostly, of course, they are quite short, and have always necessarily been so, for the attention span of human beings is limited, though they are rarely as short as General McAuliffe's reply to the demand for surrender of his troops at Bastogne in 1945 ("Nuts!") or the operating instructions of Thomas J. Watson to his employees at IBM ("THINK").

Just as important as what is said in a sound bite is when it is said. When Prince Hamlet, one of the most prolific producers of sound bites ever, said, "There's nothing either good or bad, but thinking makes it so," he might with no loss to either the rhythm or the sense have substituted "timing" for "thinking." For what seem like the best sound bites may fail if produced at the wrong moment. "I shall return," uttered in 1942, became a brilliantly successful sound bite only when General MacArthur did wade ashore in the Philippines in 1944. Later he tried another one, after being relieved of his command in Korea in 1951: "In war, there is no substitute for victory." But since that war ended in a draw, the phrase has gone into the old curiosity shop of history along with "Disperse, ye rebels" (reportedly shouted by a British officer to the minutemen at Lexington in 1776), "Hang the Kaiser" (a rallying cry in the first World War) and "Mother of all Battles" (fight talk by Saddam Hussein in 1991).

In this field as in so many others, quantity is no substitute for quality. Today there may be more sound bites than were ever before dreamed of hovering through the fog of TV and the Internet, but when did you last hear one that could move a mountain or even win an election? Past ages have produced a rich garland of colorful sound bites that changed the world and echoed down the years (William Randolph Hearst to artist Frederic Remington in Cuba in 1898: "You furnish the pictures and I'll furnish the war"; Louis XIV to Parliament, and the world in general: "*L'état c'est moi*"; the cool Yankee, wise in the unreliable ways of 18th-century muskets, to the recruits at Bunker Hill: "Don't fire until you see the whites of their eyes"). But the recent record is one of almost unrelieved dreariness. Look through all the files of news magazines and *60 Minutes* and spin doctors and media consultants of the past ten years, and you will come up with nothing more memorable than George Bush's appeal in 1988 to "Read my lips: No new taxes," which of course blew up in his face in 1992 when Democratic strategist James Carville fired back into the whites of his eyes with his war room slogan, "The Economy, Stupid."

If this is the best that our generation can do, what are our great-grandchildren, and future historians, going to think of us? It is true that such a poverty of invention is not necessarily fatal to the republic. The America of the late 19th century, held up to us as a model in some of the unsoundest bites of modern politi-

174

cians, was a land faced with racial and sectional enmities, unbridled immigration, greed, rape of the environment, growing disparity between rich and poor, rampant criminality, homelessness. The statesmen who tried to deal with those problems won their elections more often than not by using a set of undistinguished and by now completely forgotten sound bites known collectively as "Waving the Bloody Shirt," the message of which was a claim to represent the heroes of the Civil War and an implication that the opposing candidate was a traitorous rebel at heart. Somehow the country survived, and perhaps we will, too.

Still, we are more prosperous, better educated and better informed than our great-grandparents were. Is it not time for the critics and commentators to stop whining and wailing about the nefariousness of sound bites, and devote their considerable energies to raising the level of public discourse by turning out a few good ones of their own? It would require some literary talent and a good sense of timing. But that has been the way of sound bites since God said, "Let there be light."

Smithsonian (August 1996), pp. 62-65.

Hebrew to Her is Greek to Me (1997)

Nick auf der Maur

Maintenow, we're going to have a language lesson. Pourqwhy? you might demand. Because. Just parce que. Don't be inquiet.

It's snowing out, put on your coat de neiges.

I just love the way our English sometimes gets mangled here in Montreal. Sorry, I didn't mean to derange you. Sorry, I was retarded.

It's the Frenglish we speak. Naturally, it works the other way, too, not just Franglais, but mixing metaphors and such.

The other day, I was at the hospital for an appointment, and I was checking in at the desk.

I gave the French-speaking woman my card, and in response, she sort of gagged.

She had to swallow and then said: "Excusez-moi, I've got a cat in my throat."

" You mean a frog," I said.

"What?" she asked in her French accent, looking at me as if I had insulted her. "A frog?"

Uh-oh, I thought, this is one of those things that gets worse when you try to explain it.

"In French, you say un chat dans la gorge," I tried, "but the expression in English is a frog in the throat. It has nothing to do with frog or bloke – French or English – I mean – "

She looked at me dubiously.

I thought furiously. I tried to remember other translations of expressions, to illustrate what I was saying. Of course, I couldn't remember any, so I was reduced to stammering and saying, well, umm, ah.

And then one came to me: "Un chien dans un jeu de quilles. That translates as a dog in a bowling alley. But in English we say a bull in a china shop to mean the same thing.' "

Still she looked dubious.

I couldn't remember any more examples. We finished our business and I shuffled off and saw my doctor.

On my way out, I remembered another one, so I went by the woman's desk.

"C'est de l'hébreu. It's Hebrew. But in English, we say it's all Greek to me if we don't understand something."

Her dubious look changed to a what-are-you-some-kind-of-a-nut? look.

Then it occurred to me that maybe she didn't even know the expression c'est de l'hébreu in French, let alone the rest of it, in which case she would not have a clue what I was talking about. Which was funny, because then she could legitimately have used the expression, in French or English, to signify that it was all Greek to her. So I continued my explanation.

The reason we use that expression is not only that Greek is a foreign language, but it's written in a different alphabet, so we can't decipher it. Presumably, that's why the French use Hebrew in the same context.

Anyway, this thing was getting out of hand, as I was trying to explain this to the woman at the hospital. Obviously she thought I was a lunatic.

She might have been thinking about calling security when I decided to drop the windy explanation, say Joyeux Noël and leave.

She looked more dubious than ever as she watched me shuffle down the hall.

What are some of those other odd translations?

When I got home, I rummaged through my papers and found a list of translations provided by a French-Canadian advertising executive many years ago. Unfortunately, I forget his name. But here are some common expressions and their French equivalents.

Unable to make head or tail of it is perdre son Latin (to lose one's Latin).

Not working for peanuts – pas pour des prunes (plums).

Chicken-hearted – avoir du sang du navet (to have turnip blood).

To make a mountain out of a molehill – se noyer dans un verre d'eau (to drown to a glass of water).

The straw that breaks the camel's back – la goutte qui fait déborder le vase (the drop that overflows the vase).

To cry in one's beer – avoir le vin triste (have sad wine).

Take someone to the cleaners – plumer quelqu'un (to pluck someone).

A little birdie told me – mon petit doigt me l'a dit (my little finger told me).

Shoot your mouth off – perdre une belle occasion de se taire (to miss an opportunity to keep your mouth shut).

Snug as a bug in a rug – heureux comme un poisson dans l'eau.

Two peas in a pod – deux gouttes d'eau (two drops of water).

A fly in the ointment – une anguille sous roche (an eel under the rock).

Dumb as an ox – bête à manger du foin (stupid enough to eat hay).

A horse of a different colour – une autre paire de manches (another pair of sleeves).

To beat about the bush – aller par quatre chemins (to go four ways).

To have too many irons in the fire – courir deux lièvres à la fois (to chase two hares at a time).

Not to know which way to turn – ne plus savoir sur quel pied danser (not to know which foot to dance on).

Nothing to sneeze at – ne pas cracher dessus (nothing to spit on).

To sit on the fence – nager entre deux eaux (to swim between two currents).

Can't teach an old dog new tricks – on n'apprend pas à un vieux singe à faire des grimaces (can't teach an old monkey to make faces).

Well, you get the picture.

The Montreal Gazette (December 10, 1997), p. A4.

Proverbial Wisdom (1998)

Robert Lacville

My old friend Souleyman Touray [of Mali] said: "I have just understood something my grandfather told me, some 30 years ago." Souley's grandfather was a speaker of proverbs and a famous hippo-hunter who died at the hands (or, rather, at the teeth) of a hippo. He had been a spiritual leader and source of wisdom for the whole community – until the hippo got him.

All elders and community leaders speak in proverbs and parables. I love them. Proverbs are very picturesque in translated language, but they often make it horrendously difficult to understand what elders are actually saying. First you have to understand the proverb; next you have to understand what it means. And even then you are not out of the mud: for behind the meaning lies a wisdom. The best proverbs have multiple meanings with varying interpretations and wisdoms. All this is part of West Africans' love of word-play and debate. It explains why it took Souleyman 30 years to understand his grandfather's wise advice. And it goes some way towards excusing strangers like me who have difficulty in mastering African languages.

African conversation is full of enigmatic observations. Silence is admired as much as proverbs. Silence is also a sign of wisdom. Once wisdom is dispensed, elders usually relapse into silence. Village conversation is punctuated with companionable silence and thoughtfulness. If a younger person does venture to ask the meaning of a proverb, the usual response is: "May God give you long life, my son!" Time, experience, and your own growing wisdom may allow you to understand the meaning some day.

African proverbs often use animals. Here are a couple of examples from the Dogon country on Mali's eastern border, home of famous animal masks and ancestor death dances. The symbol of Dogon culture is the kanaga, a mask which represents the antelope. The dancers hold the mask in their teeth, sweeping their bodies down and round so that the antlers brush the dust in front of them. At the same time, the mask represents the universe as perceived by the Dogons, a unity between sky and earth, between those who are here, those who came before us and those who are yet to come. In Africa, there is no fear of death because life is part of a continuous birth.

179

The Dogon village is ruled by the ancestors. Their venerated remains are pulled up the cliff and laid to rest in caves, or in the troglodyte dwellings of the Pygmies who once lived in these cliffs. The oldest man in the community, the Hogon, also lives up in the cliff: "He is so old, he is almost dead," a younger Dogon once explained to me, with awe in his voice. Once the Hogon is up there, he never comes down. Other elders climb up the cliff to consult him and bring down his instructions: an agreeable example of African constitutional monarchy, so much more peaceful than dealing with elected presidents!

When he is not receiving visits, the Hogon spends his time in meditation and looks after the ancestor fetishes. Or he sleeps. Once each day, an elderly woman takes food up to the old man. Who looks after the Hogon? I wondered. "He never washes," I was told. "A serpent licks him clean." My informant was amazed by the magic of the serpent. With the wisdom of 40 years in Africa, I know that the old woman is the serpent. This is her title, an honour for the wisdom she carries. She has the wisdom of the serpent, whose ancestors lived in these cliffs when men had not yet evolved into bipeds. It takes time and maturity to understand the code: "May God give you long life, my son!"

The French fable-writer La Fontaine used the same literary conceit. His fox and cat show cunning, the raven illustrates stupidity or cupidity. In Africa hyenas are stupid and mean, while the rabbit (actually a hare) shows cunning and wit. Brer Rabbit, hero of American folklore and grandfather of filmstar Roger Rabbit, was African. He came to America with the slave ships. The African hare took over humour just as African singing took over the churches and jazz came to define American music.

Souley told me another African story which illustrates how wisdom and initiation come only with age. In an African jungle, the baby monkey asked his mother: "Mother, why do you have such big red buttocks?" To which his mother replied "May God give you long life, my son!"

Guardian Weekly (August 23, 1998), p. 25.

Proverbs and Mystery Fiction (1998)

Gordon Magnuson

Recently I was browsing through a collection of proverbs. Nothing unusual there, as any book on words, phrases, idioms or such is of interest. But here I was struck by the number of illustrative quotations that were drawn from mystery fiction.

The book, *The Concise Oxford Dictionary of Proverbs*, published in 1982, is edited by John Simpson. It is organized alphabetically by key words. For each proverb Simpson provides a date and quotation for the first known occurrence and then follows with a number of further examples listed chronologically, ending with a quotation from modern literature. It was the last that attracted my attention.

The first proverb listed under A, "Absence makes the heart grow fonder," had its final illustrative quotation from Christianna Brand's *Rose in Darkness*; the second, "Accidents will happen in the best-regulated families" ended with a quotation from Jeremy Scott's *Angels in Your Beer*, the fourth with Catherine Aird. Intrigued, I began looking at the examples from modern literature that ended each entry.

I found, for instance, that of the 24 proverbs listed under letter A, seven ended with quotations from mystery novelists, not counting an entry from J.I.M. Stewart. This seemed an unusually high percentage. I began to count in earnest. Under B, 22 mystery novelists appeared in 84 entries. Still interested, but bored by such methodical plodding, I skipped to letters with few entries. I: 4 of 13 entries; J: 2 of 8; O: 11 of 24, not counting two examples under one proverb; Q: 2 of 3; finally U: 0 of 3. So far 48 mystery novelists in 159 entries: even my rudimentary arithmetic figured that almost one-third of all entries illustrating proverbs in modern literature came from mystery fiction. Strange. But I wasn't planning to count the whole book. Perhaps I'd better count one more large entry before speculating about the why. Statistics and their use, after all, are strange too. I tried also to remember that I did not have the name of every mystery novelist in my head; I might have missed some, although I had conscientiously omitted Graham Greene and P.G. Wodehouse. I'd try M, a fat, middle-of-the alphabet letter.

22 of 62. The percentage was holding. What did this mean? Why had the editor drawn almost one-third of all contemporary

examples from detective fiction? No doubt many of the writers were well-known: Chandler, Christie, Francis, Block were household words and easily accessible for those who scout books for proverbial sayings. But were these writers also to be respected for their transmission of gnomic literature, as serious preservators of past wisdom?.

Was a new dimension of detective literature being revealed to me? Should I rush to examine several more recent collections of proverbs as a control, and reality, check? Conflicting thoughts rushed through my mind. It was disturbing to think that there was some mysterious connection between proverbs and murder. Had mainstream fiction become such thin milk, or so mannered in its modernity, that traditional phrasing was heretical? Perhaps the data simply showed that mystery novelists were easy sources because they tended to use clichéd, easily found phrases. Should one infer that the collection was a not-so-subtle criticism of mystery fiction? There was plenty of bad writing and thinking among recent mystery writers, but not more, surely, than in most of the books that appeared each year, and I hated to think that mystery novelists were being singled out. Anyway, I liked the idea that proverbs, containing the nugget of some ancient wisdom, ought to be preserved.

But as I reflected that one should look first for the simple explanation, not the most complicated or complex, the answer suddenly seemed obvious: Mr. Simpson, the editor, simply liked to read mystery novels. Of course. And he was (and is, as far as I know) associated with Oxford University Press and therefore with Oxford University itself. We all know that academics of the highest intellectual order read mystery novels. Sometimes they even write them. It confirmed what I had long read and been told: mysteries are read by the intelligentsia. This was a consoling thought, especially to a former professor, but even more rewarding is believing that here is simply another lover of mystery fiction.

Deadly Pleasures: A Mystery Magazine, no. 22 (Autumn–Winter, 1998), p. 26.

Editors' note:
Bartlett Jere Whiting (1904-1995), professor of English at Harvard University and editor of the massive dictionary of *Modern*

Proverbs and Proverbial Sayings (Cambridge, Massachusetts: Harvard University Press, 1989), also was an avid reader of murder mysteries. His compilation is therefore replete with references from this type of fiction as well.

Our colleague George B. Bryan (1939-1996), professor of Theatre History at the University of Vermont, was equally fascinated by detective novels, as can be seen from his book *Black Sheep, Red Herrings, and Blue Murder. The Proverbial Agatha Christie* (Bern: Peter Lang, 1993).

Do Consultants Rot From the Head Down? (1999)

Anna Muoio

What is it about fish and consultants? First there was "Fish where the fish are" ("This Advice Sounds Fishy," August 1998). Then, last month, we learned about the myth of the sea squirt that eats its own brain. Now we arrive at the biggest, oldest, and most frequently cited fish tale of all: "A fish rots from the head down." It is, of course, the ultimate consultant concept. The topic is leadership (a perennial favorite among the consulting corps) – in particular, the failure of leadership. And, perhaps best of all, it's about fish – a fact that guarantees it a spot in every consultant's bait box.

All of which is enough to get the FAST COMPANY Consultant Debunking Unit (CDU) on the case.

To learn the history of this phrase, the CDU spoke with Professor Wolfgang Mieder, chairman of the department of German and Russian at the University of Vermont, author of *The Politics of Proverbs: From Traditional Wisdom to Proverbial Stereotypes* (University of Wisconsin Press, 1997), and one of the world's foremost authorities on proverbs.

According to Professor Mieder, the fish-rot proverb dates back to 1674, when it appeared in a treatise called *An Account of the Voyage to New England*. Today the saying exists in an estimated 36 European languages. "The proverb is based on the fact that fish do begin to spoil at the head," explains Mieder. "As a figure of speech, it means that any problem in an organization can be traced back to the boss."

To find a more recent rotting-fish application, the CDU turned to Bob Garratt, professor of corporate governance at London University's Imperial College, chairman of Organization Development Limited (one of Hong Kong's largest management-consulting firms), and author of *The Fish Rots from the Head: The Crisis in Our Boardrooms – Developing the Crucial Skills of the Competent Director* (HarperCollins Business, 1997). Garratt explains the utility of the fish-phrase this way: "I use the metaphor a lot to describe a failing company or a company that is going nowhere – because of a 'rotting head.'"

Garratt argues that the phrase is organizationally, semantically, and biologically correct. "I've been assured by my various

184

biologist friends that the first thing that starts to disintegrate in a fish is the brain," he says.

Not according to David Groman, a fish pathologist at Atlantic Veterinary College, which is part of the University of Prince Edward Island, in Charlottetown, Prince Edward Island. Groman may not be the Quincy of fish (he's not a *forensic* fish pathologist), but he does make it his business to know how and why fish die. Which means that he knows how and why fish rot.

Groman found time between his fish autopsies to comment on the rotting-fish metaphor. "I don't know where that proverb comes from," says Groman. "But it's a poor metaphor. And, I must say, it's biologically incorrect. When a fish rots, the organs in the gut go first. If you can't tell that a fish is rotting by the smell of it, you'll sure know when you cut it open and everything pours out – when all the internal tissue loses its integrity and turns into liquid."

Having learned about dead fish, the CDU next went looking for information about fresh fish: The call went to Richard Yokoyama, manager of Seattle's famous Pike Place Fish Market, which has been in operation since 1930. "Before I buy a fish from one of our dealers, I always look at the belly," says Yokoyama. "On a fish, that's the first thing to go. That's where all the action is – in the gut. If the belly is brown and the bones are breaking through the skin, I toss the fish out. It's rotten."

The CDU couldn't wrap up this fish tale without making one last stop: a visit with the wildly popular rock band Phish. The question: Does Phish rot from the head? To find out, we asked the "fish" of Phish, drummer Jon Fishman. "There's the band Phish, and then there's the man Fish," says Fishman. "My whole life, I've been Fish-something-or-other: Fish-monger, Fish-face, Fish-head. And I've had a lot of experience with rot. For instance, during camp one summer, I got a really bad case of impetigo – a highly contagious skin rash that turns into a gross, scabby flesh wound. And just now, I'm getting over a truly treacherous case of athlete's foot on the pinky toe of my right foot. Not counting the really bad case of dandruff that I'm recovering from, I'd have to say that this Fishman rots from the foot up," admits Fishman.

"But the band is a different matter," he adds. "We're a multiheaded beast. As the CEO of Phish Inc., I'm the head on paper. But Trey [Anastasio], our guitarist and vocalist, is the head onstage. And Mike [Gordon], our bassist, is the pure musical head. We all know that if Mike is having a rotten night, the whole band will suck." Phish's Fishman's response to learning that real fish rot from the belly? "Hey, maybe that explains the bad case of indigestion that I've had lately!"

Fast Company (June 1999), p. 58 and p. 60.

Not-so-Ancient Chinese Proverb:
Glib Truisms Gloss Over Reality (1999)

Seth Faison

A few years ago, when I took a visiting editor out to the Chinese countryside for a taste of rural life, I had an opportunity to show off my proficiency in Chinese – or thought I did. We came upon a peasant working a field 50 miles outside Shanghai, and struck up a conversation. The farmer spoke of how things had changed in his village thanks to the arrival of television and, more recently, a video store. His thick rural accent proved no problem: I proudly translated for my boss.

Then the farmer threw me a curve. "No knowledge deer dead who hand," he said.

Huh? I looked around, half expecting to see a doe grazing in the field. I stared at the farmer blankly, probably resembling a deer myself, eyes transfixed by headlights. Then I recovered, nodded knowingly and swiftly changed the subject.

I said nothing to my editor, preserving (I think) the illusion of complete fluency resulting from years of studying the language. But in the privacy of my office later, I looked up the phrase in a book of Chinese proverbs, and found the saying the farmer had used. The explanation for it was a long, roundabout story about how a general in ancient China struggled to predict the future, saying to an aide something that can be roughly translated as, "You never know at whose hand a deer will die."

Of course it is hard to predict the future, I thought. But why bring deer into it?

Chinese is a difficult language for any Westerner to master, with its four different tones giving different meanings to the same sound, a mind-boggling number of synonyms and the meaning of each word, or written character, discerned only from the context in which it is used.

But the real killer, for me at least, is learning the proverbs that Chinese pepper their language with every day. Generally four to eight characters long, a proverb is often so cryptic as to be incomprehensible to me upon first hearing it. And almost every time I take the trouble to learn a proverb, I forget it the following day.

Virtually all Chinese who have been to school, and many who have not, can and do spout proverbs; farmers, street cleaners and postmen employ them as readily as professors and writers.

"A thousand dollars buys a neighbor; eight hundred buys a house" is a proverb that wisely reminds the avaricious that friendship can be more valuable than property.

For the Chinese, such verities are a proud reflection of their ancient culture (and some relish the chance to tell confused outsiders, in a tone of superiority, the long and arcane story behind this or that proverb). But beyond their actual meanings, proverbs also say something about today's China: They often serve not just as timeless truths but also as pat homilies to gloss over or explain away the unpleasant realities of the present.

"Feeling stones while crossing a river" is a proverb that Deng Xiaoping, China's paramount leader until his death in 1997, often used in describing the uncertain nature of China's ambitious but unwieldy efforts to use capitalist methods in a socialist state. For mid-level officials and company managers who grapple with the challenge of making decisions in a nominally Communist land that in fact lacks an ideology, one utterance of "feeling stones while crossing a river" can excuse a multitude of hard-to-explain actions, virtuous or otherwise.

In a society that stresses deference to authority, proverbs are one of the more subtle tools used to maintain and reinforce those in power. Political leaders often trot them out to placate or simply distract underlings with the implication that problems are ages old and cannot easily be solved.

In times of political extremism, the Chinese reliance on proverbs can be manipulated to an extreme. It is hard to imagine another country in the world where so many millions of people would fall into line, as Chinese did during the leftist frenzy of the 1960's, behind slogans from the "Little Red Book" of sayings by Chairman Mao.

Yet even in more rational times, proverbs are regularly used to justify actions by the authorities. In a recent interview, a Shanghai construction executive dismissed objections to the edifices of chrome and reflecting glass now dominating Shanghai architecture – buildings erected in some cases after stately old buildings and homes were demolished to make way for them.

"Fish scale order comb comparison," the official said brightly.

188

I looked at him blankly. Luckily, my assistant was along, and he translated the proverb in what sounded to me like a random string of disconnected words: "Packed in as tight as teeth of a comb."

The official apparently meant that buildings will keep going up until they are packed in tightly. Expressing it in an ancient proverb seemed to justify the action, as though the fact that there was an ancient metaphor for such a situation made this particular action itself acceptable.

On a bad, proverb-laden day, I often become convinced that the Chinese use of these sayings is a conspiracy to keep out ignorant interlopers. I have come to dread the words, "We Chinese have a saying..." because I know a long lesson about a Chinese proverb is about to begin, and with it will come the recurring sense of helplessness that has bedeviled my efforts over 10 years to learn Chinese and understand China.

China's locomotive-like growth over the past decade has excited some outsiders, and scared others. Many visitors eagerly ask me questions about China's future, mostly about the mystery of what will happen to a country run by a Communist Party when no one believes in Communism anymore.

It's a fascinating question. It's also an unanswerable one. When it is raised, it always stumps me. Maybe I should answer with a proverb, but given my problem with proverbs, I can never remember one on the spot.

Wait – how about this one: "You never know at whose hand a deer will die."

He Who Dabbles in Cryptic Phrases ...

Chinese proverbs generally evolved over centuries from old stories offering a specific lesson. Some are easily understood; others have become cryptic over the ages, referring in some cases to long-forgotten personages. Examples:

Proverb: "When one man finds the way, his chickens and dogs ascend to heaven."
Meaning: When a man is promoted to a position of authority, all his friends and relatives benefit.

Proverb: "Eight immortals cross the sea; each shows a saintly passage."
Meaning: Different individuals can achieve the same goal in different ways.

189

Proverb: "The sky is high; the emperor is far away."
Meaning: Far from a central authority, one enjoys relative freedom.

Proverb: "When you mention Cao Cao, he soon arrives."
Meaning: I was just talking about you!

Proverb: "Never pull on your shoes in a melon patch; never adjust your cap under a plum tree."
Meaning: Don't act suspicious if you want to avoid being suspected.

Proverb: "Lord Jiang casts a line, a fish wants to be caught."
Meaning: Someone who is trapped willingly.

The New York Times (November 14, 1999), p. 7WK.

If Seeing Is Believing, Looks Can Be Deceiving (2000)

Derek Thurber

"The early bird gets the worm," your mother said, waking you on a school day. "A penny saved is a penny earned," your father told you, imploring you not to spend all your money on chewing gum. "You can't teach an old dog new tricks," said your grandma after trying to use the Internet.

Such expressions are old, familiar and supposedly possessing a truth that we would be foolish to disagree with. So, do these aphorisms hold up under the microscope of modern science?

With the help of local experts, here is a guide to the literal side of some common aphorisms. (Names and dates represent the earliest written record of each.)

The early bird gets the worm (William Camden, 1605)
True. Worms prefer darkness and cool temperatures, so in the summer they are more likely to be at or near the surface In the morning. Songbirds such as robins – the most common worm predators in the eastern United States – must wake up at first light to find exposed worms before their competitors, and before the worms burrow deeper underground. On the morning after a rainstorm washes worms to the surface or after a farmer's field is plowed, hunting for worms can be highly competitive, so starting late won't do.

In woodland areas, woodcock are worm-hunters that are crepuscular, meaning they are most active – and frequently catch worms – at dusk as well as at dawn. If you really want to sleep in, you might rebut this aphorism by claiming that, like a woodcock, you are also adept at "catching worms" in the evening.

A penny saved is a penny earned (Ben Franklin, 1732; orig., 16th century)
For the past four years, whenever Odenton resident Gwen Jones has found coins on the floor or sidewalk, she has put them in a pink piggy bank covered with polka-dotted pigs. Although her piggy bank still is far from full, Gwen, 8, estimates that it now contains about $2.

Gwen says such saving is important because "you could get something if you save your money. ... I could buy stuff from a bubble gum machine." Once, she took money out to buy some ice cream.

191

Saving pennies allows Gwen to buy more than any individual pennies could buy. However, since piggy banks provide less--than-competitive interest rates, she isn't keeping up with inflation.

Even adult savings accounts don't beat inflation by much. The yearly inflation rate during 1990-99, as measured by the consumer price index, averaged 2.93 percent-more than the 2.57 percent yield offered by today's average checking account, and only 1.47 percent less than the 4.40 percent yield offered by today's average money market account under $10,000.

If one defines saving as putting money in the bank, people usually can earn far more by investing – or in some cases, spending.

Chevy Chase economist Mana McNeill says, "Say you finished high school and were trying to decide whether to go to college. Should you spend money to go to college or stay home and put money in the bank? Your human capital would be improved by spending the money to go to college. Even traveling could expand your horizons, make you a more well-rounded person."

You can't teach an old dog new tricks (Anthony Fitzherbert, 1523)

All seven of the dog trainers contacted disagreed with this saying. Allie Lee, owner of Greenbelt Dog Training, says, "As long as the dog is physically and mentally fit, [it] can learn anything you teach it. I haven't found a dog [that can't], unless it has arthritis.

"[Dogs are] willing to please you whatever it takes. All they need to know is what it takes to please you and they'll do it."

In March of 1999, Lee began working with Maureen Kelley, 54, of Silver Spring, and a rescued golden retriever named Rusty that she had adopted at age 8 1/2. Rusty, who had been tied up in a backyard for his whole life, was not trained or even housebroken, and had a habit of chasing little dogs as if they were squirrels.

After a year of daily training by Kelley and weekly one-hour sessions with Lee, Rusty had overcome his problems enough to earn a Companion Dog obedience title from the American Kennel Club. Now Rusty not only sits, stays and heels, but also competes in Canine Freestyle, a new sport in which a dog and its owner perform stylish moves to music.

Pam Watson, an instructor at Capital Dog Training Club in Silver Spring, says dogs that have been trained as puppies can learn quickly because they have developed the habit of thinking. However, she says many older dogs that have not been trained have actually used their brains quite a lot.

"Even a dog that's a family pet, a 'couch potato,' hopefully that dog has learned a lot and people don't realize it," Watson says. The dog has learned manners, or how to live in society. ... [It may] have you wrapped around [its] paw."

Lee concluded that although nearly all old dogs can learn new tricks, "there are a few owners that are hard to get through."

All that glitters is not gold (Geoffrey Chaucer, 1380; orig. Latin proverb)

Xiangdong Ji, associate professor of physics at the University of Maryland, says an object often glitters or sparkles if it has many flat, reflective surfaces that are oriented in different directions.

Much that is not gold could glitter, including other metals, water, jewels or a new car. Whiter metals, such as silver, platinum and nickel, are more reflective than gold.

So why does this saying exist? With the help of Ji and his colleague, assistant professor of chemistry Andrew Morehead, I came up with four reasons.

First, gold is the most "noble," or unreactive, of metals, so it resists oxidation – or bonding with oxygen to form a new (usually nonreflective) compound like rust. Rather than polishing their silver, it may be easier for people to make up sayings about how shiny gold is.

Second, gold is the most malleable metal, able to be made into sheets just one 100,000th of a centimeter thick. Because of this property, gold has been intricately worked since at least 5,000 B.C., creating many different reflective surfaces.

Third, gold tends to absorb the blue spectrum of the light that strikes it. As a result, the light we see reflected from gold is a rich, attractive shade of yellow (especially important to sun worshipers such as the Incas and the Aztecs).

Fourth, gold is expensive.

An apple a day keeps the doctor away (Orig. 17th century, incl. John Ray 1670)

In January, researchers at St. George's Hospital Medical School in London published a study showing improved lung function among middle-age men who eat five apples a week.

In April, researchers at the University of California at Davis published a study showing that apples contain significant amounts of antioxidants – chemicals that mop up unstable "free radicals" – and that these antioxidants may reduce the buildup of low-density lipoproteins (or "bad" cholesterol) on artery walls.

In June, Cornell food scientists published a study showing that eating apples may slow the proliferation of cancer cells.

And apples contain about three grams of fiber each.

Bill Harlan, associate director for disease prevention at the National Institutes of Health, says almost all fruits and vegetables have antioxidant properties, and many fruits and vegetables contain some of the same beneficial substances, including fiber, potassium, Vitamin C, carotenoids and folic acid. All of these have been linked with such benefits as reduced blood pressure or reduced risk of heart disease or cancer.

"A single apple is not going to meet the requirement of 5-7 fruits and vegetables a day," Harlan says. "While this saying is on the right track, an apple a day is not enough."

Mark Kantor, assistant professor of nutrition and food science at the University of Maryland, suggested that the expression might have come about because eating an apple a day keeps some people regular.

One of Kantor's colleagues, Elizabeth Boyle-Roden, suggested that the expression might be popular because apples store well and are available year-round.

Boyle-Roden added that despite her doubts about the saying, her husband, who eats an apple a day, "seems to be an extremely healthy individual."

Early to bed and early to rise makes a man healthy and wealthy and wise (Franklin, 1757; orig. Dame Juliana Berners, 1496)

The Dalai Lama – spiritual leader of Tibet – wakes up at 4 a.m. to recite mantras and make prostrations in salutation of the Buddhas. Alan Greenspan – spiritual leader of the U.S. economy – rises to take a bath at 6 a.m., during which he ponders world affairs and writes speeches or testimonies.

194

Could these men have achieved wisdom through proper sleep schedules? Research has shown that adequate sleep improves overall health by boosting immune functions and a variety of psychological functions, including intellectual performance. Such health benefits might also increase "wisdom" and even wealth.

But as for the correct times to sleep, Franklin's saying applies only to some people. Samuel Potolicchio, director of the George Washington University sleep center, says that for both genetic and environmental reasons, some people tend to be early-morning "larks" whereas others are "night owls."

"'Early to bed and early to rise' would fit the lark," Potolicchio says. "But what kind of expression would fit the night owl? 'Sleep in and you'll feel more fit.' The night owl would have to sleep later given that he goes to bed later."

Whether people are night owls or larks is determined by their circadian rhythms, cycles of sleep and waking that regulate body temperature and hormone secretions during different parts of a 24-hour period. The body warms up in the morning and cools in the evening, reaching its lowest temperature during deep sleep. One important hormone controlled by the sleep cycle is cortisol, an alertness-increasing chemical that is secreted at the end of the sleep period.

"You may blunt cortisol secretion if you're waking up early and not completing the cycle as you could," Potolicchio says. "If you wake up sluggish, and you can't function, your sleep schedule is probably not tuned [to your circadian rhythms]. ... The most important thing is when you wake up early in the morning you are chipper, ready to go."

A bird in the hand is worth two in the bush (Aesop, 600 B.C.)

For people who hunt ruffed grouse and woodcock – the primary bush-dwelling game birds in the eastern United States – a bird in the hand is worth about 16 birds in the bush. Dan Dessecker, the senior wildlife biologist for the 25,000-member Ruffed Grouse Society (based in Coraopolis, Pa.), says, "You see about every other [ruffed grouse or woodcock] that you flush [out of cover]. The other bird you simply hear. You get a shot at half the birds you see. You bag one out of four that you shoot at. ... [One in 16] is probably typical."

For scientists wishing to track birds, a bird in the hand may be worth more than 200 in the bush, according to biologist and former Virginia Society of Ornithology president Thelma Dalmas. Dalmas says that East Coast migratory birds are fitted with bands or radio transmitters at "banding stations." Birds are captured in 50 or 60 "mist nets" – thin string nets 6 feet high and 30 to 40 feet long that at dawn are stretched across "lanes" bordered by shrubbery and bushes.

Dalmas says that probably less than 1/2 of 1 percent of the birds flying in the area of a banding station become tangled in the mist nets and are subsequently examined, banded and released.

A stitch in time saves nine (Thomas Fuller, 1732)

Alice Jones, who owns a tailor's shop on P Street NW, says this expression is most literally true for the chain stitch, a stitch comprising tiny interlocking loops that pull apart almost as easily as a zipper after one stitch is severed. Chain stitches often are used decoratively; they also may appear in the crotch and seat of pants, or in sports jackets.

For other stitches, such as the straight stitch or blind stitch, a stitch in time might save two or three, but it could take a while – or some vigorous physical activity – to make it save nine.

The Washington Post (October 19, 2000), p. C4.

Fifth-Graders Find Fun in Proverbs: Teacher, UVM Professor Collaborate on Successful Adage-- Based Learning (2000)

Modisane Kwanza

If the proverb fits, use it.

So says a group of fifth-graders at Milton [Vermont] Elementary School, who studied quotable pearls of wisdom last year.

"Every day I'll just blurt out this proverb," said Will Noel, 11.

"He will!" said classmate Heather Little, 10.

"I feel like I'm showing off," Will said, "but I can't help having the wisdom."

Milton fourth-grade teacher Deborah Holmes and Wolfgang Mieder, University of Vermont professor of German and Folklore, imparted the wisdom to Will and his classmates in a year-long project. Holmes and Mieder, with funding from The John Templeton Foundation, wanted to demonstrate that 9- and 10-year-olds not only could memorize proverbs, but also learn their meaning and apply them to their lives. The children worked with 150 common Anglo-American proverbs that were incorporated into their regular studies.

The project was a rousing success, the two project leaders said. Parents told them their children were using proverbs at home.

The group even published a book of the students' work.

"We were able to show that if you teach children proverbs and discuss the meanings and give explanations, their minds are capable of dealing with the metaphors," Mieder said.

"The children were excited to learn the proverbs" Holmes said.

Last month, Holmes, Mieder and their 20 proverb-quoting charges reunited at a book-signing for "Children and Proverbs Speak the Truth," a paperback compilation of the students' writings and illustrations from the project. The book was published as part of "Proverbium," an international yearbook that is one of over a hundred edited and written by Mieder. The book, available at the UVM bookstore, serves as a record of the project and as a guide for teachers.

The children's excitement hadn't subsided by Thanksgiving break, as seven of them came to school to answer questions about the project. The "Golden Rule" was their favorite proverb: "Do unto others as you would have them do unto you."

"I use it almost every day, everywhere," Heather said.

Carl Affinati, 10, was partial to "you don't miss the water until the well runs dry," saying people shouldn't take things for granted.

Emma Ruopp, 11, said her favorite proverb is "every cloud has a silver lining." For her it means, "there's always hope."

"My mom has a different meaning for 'every cloud'," said her sister, Maggie, 10. "Why not a gold lining? She thinks it means there's always something good even if it's not the best thing."

Holmes, an award-winning teacher who has been at the school for 15 years, said the children learned to accept that proverbs mean different things to different people – or to put it proverbially, "different strokes for different folks."

For example, Will said, "Never turn your back on a tiger," spoke to always being on the lookout for danger. However, Kelly Simollardes, 10, said it could mean we should be willing to help anyone.

"Even a tiger should be respected," Kelly said.

The students admitted it irks them when they hear a proverb that's worded incorrectly or changed around – especially in TV commercials.

"I know what they're trying to say," said Emily May, 10, "it really sticks out."

Mieder and Holmes are working with a new set of eager fourth-graders – without the foundation funding.

"The new students have the same enthusiasm," Holmes said.

The fifth-graders said they still use the proverbs they've learned and probably will "until we get to high school."

"I feel wiser," Emma said.

The Burlington Free Press (November 29, 2000), P. 4B.

Clichés Are Here to Stay –
Tired Phrases Put Talkers on Common Ground (2001)

C. Ray Hall

This happened on television, midway through a recent episode of "Sex in the City."

Charlotte, the nice one, was in bed with her husband, Trey, who has finally overcome his shortcomings in the sack.

"Houston," he declares smugly, "we don't have a problem."

On the same weekend ...

The term "proof is in the pudding" turned up on a baseball game and in a discussion among eggheads on National Public Radio.

On other baseball broadcasts, thinking caps were put on in the late innings. Bullets were dodged. Baserunners decided it was better to be safe than sorry. And fish were out of water.

A computer whiz on TechTV resorted to the term "straight from the horse's mouth."

On a PBS documentary, a Stanford University student (by definition the best and brightest) spoke the word "like" a few dozen times. ("I only had, like, one fight ...." "Do you think they, like, hate you?" Or words to that effect.)

"Like" is already trite, but it's too new to rise (or fall) to the level of cliché. An irritant, but not yet a cliché. It's not old enough.

The jury is out (cliché alert) on "like" and other recent inventions, such as "fallen and can't get up."

Allan Metcalf, a MacMurray (Ill.) College English professor who is executive secretary of the American Dialect Society, says: "You can't be sure that they will stick around the language until they've gone through two generations – by rule of thumb. And of course, 'rule of thumb,' there's another cliché."

Could there be such a thing as a fresh cliché?

"The term 'fresh cliché' seems almost oxymoronic, like 'jumbo shrimp,'" says Stephen Watt, chairman of the English department at Indiana University. "The typical connotation of the word 'cliché' is that it is trite and hackneyed and hence overused. And to be overused, it would have to be around for a while."

Watt has been teaching 28 years, long enough to see some expressions enter pop culture – and stay.

"'Float like a butterfly, sting like a bee' – I've heard that a zillion times, it seems to me, since Muhammad Ali first used that expression."

But then, clichés – even the oldest and most world-weary – do have their uses.

Metcalf, author of several books, including "How We Talk," says: "One of the basic principles of language is that people don't say things that they don't find useful. If you use a word or phrase that's not familiar, then maybe you'll have a strikingly poetic expression that others will be amazed at – or maybe you won't be so well understood."

"You have to use words and phrases on whose meanings people happen to agree, or else you'll be very confusing."

Somewhere there's a (cliché alert) happy medium, we presume, where clichés are kaput and originality isn't obscure.

"As English teachers, our typical advice to students is to try to avoid clichés," Watt says.

And yet even smart, articulate people who deal with words all the time lapse into clichés. You've got to say this for clichés: They enable regular folks to quote Shakespeare, whether they mean to or not.

Suspected origins:

Damn with faint praise: Alexander Pope in "Epistle to Dr. Arbuthnot" (1733).

Gone to pot: Perhaps from the idea of being cannibalized after death; also, from having one's ashes put into an urn.

Happy as a clam: The full saying is "happy as a clam at high tide" (and therefore safe from human predators).

Kick the bucket: To die; perhaps from the twitching and kicking of slaughtered hogs, kicking an 18th-century wooden framework called a "bucket." Or perhaps from the notion that a person about to be hanged might stand on a bucket, which was kicked away, bringing prompt relief from life's travails.

Let the cat out of the bag: From the fairground trick of selling a "pig" in a sack; the pig turned out to be a cat.

Necessity is the mother of invention: From playwright William Wycherly, "Love in a Wood" (1671).

Off the cuff: From some speakers' habits of writing notes on the cuffs of their shirts.

Pay through the nose: According to folklore, the Irish had to pay a stiff tax or have their noses slit by their 9th century conquerors, the Norse. Or the Danes. It's folklore, after all.

Pleased/proud as Punch: From the full-of-himself character Punch (of the old Punch and Judy puppet shows).

Know the ropes/learn the ropes: Probably nautical; sailors have to know their ropes, or learn them.

Seventh heaven: In Islamic belief, the abode of God – the heaven of heavens.

The Burlington Free Press (July 13, 2001), p. 4C.

Proverbial Punch Line – Scrambled Sayings Express Our Satirical, Humorous Sides (2003)

Sally Pollak

There's no scholar like the proverbial scholar. Where there's a Wolfgang, there's a way with words. Don't put all your proverbs in one book; put them in 100 books.

Let the record show that Wolfgang Mieder, connoisseur and arbiter of all things proverbial, washed his hands of the above selection of "fractured proverbs."

The University of Vermont scholar of the proverb, master of the metaphor, and chairman of the German and Russian department had nothing to do with devising these proverb parodies – take-offs on traditional proverbs that might change the meaning of the saying but adhere to its formulaic language.

Mieder isn't the cook who spoiled the broth in an effort to devise proverbs that describe the prof. But he is the master chef: Mieder inspired these fractured proverbs, also called anti-proverbs and proverb parodies, with his new book, "Wisecracks! Fractured Proverbs." (The opening samples, scribbled by a scribe, do not appear in Mieder's book).

The slim volume is the latest of more than 100 books that Mieder has written or edited. It contains about 150 traditional proverbs and the 1,000-plus variations that they have spawned.

"This book is a way of communicating my scholarship to the general public," Mieder said. The vast majority of his books are scholarly texts – thick tomes packed with references, derivations and sources.

By contrast, "Wisecracks!" consists of literary gems including: "Two heads are better than one – except during a hangover" and "Better mate than never."

"This little book is meant for entertainment or for saying, 'This is the wisdom we use in Vermont,'" said Mieder, 59, who has been on the UVM faculty for 32 years and head of the department for 26.

"If you quote proverbs all the time, eventually there's a tendency to play with formulaic language," Mieder said. "What people enjoy doing is playing with the juxtaposition between tradition on the one hand, and innovation on the other hand."

The anti-proverbs collected in "Wisecracks!" are sayings that Mieder has come across over 30 years in the course of his wide-reaching research on proverbs. Some people are inspired to invent variations on proverbs by a sense of humor and fun, or because they enjoy manipulating language, Mieder said.

Another source of such manipulation is the mass media – from editorial cartoonists commenting on politics and culture to advertising copy writers drawing attention to a product, Mieder said. An example is an ad for exercise equipment that reads: "No body is perfect."

Not all the fractured proverbs are humorous, Mieder said. A variation of "Old soldiers never die, they simply fade away" is particularly apt these days: "Old soldiers never die – just young ones."

Recently, Mieder came across a newspaper cartoon that spins off the soldier proverb. "Old soldiers never die," says the caption, "they just go on television."

"We use proverbs to communicate," Mieder said. "We use them to communicate indirectly. That is the purpose of all folklore." Fables, for example, are stories about animals, but the animal tales say something about human nature.

Lincoln used a proverb to brilliant effect in June, 1858, Mieder said. Lincoln proclaimed: "A house divided cannot stand."

Backed by the authority of the Bible and using words easily understood, Lincoln chose non-threatening language to tell Americans: The nation must stay together.

Churchill coined a fractured proverb to urge Roosevelt to join the war: "Make hell while the sun shines," implored the British prime minister, a variation on the traditional, "Make hay while the sun shines."

Mieder, a native of Germany, has lived in the United States since 1960, when he arrived in Michigan to attend high school. "I loved America so much I didn't go home," he said.

His interest in proverbs dates to graduate school, when he earned a Ph.D. in German and folklore at Michigan State. He is devoted to UVM and its students, and thinks that Burlington doesn't appreciate its university as do other college towns where he has lived.

In fact, Mieder can provide a cautionary proverb for those who are apt to condemn the university after a particularly rowdy weekend: "Don't throw the baby out with the bath water."

Mieder can provide a proverb – which is essentially a metaphor or imagistic phrase that contains wisdom, such as it is – appropriate to virtually every circumstance, event or person.

But he comes up short suggesting one that applies to him. In search of such a proverb, Mieder scans the index of an anthology, beginning with the word "fool." Then he tries "work" and "bee" (as in busy).

His colleague Janet Sobieski suggests a proverb that originated with Benjamin Franklin: "There will be sleeping enough in the grave."

Until then, Mieder will teach and read and research and write – as busy as a bee and as curious as a cat in his search for rhyme and reason.

Fractured Proverbs from 'Wisecracks'
Excerpts from "Wisecracks!" by Wolfgang Mieder:

"Make hay while the sun shines."
Make hay while the sun shines, and make rye while the
    moon shines.

"Familiarity breeds contempt."
Familiarity breeds.

"Charity begins at home."
Charity begins at home and ends on the income tax re-
    turn.
Charity begins at home and usually winds up in some
    foreign country.

"Children should be seen and not heard."
Children should be heard and not seen plastered to the
    TV.
Children should be seen and not had.
Children should be seen and not hurt.
Graffiti should be obscene and not heard.

"Old soldiers never die, they simply fade away."
Bankers never die; they just lose interest.
Old accountants never die; they just lose their balance.
Old fishermen never die; they just smell that way.
Old female lawyers never die; they just lose their appeals.

The Burlington Free Press (March 29, 2003), pp. 1D-2D.

Words We Live By:
What Do Proverbs Really Mean to Us? (2003)

Peggy Noonan, Jacquelyn Mitchard, and Christopher Buckley

We learn proverbs from the Bible, from literature, from our wise old grandma. But what do they really mean to us?

On these pages, three high-profile writers offer inspiring and amusing reflections on their favorite sayings.

Peggy Noonan: *This too shall pass*

"This too shall pass" is at the heart of my understanding of things. I pair it in my mind with the words of the wise old man of Ecclesiastes, who said, "There is nothing new under the sun." Good times, bad times, the seven fat years, the lean ones, break-throughs and setbacks: It's not "new," any of it, it's the story of life on Earth. The story of the big revolving drama.

Someone once said that at the heart of each victory is future defeat, and at the heart of each defeat is a future victory. Every-thing changes. It is instructive, and somehow comforting, to know that. Everything moves onward, nothing is "stable." Yes-terday's dead leaf is mulched into soil that produces tomorrow's garden. The garden's flowers will bear leaves that will fall, and be mulched.

We can rely on just one unchanging thing: the inevitability of change. This perspective can help you get through the bad times. People tend to think, "This too shall pass," in bad times. But it applies to good times, too, and perhaps more valuably. It helps sharpen your pleasure in the moment. Good luck and good times should be seized, enjoyed, reveled in, for they won't be here forever, and it would be ungrateful not to appreciate them while they are.

My career was kind of low and depressing for a while. Noth-ing that I was doing was working. I thought, "This is a bad time. I have to keep doing my work, keep attempting to produce some-thing that is meaningful and that I respect." This lasted years. But I became so engaged by my work and my thoughts that I sort of forgot to remember that I was in a bad time. I started believing I was in a peaceful time, with fewer demands. I could find more coherence, more depth, in the other spheres of my life.

Then good times came, as good times will. I thought: "Great, keep going, and by the way, let's go to a nice restaurant and toast my good fortune." But when you know this too shall pass, it has a way of tempering your ego. You're not doing well because you're the best at what you do. You're doing well because you're still trying to do good work, and a good time came and lifted it up. All this applies in one's personal life, of course. Are you alone? People will enter your life. Are you surrounded by friends? Someday it will be less crowded around you. Did you ever have a broken heart? It will heal. Everything changes. Take the good times and enjoy them, take the bad times and use them. You can really savor them when you know that they're fleeting and will turn – on whatever schedule and in whatever way – to something different.

All you have to do is the best you can. A high wave comes, a crushing wave comes, a gentle swell follows. Whatever comes, stay in your boat. And enjoy the ride. And row.

Jacquelyn Mitchard: *Never put off until tomorrow what you can do today*

My entire life has been an exercise in overcoming the as yet un-mapped gene for procrastination.

Now, no one I know would ever call me a procrastinator. I arrive early for engagements; I invent deadlines far ahead of the actual ones. I hang up my sweaters –and button them – at the time I take them off. I keep my travel kit stocked so I never have to rush out for supplies. All this is a facade, however, born to defeat the true nature of my nature, which is to put off every-thing and spend my time reading juicy novels and taking naps.

Even so, invitations to procrastinate lurk everywhere: Love is a huge lure. Whether for a child, a sweetheart, or a garden, performing a delicious task can make it ever so much easier to postpone a distasteful one.

Fear is another.

Once, at college, I had a bed with three legs. During the sec-ond week of honors psychology I checked out the books I would need to write the final paper – which you could do instead of taking the final exam. I left those books propping up the bed for an entire quarter, and ended up taking the exam – renowned for its Herculean difficulty.

Did I believe that by sleeping on the books I would some-how absorb the knowledge I needed to write that paper? Did I think my professor would be too preoccupied to notice, or I would meet a boyfriend so smitten by my charms he would explain statistical analysis to me?

No, I was so terrified at the prospect of writing about facts I couldn't grasp that I put up the procrastinator's shield: avoidance. It was the worst possible choice I could have made.

I got a D on the exam. I lost my scholarship for an entire year. Instead of taking the photography elective I craved, I ended up waiting tables at a sorority to pay my tuition. My late fee at the library was equivalent to the cost of a Volkswagen. The disappointment of my parents was heartbreaking. Echoes of my choice to postpone reverberated for years.

What envy I feel for people who truly can procrastinate gracefully, who can enjoy a movie amid rank piles of dirty laundry. For me, a task deferred quickly grows fangs. It gets larger and more daunting than it ever actually was. Pretty soon, it is hunched in the closet, waiting to devour me. The things I do instead have no savor as the monster of accountability follows me everywhere, leering. When I finally face the beast, the end product – conceived in dread and executed in haste – is precisely the botched effort I so feared when I put it off in the first place.

"Put off" goes for small things as well. Put off washing your face; you'll get zits. Put off sorting your mail; you'll get collection calls. Put off seeing the dentist and you'll end up one tooth short of a set. But the unmatched exhilaration that comes from crossing a difficult task off my list literally brightens my eyes and relaxes my brow.

Eat the broccoli of life, I beg my children, the better to enjoy the mousse. If I leave them with one piece of wisdom, it will be the absolute and utter truth of the adage: Never put off until tomorrow what you can do today. In fact, I encourage them to do today's work yesterday, as a hedge against what today might bring when it turns into tomorrow.

Christopher Buckley: *En boca cerrada, no entran moscas*

It means, "Flies can't get into a closed mouth." Nor can a foot.

When I first came across this proverb coined by an anonymous Spanish sage, my mouth did the opposite. It popped open. I quickly closed it, imagining swarms of approaching moscas. This is the test of a really good proverb, that it seems to have been tailor-coined just for you.

There are variations on it: "You never have to apologize for something you never said," and "There's nothing more satisfying than writing an angry letter – and nothing more foolish than mailing it." The trial lawyers version is: "Don't ask the question unless you already know the answer." I'm 50 years old now, and it took me about 49 years to learn all this. (I never said I was a quick study.)

It would take too long to list all the ill-advised, or inappropriate, or downright idiotic statements I have made over a half century. Tempted as I am to rehumiliate myself by recounting some of my more blithering whoppers, I think I'll pass. I'm not sure I could bear it.

The worst part is that so many of them were recorded at the time and have been preserved, like flies in amber. For someone who 1) writes, 2) goes on book tours, 3) speaks frequently in front of audiences, and 4) occasionally comments on television, life is a continuing series of arrests without benefit of a Miranda warning. No one is there to tell you, "Anything you say may be taken down and used against you." If I had the money, I would hire someone to whisper it in my ear before I write an article for *The New York Times*, or go into a TV studio, or find myself in front of 1,000 people fielding questions about Iraq or literature or child-raising. I am an authority on none of these subjects, nor, indeed, on any subject, though I can claim to know something about making a pretty good chicken piccata and spaghetti carbonara.

All right, I'll tell you a couple: I was once interviewing a member of British Prime Minister Margaret Thatcher's cabinet ... it pains me even to type this ... and I asked him to explain the difference between a Tory and a Conservative. It happens that they are identical. It was a real hundred-flies-in-the-mouth moment. His look of withering disdain still comes to me at three A.M. even 24 years later.

Only a few weeks ago, I jovially asked a hometown acquaintance of many years how his wife was. I compounded things by saying: "How's my favorite girl?" He looked at me with an air of disappointed serenity and said, "She died two years ago." A fifty-fly moment.

There. And I must say, I don't feel any better for having told you.

208

I spent four years at boarding school at a Benedictine monastery. The nice thing about being taught by monks is that no matter how badly you screw up, they have to forgive you.

Inside the monastery is a sign that announces simply, "Silence." I asked one of the monks about it. This was in 1967 or so, but I still remember Father Julian's answer. He said that Saint Gregory the Great, after whom the monastery was named, "felt that we tend to get into trouble the more we talk, so it's best to say as little as possible."

This rule may not be completely practical if you don't happen to be a monk. And it may not be the recipe for a stimulating dinner party. But the more I remember it, the fewer bugs I find myself having to spit out at the end of the day.

Good Housekeeping (June 2003), p. 138, p. 140, and p. 142.

Déjà Vu: Clever Lines / Make Us Crave / Return to Days / of Burma-Shave (2003)

Cynthia Crossen

When it rains, it pours. That's every bit as true today as it was 90 years ago, when Morton adopted this slogan to sell salt. Like other trenchant lines of commercial poetry, such as "Look Ma, no cavities," "When you got it, flaunt it" and "Good to the last drop," Morton's slogan has embedded itself in America's discourse.

Some advertising slogans are so powerful that they outlast their creators, competitors and, occasionally, the product for which they were invented.

Remember the Burma-Shave slogans of the 1950s, delivered on several signs, a line at a time, along the nation's two-lane highways? "If you think / She likes / Your bristles / Walk bare-footed / Through some thistles / Burma-Shave," one read. Another: "My job is / Keeping faces clean / And nobody knows / De stubble / I've seen / Burma-Shave."

The Burma-Shave brand, an early "brushless shaving cream," would have been long forgotten except for its immortal verse.

The earliest commercial slogans tended to be wordier than the modern staccato commands: "Just do it"; "Think small"; "Have it your way." In Victorian England, for example, advertisers used slogans such as "Sold at prices which will bear comparison with any other store" and "Has risen into favor by its merits alone."

An early U.S. toothpaste maker asked, "Nine out of 10 children have defective teeth – is yours one of the nine?" Makers of patent medicine lured customers with, "Make the liver do its duty" and "Better than whisky for a cold."

Slogans became more important in the early 20th century, when the number of manufactured goods available to the general public exploded. In 1903, Pepsi promised, "Exhilarating, invigorating, aids digestion." The next year, Coke bragged of being "a delightful, palatable, healthful beverage."

"Say it with flowers" appeared in 1917, and four years later, Listerine threatened young women with the prospect of being, "Always a bridesmaid, but never a bride." In 1926, the coffee company Alexander Balart punned, "Without grounds for complaint."

For products that were otherwise similar except for their brand names, a vivid slogan was essential. Camel cigarettes came up with these two now unimaginable slogans: "More doctors smoke Camels than any other cigarette" and "I'd walk a mile for a Camel." Bonded Tobacco Co. boasted it was "Making smoking 'safe' for smokers," while Old Gold pledged, "Not a cough in a carload."

Timothy R.V. Foster, founder of Adslogans, a London consulting firm, has collected more than 100,000 advertising slogans from around the world, dating back to the 1920s. Several years ago, Mr. Foster, who learned marketing at Procter & Gamble and Merrill Lynch, became annoyed by the "banality of the average corporate slogan – you know, 'total quality through excellence' or 'excellence through total quality' or 'where quality counts.'"

Mr. Foster's slogan Hall of Fame cites many that use the brand name – "Nothing runs like a Deere," or "You'll wonder where the yellow went when you brush your teeth with Pepsodent." Exceptions abound, however, such as "Breakfast of champions," "Where's the beef?" and "We try harder."

Advertising slogans are, for better and worse, often set to music. Some jingles (Doublemint, Campbell's, Oscar Mayer) stick in the brain long after more useful material has slipped away. "In the valley of the jolly, ho-ho-ho, Green Giant," was a snappy tune, as was the Chiquita banana song, which first appeared in 1944. At its peak, the Chiquita song was played more than 350 times a day on American radio stations. The lyrics have been rewritten several times, and the changes reflect Americans' improved understanding of bananas.

The original song ended, "But bananas like the climate of the very, very tropical equator – so you should never put bananas in the refrigerator." Today, the final lines of the song are, "They're a gift from Mother Nature and a natural addition to your table – for wholesome, healthy, pure bananas, look for Chiquita's label!"

Like banana sellers, political candidates have long used slogans to market themselves. The word "slogan" comes from the Gaelic, "sluaghghairm," meaning war cry.

In 1884, Grover Cleveland's campaign taunted his opponent, James Blaine, with the rhyming, "Blame, Blaine, James G.

Blaine, the continental liar from the state of Maine." Warren Harding captured the presidency in 1920 with the dull slogan, "Return to normalcy." A Jimmy Carter slogan was "Not Just Peanuts," and the first George Bush taught many people around the world to read lips.

Because most slogans are tested before they're unleashed on the general public, the losers usually die on the drawing table. But some people may think "Subaru: Inexpensive and built to stay that way" doesn't give the assurance a car buyer wants. Spree candy promises "a kick in the mouth," which isn't always a good thing. And you have to wonder about the efficacy of this slogan for a travel agency: "Go away."

The Wall Street Journal (August 20, 2003), online.

"Put a Sock in It!"
Wacky, Worn Phrases ... Where Did They Start? (2004)

Gary Pettus

John Saleeby of Pearl was involved with this woman, he says, "until we got into a fight over whether it was Jesus or Abraham Lincoln who said, 'A house divided against itself cannot stand.'"

"And we split up."

Saleeby, of course, is joking. Probably.

But the one-time stand-up comedian does make a good point: Folk sayings, proverbs, adages, old saws – whatever you call them – are familiar and constant companions in our daily conversations, but their origins are often mysterious to us.

An argument over those origins is not, as in Saleeby's illustration, worth losing a love over (don't throw the baby out with the bath water). But, if you're willing to persevere (put your nose to the grindstone), and read on, you may become armed with enough information to win any water-cooler debate.

Because this article is the Real McCoy, covering the whole nine yards, it might just put you in the catbird seat, while obliging your antagonist to put a sock in it.

Knock on wood.

Because, as Benjamin Franklin said: Nothing is certain but death and taxes.

"I don't know the source of these sayings, but I sure use them," says State Rep. Steve Holland, D-Plantersville, who admits to trotting out herds of them on the House floor.

"A lot of them I got from my Appalachian ancestors. They're a way of communication that puts the hay down where the cows can eat it."

That's the key. Says Mississippi native Bill Ferris, history professor and folklorist at the University of North Carolina-Chapel Hill: "In Africa there is a proverb that says, 'Proverbs are the palm wine (social drink) with which conversation is eaten.'"

That is: They make the hay of human experience, and observation, easier to swallow.

"Proverbs are remembered by certain poetic devices," says Wolfgang Mieder, a renowned folklorist who teaches at the University of Vermont and has traced some proverbs back to his native country of Germany.

"Some follow certain structural patterns: "Where there is x, there is y. 'Where there is smoke there is fire.' 'Where there's a will there's a way.'"

"Many times proverbs rhyme, as with my favorite: 'Different strokes for different folks.' That is one that almost had to grow on American soil. It says, 'Be yourself. Give me a chance to be myself. If I want to mow my lawn at 3 in the morning, then give me a break.'"

"You couldn't do that in Germany; that's the quiet time."

Proverbs, treasured phrases and sayings also "use certain rhythmic patterns, or alliteration that help you to remember them," says Mieder, who has written an entire book on one: *Grosse Fische fressen kleine Fische*, or: Big fish eat little fish.

"I traced that back to 800 B.C. ... It's basically Darwinism: 'The stronger overcome the weaker,'" Mieder says.

"Today, with bigger companies taking over smaller ones, hardly a week goes by where you don't see that in a headline."

Some sayings, however, seem made up on the spot. And highly provincial.

Take this one from Thurman Boykin of Ridgeland: "We here in Mississippi count time beginning with the night Mary Ann Mobley was crowned Miss America!"

Or this one from school teacher Becky Bach of Petal, who got it "from an AOL friend": "'If I tell you a chicken dips snuff, you look under his wing for a can.'"

From Bach's co-worker, Gabriella Pervel: "If a frog had wings, it wouldn't bump its butt."

And this one from Lindy Tolar of Oak Grove: "You can put a $700 suit on a hog and it's still a hog."

Then, there is the old Southern standby, "He's as drunk as Cooter Brown."

Boykin has a theory about that one: "Cooter Brown was a fraternity brother of mine at Ole Miss whose name wasn't really 'Cooter' Brown."

"After big parties we would be cleaning up and dumping all the warm liquor and beer left standing in plastic cups into one huge container. One of the girls who had stayed to help us clean up noticed what she mistook as a 'coot' (cute) pledge upturn the huge container of rancid refuse and drink it down, all four gallons of brown (stuff)."

214

Down South, sayings seem to take on a life, and a rural one at that, of their own.

"In the South, proverbial sayings come from Africa and Europe," says Ferris, co-editor with Charles Reagan Wilson of the *Encyclopedia of Southern Culture.*

"The proverb is really the foundation for the blues verse. B.B. King sings: 'Nobody loves me but my mama, and she may be jiving too.' It's call and response."

Call and response is right. The call for proverbs and colorful, commonly-used phrases is a response to more than one human need.

The human need to give wondrously sage advice, for one. "It's shorthand for wisdom," Ferris says. "Someone who's good with proverbs can give the appearance of being enormously smart."

And, there's the human need to speak colorfully and compactly.

"Proverbs are ready-made linguistic signs that we choose at any given moment when they suit our purpose," Mieder says. "They're a kind of automatic retrieval system that you pull out when your mind thinks, 'Wow, I can drive home that point with an idiom here or proverbial phrase to add a little bit of flavor to what I say.'"

"They are not clichés if you use them at the right moment, say, in a political debate. They prevent speeches from being very dry."

"Ross Perot was very good at this. Winston Churchill was very good at this. Unfortunately, Adolf Hitler was very good at this."

In fact, folk sayings can be used as a form of social control – for good or evil.

"As an anti-Semite, Hitler used them for manipulation and mind control," Mieder says. "But you can also use them to instruct youngsters: 'Honesty is the best policy.' 'Look before you leap.'"

"We use them to advance our designs. If you are a skillful linguist, it's amazing how you can influence a person's behavior, negatively or positively."

And they can advance the cause of humor, particularly in one of their less lofty forms: graffiti, such as this questionably instructive message from the men's restroom in Jackson's old Cherokee Inn: "Eat Spam with mayo."

"Some graffiti can well become proverbial," Mieder says. "You can just imagine what you can do in the bathroom."

Often, graffiti poets play with well-known proverbs, although many cannot be reprinted here. One of the mildest examples, put forth by Mieder: "A condom a day keeps the doctor away."

So much for apples.

"But you better know the original proverb or it doesn't make sense," Mieder says.

Bach, the schoolteacher, can testify to that. "One of my first graders interpreted the saying, 'Don't judge a book by its cover', this way: 'That's because you read a book under the cover.'"

"'Sometimes I read a book under the cover.'"

Phrase be!: Proverbs and their origins.

A house divided against itself cannot stand: From the Bible, Matthew 12:25. "And Jesus knew their thoughts, and said unto them, 'Every kingdom divided against itself is brought to desolation; and every city or house divided against itself shall not stand.'"

Put a sock in it ("Be quiet!"): Gramophones (primitive phonographs) at first had no volume controls. You had to stick a sock in the trumpet to tone them down.

It's raining cats and dogs: Supposedly, in 17th century England, city streets were so filthy a heavy rain would sometimes carry away dead animals.

The pot calling the kettle black ("Look who's calling who what!"): From Cervantes' *Don Quixote*.

Three sheets to the wind (drunk): From a nautical expression. "Sheets" refers to the ropes that held the sails, rather than the sails themselves. If these ropes were too loose, the boat or ship would flounder and sway like a pie-eyed sailor in the wind.

Drunker than Cooter Brown (really drunk): Not provable, but this well-known Southern saying may have come from another phrase, "drunk as a cooter," which probably originated in the early 1800s. "Cooter" is Southernese for a turtle or tortoise, although no one seems to know exactly how a turtle manages to make it to a bar before closing time.

Once in a blue moon (the occurrence of a rare event): Possibly comes from *The Maine Farmer's Almanac* which, when two full moons appeared within the same month, illustrated the first in red, the second in blue.

Knock on wood (an invocation for good luck): Possibly derives from the association of wood and trees with good spirits in mythology, or with the Christian cross.

Keep your nose to the grindstone (work hard): Human knife sharpeners in Victorian England lay prostrate while applying the blades to grindstones.

In the catbird seat (sitting pretty): From the Southern legend that the catbird dominates other species; also: the catbird tends to perch high up in the trees.

The Real McCoy (the genuine article): At least eight theories exist, one of the oldest of which is that "McCoy" is a corruption of "Mackay," a reference to a family of 19th-century Scottish whiskey makers who at one point touted their product as "the real Mackay."

The whole nine yards (the full measure, the whole enchilada): Several proposed theories exist, but there's no hard evidence that it appeared in print before 1967, when Elaine Shephard used it in *Doom Pussy*, her novel about the Vietnam War. Apparently, the phrase has military and shipyard associations related to measures of area and volume or even the size of certain ordnance. One other explanation says it comes from a tailor's need for nine yards of material to make a top-notch suit.

Different strokes for different folks: Folklorist Wolfgang Mieder believes it may have originated in the United States; he traces "different strokes" to Southern blacks in the 1950s.

Don't throw the baby out with the bath water: Mieder says this admonition is an Americanization of a very old German proverb. As he writes in his electronic book, De Proverbio: "It had its first written occurrence in Thomas Murner's (1475-1537) versified satirical book *Narrenbeschwoerung* (1512) which contains ... a treatise on fools who, by trying to rid themselves of a bad thing, succeed in destroying whatever good there was as well."

Don't judge a book by its cover (don't judge things by their appearance only): Originated in the United States; appeared in the journal *American Speech* (1929), and has been used in Britain since 1954.

Sources: The Phrase Finder (phrases.shu.ac.uk/meanings/proverbs.html), www.word-detective.com, folklorist Wolfgang Mieder, and *Random House Dictionary of Popular Proverbs and Sayings*.

The Clarion-Ledger [Jackson, Mississippi] (March 7, 2004), pp. 1F-2F.

Counting Chickens, Milking Cats:
The World's Timeless Proverbs Offer Great Wisdom –
Which We Sometimes Turn into Folly (2004)

Fred Baldwin

Whenever I find myself banking on future good fortune, I'm apt to think, "Don't count your chickens before they hatch." Germans express the same idea like this: "You have to catch the hare before you can roast him." The French say: "You can't sell the bear's skin until you've caught him." A Japanese version is almost identical, except that the animal to be caught is a tanuki, which resembles a raccoon.

Proverbs–bite-sized chunks of popular wisdom–abound in all languages. A few appear to be almost as old as the spoken word itself. Nearly 4,000 years ago, some Sumerian wit inscribed a clay tablet with what may already have been a popular proverb resembling those just quoted: "He has not yet caught the fox, but he is already making a neck-stock for it."

We use proverbs like these to make points more convincingly and more memorably than most of us could otherwise manage. Without relying on a proverb, I can explain why it's unwise to act as if some future benefit is a sure thing, but I can't improve on that proverbial warning about counting chickens prematurely.

Proverbs are short and rarely wishy-washy, which is one reason we like them. "He who hesitates is lost" has a no-nonsense ring to it. I also like its German counterpart: "A little too late is much too late." I like even better an East African proverb on the same theme: "He who waits for the whole animal to appear will spear only its tail."

We also use proverbs because they lend a measure of authority to our opinions, suggesting that what we are saying is simply common sense. Paul Hernadi, professor emeritus in the English department of the University of California, Santa Barbara, comments, "The internalized proverb is a marvelous way of rationalizing. What I want to do can be justified with communal approval and maybe as age-old wisdom."

Yet proverbial wisdom can be contradictory. We warn the cautious against hesitation, but we also warn the bold, "Look before you leap." We may say that "Absence makes the heart grow fonder," but we also say, "Out of sight, out of mind."

When we want help, we say, "Many hands make light work." When we don't want it, we grumble that "Too many cooks spoil the broth."

"Proverbs are not universal truths," says Wolfgang Mieder, professor of German and folklore at the University of Vermont. "Proverbs represent life; therefore, there will be contradictory proverbs. You and I will always choose that particular proverb that fits the specific context. I always say to my students, 'If the proverb fits, use it.'"

Mieder may well be the world's leading scholar in paremiology, the systematic study of proverbs. He is also editor of *De Proverbio* [Baldwin means *Proverbium*], an international journal [yearbook] on proverb studies, and has written or edited well over 50 books and a few hundred articles. He's published proverb collections on special topics (such as gardening), and he's analyzed the political uses of proverbs by leaders like Lincoln and Churchill.

According to Mieder, most European languages have a core set of about 300 widely used proverbs. Of these, something like 100 occur in similar form in all these languages, thanks to the influence of three sources: the Bible, Greek and Roman classics, and Medieval Latin, which for centuries served as a common language among educated people, much as English does today. When we read about a large corporation swallowing a smaller firm, we may think, "Big fish eat little fish." That's the English translation of a proverb from Greek and Roman times. (There's a similar Chinese saying: "The mantis seizes the locust but does not see the yellow bird behind him.")

Proverbs continue to evolve. Mieder remarks that "Garbage in, garbage out" has outgrown its origins in computer programming and that the spread of fitness centers has given new muscle to "No pain, no gain," variants of which go back to the 16th century. He adds that all around the world, today's image- and Web-oriented youth are multiplying local adaptations of "One picture is worth a thousand words" (often described as ancient Chinese wisdom, but in fact coined by an American advertising executive in the 1920s). And a word-by-word translation of the Anglo-American proverb "The early bird catches the worm" is catching on in Germany because it's easier to portray visually than its older German equivalent: "The morning hour brings gold in its mouth."

Yet the proverb about "the morning hour" remains popular, no doubt because in German it's a catchy, compact couplet: *Morgenstund hat Gold im Mund.* A memorable proverb sometimes outlives its metaphorical source. Mental images of the village blacksmith may fade, but "Strike while the iron is hot" endures. Hernadi, after quoting "A stitch in time saves nine," says, "Nobody mends socks any longer, right? But we all know that if we don't see the mechanic about the little noise in our car, sooner or later there will be a bigger problem. We still convey this advice through the somewhat dated vocabulary of mending clothes."

That proverbs serve as small, prefabricated parts to conversation makes them useful to travelers. If your fluency in a language is limited, a memorized proverb can come in handy when encountering situations likely to occur on any trip–a late arrival, an unexpected turn of events, or perhaps the need to acknowledge a blunder. "Proverbs," Mieder says, "are complete sentences that are easy to memorize. When you go to the country with the language you happen to have studied, you can once in a while pop up with a piece of wisdom that relaxes people at the table. And you can actually shine with them."

I've done this–popped up, at least, if not always shone. Even when my command of a language other than English is adequate for asking directions, it's never good enough for much in the way of small talk. So, when traveling to non-English-speaking countries, I've tried to pack my mental bags with a few folk sayings–the linguistic analog of a few small granola bars. Necessity is the mother of invention. Or, as a German proverb has it, "Who has no cow must milk the cat."

It's easy to find collections of proverbs in many languages in libraries and on the Internet. Do be aware that these are likely to include proverbs no longer in current use. And you can't assume, that just because a proverb is in Spanish, that it will be familiar in Mexico or South America. If possible, before leaving for some foreign destination, have a native speaker suggest a popular saying you might find useful.

You'll be surprised at how often you'll use what you've learned. Suppose, for example, that you want to decline a second or third drink without sounding abrupt. Every language has applicable sayings. There's a nice Spanish rhyme: *El vino y* el tino no andanpor un camino. (Wine and wit don't walk the same road.) German has a similar bit of doggerel: *Ist das Bier im Manne, ist der Verstand in der Kanne*. Loosely, that's "Beer in the man, brains in the can." These may not be knee-slappers, but they beat trying to remember how to stammer out, "I'm afraid that one more will put me under the table."

I admit, however, to having once spent several uncomfortable minutes in Japan after having come out with "The child of a frog is a frog," the Japanese version of "The apple doesn't fall far from the tree." Although my Japanese vocabulary doesn't go much beyond counting to ten, I'd found this phrase in a Japanese proverb book and was sure I could somehow work it into dinner-table conversation. And so I did—only to be met with blank, uncomprehending stares. It seems that the Japanese word for "frog" sounds much like the Japanese verb "to return." My hosts must have thought that I was babbling about a B-movie—something like "The Return of Frog-Boy."

As we often say, anybody can make a mistake. Or, as a Japanese proverb has it, "Even monkeys fall from trees." When people at the table finally grasped what I was trying to say, my recitation did indeed relax them—doubled them up with laughter, in fact. It gave me a perfect opening for "Fall down seven times, get up eight." That's the Japanese version of "If at first you don't succeed...try, try again."

US Airways Attaché (October 2004), pp. 44-47.

Standing on the Shoulders of Clichés – A Key Milestone on the Way to Ordinary Language (2005)

Guy Deutscher

The season of clichés is upon us, with end-of-school speeches – perversely called "commencement" – ringing out their uplifting platitudes: "go forth," "trust your instincts," "make the world a better place." This is the time when new chapters are beginning, windows of opportunity are opening, and countless mass-produced metaphors are filling the halls of learning.

It's enough to make language mavens grimace: the more often we hear a phrase, the less forceful the impression it makes. So through over-familiarity, the currency of language is devalued.

Take this example: when in the 17th century Isaac Newton paid homage to his intellectual predecessors, he expressed his humility with an image that was still fresh and evocative. "If I have seen further than others," he wrote, "it was only by standing upon the shoulders of giants." Three centuries and many repetitions later, Hillary Clinton used the same metaphor in a Harvard Medical School commencement speech, when (twice in the same paragraph) she told the graduates they would "stand on the shoulders" of their illustrious forerunners. The once vivid image has faded through overexposure, and the words have become not much more than a flourish of meaningless rhetoric. And if it seems improbable that images can really wear out beyond recognition, the arbiters of good taste might bring as evidence that ultimate literary sin, mixing metaphors. The president of the University of Maryland Eastern Shore, for example, couldn't possibly have had the picture of a locking instrument or of a pillar on a highway in her mind's eye when she assured her seniors last month that commencement was "a key milestone." in their lives. What better proof, then, of the erosive effect of clichés?

The critics certainly have a point that images are devalued through overuse, but are they also right that this devalues language as a whole and robs us of our powers of expression? Excuse the cliché, but there is another side to the coin. Were it not for all the clichés of the past, our vocabulary today would be very impoverished indeed, for cliché is a necessary stage between new imagery and everyday vocabulary.

Suppose you wanted to avoid the danger of muddled images like "key milestone," and so opted for something safer, say, the understated "important moment" or the slightly bolder "crucial instance." Would these alternatives be any less clichéd?

Only in the sense that their original imagery is so worn out by now that it's no longer recognizable. "Crucial," for instance, originally just meant cross-shaped. The current sense goes back to a phrase coined by Francis Bacon, who used "crucial" to describe an event that makes you choose between rival hypotheses. The image he had in mind was that of a cross-shaped signpost marking a parting of a road.

But through repetition, "crucial" became a cliché that was recycled so often that all traces of the original metaphor vanished from our linguistic consciousness, and it ended up as merely a different way of saying "important." Actually, even "important" itself was once an image in its own right, as it ultimately goes back to a word meaning "carry."

So the spread of clichés in fact contributes to that great democratic process in which inspired images coined by the gifted few are appropriated as the staple vocabulary of the common man. And we stand, as it were, on the shoulders of generations of past clichéurs, whose enterprise in reproducing hackneyed images has enriched our vocabulary with so many synonyms. As the German novelist Jean Paul once remarked, language is nothing but a "dictionary of faded metaphors," or in other words, our vocabulary is a treasure-hoard of worn clichés.

Those who would bar us from using our "keys" and "milestones" today are in effect depriving the next generations of their fair share of "crucials" and "importants." And isn't that rather mean? So go forth, class of 2005, trust your instincts, churn out clichés by the bucketload, and make the world a better place.

The New York Times (June 18, 2005), p. A13.

The Upside-Down World – When Maxims Mislead (2005)

Eduardo Galeano

"NEW YORK, MADRID, LONDON: TERRORISM STRIKES ANEW."

Versions of this headline adorned many of the world's newspapers on July 8, the day after the explosions in London. They didn't mention either Afghanistan or Iraq. Weren't – aren't – the bombings there also terrorist attacks, which in the case of Iraq occur daily? Isn't it always, or almost always, the working class that suffers casualties in these attacks and in war? Don't they deserve the same respect and the same compassion as the victims of any expression of disdain for human life?

In 1776, the Declaration of Independence of the United States affirmed that all men are created equal. Then a few years later the first Constitution refined this notion, establishing that for the purposes of the census, each black would be counted as three-fifths of a person. What fraction of a person are Iraqis counted as today?

Some people are more equal than others? So they say.

State terror, the prolific father of all terrorisms, finds the perfect alibi in the terrorisms that it generates. It sheds crocodile tears each time the shit hits the fan, then feigns innocence of the consequences of its actions. But the owners of the world do not need to worry: The atrocities that the fanatics and madmen commit provide them their justification and grant them impunity.

"Lies have short legs." Not so: lies have very long legs. So long they outrun the denials of the liars. After shouting to the four winds that Iraq was a danger to humanity, Bush and Blair admitted publicly that the country they invaded and annihilated had no weapons of mass destruction. In subsequent balloting in the U.S. and U.K., the people repaid them with reelection.

"Crime doesn't pay." Alas, not even such proverbs know what they are saying. The world spends $2.2 billion per day – yes, per day – on the military industry, that industry of death, and day by day that figure rises. Wars require weapons, weapons need wars, and wars and weapons need enemies.

There is no more lucrative business on the face of the Earth than this practice of industrial-scale assassination. Its subsidiary, the industry of fear, devoted to the manufacture of enemies, is today the primary source of profits for entertainment and communications companies. In Hollywood, screenwriters pile fright upon fright: as if earthly terror were not enough, they add threats from other planets.

The military industry needs to produce fear to justify its existence. It is a vicious circle: The world becomes a slaughterhouse that becomes a madhouse that becomes a slaughterhouse...Iraq, bombarded, occupied, humiliated, becomes the preeminent school for crime of our day. Its invaders, who call themselves liberators, have set up there the most prolific nursery of terrorists, fed by hopelessness and desperation.

"The early bird gets the worm." Does this mean the guerrilla leaders? The successful bankers? In reality, the saying calls on the poor laborers to wake up early, and comes from the times when it was work that paid. But in today's world, work is worth less than garbage.

Greed and fear were the two motors of the universal system of power – the system that was called capitalism back when I was born. But only one works now; greed has disappeared, at least for laborers. Today, no one has the faintest hope of getting rich by working. The twin engines of power now are fear and fear: fear of losing one's job, fear of not finding a job, fear of hunger, fear of homelessness.

The unions used to defend the workers, back in times that now seem prehistoric. But the most famous multinational companies, Wal-Mart and McDonald's, openly and unapologetically deny workers their right to unionize and throw into the street whoever dares to attempt it. For the international organizations that fight for human rights, this scandalous violation provokes little response. The atrophy of the unions, or their outright prohibition, has started to become normal.

The labor movement, the fruit of two centuries of workers' struggle, is in crisis around the world, as are all the instruments of collective and peaceful defense of people who live off their labor. And now, abandoned to their fates, people are obliged to accept whatever their employers want: twice the hours for half the pay.

The unions, weakened and persecuted, can do little to help, and God, it would seem, is busy elsewhere. President Bush needs Him day and night for his divine mission of planetary conquest, in which God guides his every step. How do they communicate? By mail, fax, telephone, telepathy? That is a state secret.

226

"The devil provides the weapons." At last a true saying. God couldn't be such a bastard. It must be the devil that provides the weapons, or at least the weapons of mass destruction, the real ones, the ones Iraq didn't have and that are ripping the world apart.

The bombardment of lies from the factories of public opinion.

The chemical weapons of consumer society that are maddening the climate and polluting the air.

The poison gas from the factories of fear that make us accept the unacceptable and turn indignity into a feature of destiny.

The deadly impunity of the serial killers who are heads of state.

The endless multiplication of armaments versus the dwindling attention to poverty.

The sowing of anti-personnel mines and then the selling of prostheses.

The raining of bombs and then the doling out of contracts for the reconstruction of the countries they annihilate.

The Progressive (September 2005), pp. 22-23.

My Survey Results Are Fascinating, but Then Ignorance Is Bliss (2006)

James Gorman

I have been inspired recently by the way science challenges the conventional wisdom. This year, two surprising stories have come out of the Women's Health Initiative, a huge study of 49,000 women, one on fat and the other on calcium.

It turns out that a low-fat diet didn't live up to its advance billing as a defense against cancer and heart disease. And calcium didn't prevent broken bones the way it was hoped it would.

These findings are causing a big debate and getting lots of attention. So I've decided to do a major study of my own, part of my continuing effort to bring the world of science and culture together. So far, I can't say that either world appreciates it much. Never mind.

I already have some important findings. Although I didn't realize it at the time, I've been doing a retrospective study my whole life. It just needed a name. So I'm calling it the Liar, Liar, Pants on Fire Survey of Annoying Sayings. My first surprising finding concerns this well-known saying: *"Practice makes perfect."*

Really? What kind of practice would that be? Batting practice? Batting is something baseball players are always practicing, and the best of them are nowhere near perfect. Any hitter would kill for a .400 average, meaning 4 hits in every 10 at bats. Perhaps the saying refers to practicing on a musical instrument. I am told that even the most brilliant musicians are not perfect, although, because of the depths of my own musical imperfection, I can't tell. But even if, say, Joshua Bell did happen to achieve perfection once, we use this saying to browbeat average children into scratching violin strings and banging on pianos. But we know perfectly well none of those children will end up perfect. That's just cruel.

Kids, are you reading this? Adults are lying to you. Nobody's perfect. Practice can make you pretty good, or if you have talent, really good, but try to relax, and remember this saying instead: *"The perfect is the enemy of the good."*

Another proverb I have discovered to be wrong is: *"It's not the size of the dog in the fight. It's the size of the fight in the dog."*

You'll notice that the people who say this are coaches, not dog owners. No one who has actually watched dogs fight would say such a thing. True, size isn't everything. But it's something.

I have had three Cairn terriers and a Pomeranian, all full of fight. The Pomeranian, in particular, was incapable of backing down. He may have looked like an animated pillow, but he was a lion in his own mind. Once, he was hurt badly by a bearded collie that also attacked one of our terriers.

The terrier was no pushover. She had flunked obedience school because of excess aggression, usually directed at a stolid Rottweiler from Westchester who often walked behind her as the dogs and owners tried to grasp the mysteries of heeling. But she had already been bitten once by the demented collie, and so was twice shy. She hid under the porch. Not the Pom. I wasn't there, but I suspect he was too busy barking obscenities to look for a good place to hide. Here's what I tell my dogs now: *"Discretion is the better part of valor."*

I anticipate a lot of criticism of the Liar, Liar, Pants on Fire Study. I have no charts, for one thing. My sample size is unknown, even to me. And my experimental protocols have been to take everything with a grain of salt and not to buy a pig in a poke.

My answer to this is: Replication! Go ahead, experiment. Practice something. I cannot, for legal reasons, encourage fighting. But anyone can go someplace that has lots of dogs, and watch.

The biggest criticism will probably be that none of these sayings have anything to do with science. I have an answer to that too, my last annoying saying: *"Today is the tomorrow you worried about yesterday."*

It doesn't matter if you have never heard this one. I have. I used to think it was true. But science, theoretical physics no less, has shown it to be unprovable at best.

Even if we stipulate that you were indeed worried yesterday about what at the time you expected to be "tomorrow," a lot of really, really smart theoreticians say that linear, day-follows-day time is an illusion. Time is actually all happening at once, like space, although "happening at once" is probably imprecise.

Besides, there could be a zillion alternative universes. Maybe the tomorrow you worried about is not today, not this today here, but one in a different space-time. As in the old Superman comics, Bizarro Tomorrow could be the one you were worried about, or actually, since we're talking about it today, Bizarro Today. Obviously, time is better dealt with by songwriters, like the great Sandy Denny, a member of Fairport Convention, a group that was popular in a yesterday that few people remember today, let alone tomorrow. As she so presciently wrote: *"Who knows where the time goes?"* I certainly don't.

The New York Times (February 21, 2006), p. F4.

Getting a Grasp on Idioms: L.A. Waitress Compiled Book to Help Foreign Students (2006)

J. Michael Kennedy

After all those years of slinging hash and refilling coffee mugs, May Pare found herself "up to her eyeballs" with a collection of sayings that would "blow the mind" of someone trying to learn English.

They were the likes of "pay through the nose," "using elbow grease," "having a hollow leg" and "being lower than a snake's belly." There was "heads will roll," "press the flesh" and "keeping your eyes peeled."

She had hundreds of these sayings, many of them overheard and scribbled down while she was waiting tables at Shakers restaurant in Glendale, north of Los Angeles, where she's worked on and off – but mostly on – for the last 30 years.

The result of her work is a self-published 363-page book that deals exclusively with body part idioms, in chapters ranging from butt to breath and head to toes. Not only is Pare one of the restaurant's most popular waitresses (many customers wait until they can get one of her tables), she is now something of a celebrity in her small world.

The book, "Body Idioms and More," is designed to help foreign-born students who would otherwise "throw up their hands" in dismay at the odd sayings, some of which give no clue to their real meaning. Think how "having a frog in my throat" would sound to the uninitiated.

Pare (pronounced Paray) is a scholar of the English language, her specialty both as a student and as a college teacher in her native Thailand. Later, she earned her master's degree from the University of California, Los Angeles, with a specialty in English as a second language.

She never bandied that talent around at the coffee shop, even among the regulars. She just took notes.

"I've learned a lot from just being here at the restaurant," Pare said as she took an afternoon break from waiting tables. "I picked up a lot of expressions from customers and co-workers."

Over the last few months the book has evolved into something of a coffee-counter project, with customers helping edit the latest edition and waitresses checking the manuscript for spelling errors.

Pare hopes to parlay her modest success (she'd like for the book to be picked up by language classes) into a shot at doing something other than jotting down food orders.

"I knew there was a need for it," she said of her book. "And I needed to do something else so I could get another job. I didn't have anything I could put on my resume."

Pare first sensed the need to define idioms about 10 years ago when she told one of her cousins a joke with an idiomatic punch line. When the cousin looked baffled, Pare told him she was just "pulling his leg."

The look did not change.

"He didn't get it," she said. "I told him this is the way people talk."

So began her research into idioms. Over the years she collected enough to compile a book, which she had printed in Thailand during one of her visits there.

That small order turned out to be a mere first draft of her anatomical opus.

It was about then that Shakers regulars like Jim Oliver and Japhet Ward came on the scene to help Pare prepare the book for its second printing.

Oliver, a 68-year-old artist, drops into Shakers ("Breakfast All Day") about once a week, usually Sunday. He'd known Pare casually for years, but they had not become good friends because he always ate at the counter, while Pare waited tables.

"I had no idea of her background except that she was a good waitress," Oliver recalled. "Then one day she said she wanted to show me her book, the first edition. I took it home and started reading it and when I noticed some mistakes I started taking notes. And then I began taking the notes in to her and she was very appreciative. I just sort of fell into being a help to her."

One example of Pare's being slightly off point was the definition of having "a stone face," which in the first edition was described as an "ugly face."

"I showed her that it meant immobile or without expression," he said. "When she saw the difference, she was just thrilled." New definition in the second edition: "Like stone, i.e., without expression, cold, granite-like, hard, immobile."

The story was much the same for Ward, who studied music at UCLA but spent the better part of his 76 years as a clocker during early morning workouts for thoroughbreds at Hollywood

Park racetrack. He'd been coming to Shakers for years, and had known Pare for 19 of them.

"I sit at tables, a lot of times with May as my waitress," he said. "We've been friends for a long time, so if she had a question about a certain word or sentence, I'd tell her what I thought was correct."

Meanwhile, news of the book slowly spread through Pare's circle of customers. Susan Dougherty, the retention coordinator at Glendale Community College, bought a copy and sent it to the head of the college's English as a second language program.

"We have a lot of sayings that don't make any sense," she said. "A lot of people come here from other countries who are educated, but not in our colloquialisms. I found it fascinating to see a whole book just on body parts. I didn't know there were so many."

Pare, meanwhile, is beginning to think about her next idiomatic project – perhaps clothes or food – even as she hopes that an English as a second language program will include her book in its curriculum.

Pare has ordered 7,000 copies of the book's second edition and has vague plans for the new year. With luck, that does not include Shakers, despite all those years of taking orders.

"I shouldn't have been here this long, but time goes so fast," she said. "I appreciate having this job. I'm thankful. But I should move on."

She said she'd like to do workshops with foreign-born students trying to learn English and its many shadings. A good example, she said, is the English-language idiom "from your lips to God's ears."

The closest she could come in Thai was: "I hope it turns out to be true."

Body language

May Pare, a Southern California waitress who earned a master's degree from UCLA specializing in English as a second language, wrote a book dealing exclusively with body part idioms. Here is a selection of her entries and definitions:

Fire in your belly (expression): Enthusiasm/driving force/passion for what you are doing.
Rub elbows with (verb phrase): To interact socially with.

Face the music (verb phrase): To suffer the unpleasant consequences, especially of one's own actions.

A hair-trigger temper (noun phrase): A tendency to become angry very easily.

Lose your head (verb phrase): To become confused or crazy about, to lose emotional control over something.

A six-pack (noun): Toned stomach muscles.

Powder your nose (verb phrase): A polite or humorous way of saying "to go to the toilet."

On your toes (adjective phrase): Alert, ready to act.

A sharp tongue (noun phrase): A tendency to reply sharply or sarcastically.

Love handles (noun phrase): Extra flesh around your waist.

The Burlington Free Press (March 12, 2006), p. 6D.

Say What? (2006)

Claire Sulmers

We know not to call animal control if it rains cats and dogs, and even the most literal person won't reach for a broom if someone spills the beans. Why we say what we do seems like a mystery, but most of the colorful phrases in our collective speech are rooted in history, fable, or myth. A few with surprising back-stories:

Scholars think "spill the beans" originated in ancient Greece, where voters cast ballots with white and black beans. If a clumsy voter knocked over the jar or helmet that held the beans, the secret was out.

The origin of "raining cats and dogs" is a little murky. According to one account, heavy rains in 17th-century England turned city streets into rivers that carried trash, along with dead cats and dogs. A less grisly story attributes the phrase to howling wind, which sounds like cats and dogs fighting.

In ancient Rome, the general and politician Pompey believed salt was an antidote to any potential poison in his food, so he added a grain of it to everything he ate or drank. That's why when people are skeptical of something, they "take it with a grain of salt."

In the Middle Ages, scholars wore a square cap similar to our graduation mortarboard. People believed the hat actually helped its owner think – and the term "thinking cap" was born.

No one knows the origin of a "skeleton in the closet," but here's one theory: Until the Anatomy Act was passed in England in 1832, it was illegal to dissect a body (executed criminals excepted), and doctors were allowed to work on only one cadaver during their careers. Those who didn't want to get rid of the skeleton kept it hidden in a dark corner or hung it in a closet.

For definitions of difficult phrases, go to www.realsimple.com/phrases.

Real Simple (September 2006), p. 74.

236

Index of Proverbs and Proverbial Phrases

As can be seen from this key-word index, journalists and free lance authors writing about proverbial matters definitely have their favorite set of examples, among them such proverbs as "Absence makes the heart grow fonder," "An apple a day keeps the doctor away," "Early to bed, early to rise, makes a man feel healthy, wealthy, and wise," "The early bird gets the worm," "Too many cooks spoil the broth," "You can't teach an old dog new tricks," "He who hesitates is lost," "Look before you leap," "A penny saved is a penny earned," "A watched pot never boils," "Out of sight, out of mind," "A stitch in time saves nine," "A rolling stone gathers no moss," and "Different strokes for different folks." But there are, of course, hundreds of other proverbs and proverbial phrases cited throughout these pages.

idleness 64
ignorance 228
illness 56
imitation 81, 160
immortals 189
independent 153
Indian 119
industry 151
injuries 152
ink 35
innocence 34
innovator 13
instincts 224
iron 163, 221
irons 178

jealousy 70
Jerusalem 158
job 126, 141, 156
Job's turkey 156
journey 25
judgment 48
jug 29
juice 165, 167
jury 199

key 69, 223, 224
kick 212
kill 67, 172
kinfolk 143
king 56, 162, 173
kingdom 169
kiss 42, 105
kit 165
knife 36, 75
knock 217
knothole 155
know 5, 9, 31, 38, 62, 83, 140, 155,
    166, 178, 187, 189, 201
knowledge 62, 71
Krakow 163

labor 21, 141
lady 32, 44
lamb 36
land 35, 161, 162
lane 76, 163
language 33
late 66, 78, 135, 163, 202, 219
laugh 47, 76, 83
law 44

lawyer 159, 160
lawyers 43, 44, 152
lazier 156
laziness 109, 120
lazy 156
leak 50
learn 64, 76, 88, 142, 201
learning 5, 9, 66, 78
leg 156, 231, 232
lend 45
length 116
liar 228
liberty 161, 172
library 144
lie 36
lies 225
life 47, 62, 66, 71, 76, 131, 136, 173,
    179, 180
lift 48
light 175
like 4, 9
line 82
linen 126
lips 115, 174, 212, 233
listen 140
little 12, 39, 76, 136
live 35, 76, 82
liver pills 159
loaf 29, 143, 160
loan 45
lock 167
locust 220
longer 136
look 2, 59, 60, 79, 88, 112, 119, 142,
    145, 163, 215, 219
looks 191
loquacity 43
Lord 112, 157
lose 89, 129
love 38, 42, 45, 47, 48, 69, 70, 104,
    105, 151, 152, 163, 234
love handles 234
loved 105
lovers 67, 70
loves 151
lower 231
luck 35, 36
lucky 39
lunch 71, 127, 157
lunge 112

247

Postscript

As the introduction and the index of proverbs and proverbial phrases indicate, this book is primarily meant for research purposes, i.e., as a basis for paremiological and phraseological studies. The production of the book was financed by *Proverbium* and generous donations. The book is not for sale in bookstores and is distributed at no charge to *Proverbium* subscribers as well as scholars, students, and libraries. Should an author nevertheless wish to receive an honorarium for the inclusion of an essay, this request would certainly be honored.

For free copies and possible inquiries please contact Prof. Wolfgang Mieder or Ms. Janet Sobieski at the Department of German and Russian, Waterman Building, University of Vermont, 85 South Prospect Street, Burlington, Vermont 05405 (USA). E-mail: Wolfgang.Mieder@uvm.edu or Janet.Sobieski@uvm.edu.